Synchronizing Science and Technology
with Human Behaviour

To B

Synchronizing Science and Technology with Human Behaviour

Ralf Brand

from Routledge

First published by Earthscan in the UK and USA in 2005

For a full list of publications please contact:
Earthscan
2 Park Square, Milton Park, Abingdon, Oxon OX14 4RN
711 Third Avenue, New York, NY 10017

Earthscan is an imprint of the Taylor & Francis Group, an informa business

Copyright © Ralf Brand 2005. Published by Taylor & Francis.

ISBN-13   978-1-84407-247-7   paperback
ISBN-13   978-1-84407-251-4   hardback

Typesetting by JS Typesetting Ltd, Porthcawl, Mid Glamorgan
Cover design by Yvonne Booth

A catalogue record for this book is available from the British Library.

Library of Congress Cataloging-in-Publication Data

Brand, Ralf.
   Synchronizing science and technnology with human behaviour / Ralf Brand.
      p. cm.
   Includes bibliographical references and index.
   ISBN-13   978-1-84407-251-4 (hardback)
   ISBN-10   1-84407-251-7 (hardback)
   ISBN-13   978-1-84407-247-7 (pbk.)
   ISBN-10   1-84407-247-9 (pbk.)
1. Technology–Social aspects. 2. Sustainable development. I. Title.
   T14.5.B697 2005
   303.48'–dc22

2005027699

Contents

List of Figures, Tables and Boxes

Figures

Tables

Boxes

List of Acronyms and Abbreviations

	Original	Translation
ADR	alternative dispute resolution	
AGALEV	Anders GAan LEVen	'going to live differently' (Flemish Green Party)
BTTB	Bond van Trein-, Tram- en Busgebruikers	Association of Train, Tramway and Bus Users
CPTED	crime prevention through environmental design	
CVP	Christelijke Volkspartij	Christian Conservative Party in Flanders
ALB	Grüne Alternative Liste Bamberg	Green Alternative List of Bamberg
GMO	genetically modified organism	
LBV	Landesbund für Vogelschutz	State Association for the Protection of Birds
MVGWV	Ministerie van de Vlaamse Gemeenschap, Afdeling Wegen en Verkeer Limburg	Department of the Flemish Community, Division for Roads and Traffic in Limburg
NKE	North Karelian Electric	
SAM	Samen Anders Mobiel	'together differently mobile' – slogan in Hasselt

SBB	Schweizer Bundesbahn	Swiss Federal Railway
SHLS	Stuurgroep Hasselt Levendig Stadscentrum	Steering Group Hasselt Lively City Centre
SNM	Strategic Niche Management	
SP	Socialistische Partij	Flemish Socialist Party
SPA	Socialistische Partij Anders	Flemish Socialist Party – Differently (successor to SP)
STS	science and technology studies	
SUV	sport utility vehicle	
SWC	Studiecentrum Willy Claes	Study Centre Willy Claes
UCI	Union Cycliste Internationale	International Cyclist Union
UNCED	United Nations Conference for Environment and Development	
VLD	Vlaamse Liberalen en Democraten	Flemish Liberals and Democrats
VU	Volksunie	People's Union (Flemish politca party)
WTO	World Trade Organization	

1

Setting the Stage

This book was inspired by unease regarding the lack of progress we have made towards sustainable development,[1] despite numerous activities carried out by government agencies, research laboratories, environmental organizations, neighbourhood councils and the like. It would be difficult indeed to defend that only little energy and thought has been dedicated to developing sustainable solutions. After all, we now have hybrid cars, e-government, Earth Days and Earth Summits, Ride Your Bike campaigns, photovoltaics and 6022 books on sustainable development in the US Library of Congress.[2] In short: much has been done, but not much has been achieved. The United Nations' General Assembly, in preparation for the Johannesburg summit *Rio +10*, enunciates the same impression much more eloquently:

> *We are deeply concerned that, despite the many successful and continuing efforts. . . the environment and the natural resource base. . . continue to deteriorate at an alarming rate.* United Nations General Assembly 55th session, 2001, p1

This book is an invitation to imagine that the problem might not rest so much with the number of activities we undertake in the name of sustainable development but – at least *also* – with the *type* of activities. 'A story of Asterix, not of Hercules'[3] as Kemp (personal communication, 26 August, 2004) describes the transition to sustainability. This is the lesson I suggest can be learned from several notable cases in which communities achieved substantial advancements with respect to sustainability, cases that are described in this book. What I encountered were not successful attempts to devise vastly more efficient technologies, nor did I find increased sustainable behaviour due to resounding awareness campaigns. These two approaches could quite rightly have been expected. After all, they represent the two poles of a spectrum I found helpful in describing the current discourse on sustainable development. It reaches from technology orientated approaches to behaviour orientated approaches. Cognate vocabularies range from modern to antimodern, from genetically modified organisms (GMOs) to eco-farming, from technophilic to sociophilic, from high-tech to back-to-the-roots. The technology orientated approach promises that smart technologies can take care of our unsustainabilities. Thus unencumbered, individuals would not have to change their behaviour, at least not to make heroic choices.[4] In contrast, advocates of the behaviour orientated approach respond that technology has proven too often to be a false promise. In this view, we should face the truth that heroic choices, such as the reduction of consumption, are unavoidable if we are to be serious about sustainability. Advocates of both camps claim to serve sustainability, which leaves not only the public in a conceptual babel, as depicted poignantly by Hellman in Figure 1.1. A more thorough explanation of these two positions is presented in Chapter 2.

Without a cartoonist to hold a mirror up to us, we are rarely aware of how immersed we are in this discourse. I, for example, grew into it as a student eager to understand what others had to say about sustainable development. I adopted their vocabulary, which subsequently helped me to categorize competently – as it seemed –the manifold voices I heard. Eventually, it appeared natural that the proponents of fuel efficient cars and the advocates of reduced consumption literally sat at different tables in community meetings and at United Nations assemblies. Chapter 2 (section entitled 'Ringing bells') demonstrates that this dichotomy is indeed a prevalent characteristic of the sustainability discourse; after all, it is clearly evident in newspaper articles, scholarly journals, national energy saving programmes and in the pamphlets of grassroots activists.

As I document in Chapter 2 (section entitled 'The seamless web'), authors of several disciplines have often criticized the distinction between the technical and the social realm as unwarranted. They argue that both are inextricably linked in two fundamental ways – whether these links are acknowledged or not. One link has come to be known as technological voluntarism; its proponents emphasize the possibility of human beings freely designing technologies according to their needs and desires. Technological determinists, in contrast, claim that existing technologies establish corridors of choices that restrict or widen the choices of individuals and of society as a whole. Science and technology studies (STS) scholars go one step further in their assertion that the relationship between the technical and the social realm is actually a constant back and forth, a circular mutual influence.

Some projects that are described throughout this book appear to have harnessed this phenomenon by proactively coordinating and synchronizing technical and social change instead of playing the oscillation game of action, re-action, re-re-action and so forth. Their designers, in most cases teams of community officials, entrepreneurs and citizens, thus managed to escape the technology–behaviour dichotomy.

While the inspiration and evidence that form the backbone of this book stem from a number of real world cases, two cases are looked at in more detail in order to learn not only *what* has been done but also *how* it has been done. Chapter 3 contains a detailed account of these cases but as a frame of reference a brief summary might be helpful at this point.

The Belgian city of Hasselt used to suffer from severe traffic related problems such as accidents, traffic congestion, low mobility for senior citizens, poor accessibility of the shopping district in the centre of the city especially for out-of-town customers, etc. Eventually, the city council opted to narrow the traffic artery

Source: Hellman, 2002, p4

Figure 1.1 *Competing sustainability bibles*

in the inner city, to increase public transport services eightfold, to radically modernize its bus fleet, to introduce a five-minute interval on some bus routes and to make bus travel free of charge. As a result, many people quickly changed their behaviour, such that bus use octupled.

In the second case, in the German county of Fürstenfeldbruck many people changed their shopping behaviour. They now buy more locally produced groceries because they are available at almost every supermarket, they are fresher than non-locally produced food products, they are easily identifiable by a uniform logo, they are produced according to strict and strictly controlled standards and they are quite reasonably priced. As a result, over 800 tonnes of bread and almost 300,000 litres of milk were sold with the 'Brucker Land' logo in 2001.

In both cases, people changed their behaviour *and* new technologies,[5] infrastructures or logistics systems were introduced. This twin change is hard to describe completely and concisely through either the technology orientated or the behaviour orientated terminology, as I demonstrate in Chapter 4. A manifest conclusion of this observation is that a vocabulary that cannot successfully describe existing cases should not be expected to excel in describing, ergo suggesting, future ones. The apparent need for a new vocabulary in this regard is met by recent developments in the field of STS, which turn the observation of a circular mutual influence between the technical and the social realm into a positive reference. Rohracher and Ornetzeder, for example, suggest the expression 'fruitful co-evolution between technology design and use' (2002, p74) and Guy and Shove talk about 'co-evolution of social and technical systems' (2000, p131). This language of co-evolution permits not only a more coherent description of the cases in Hasselt and Fürstenfeldbruck, but also enables us to semantically and conceptually grasp the condition of unsustainability in a different way. From this new outlook, fresh options for action become visible that harness the insights of both theory and empirical research and proceed from disavowed to strategic co-evolution, from an unavoidable relationship between technology and behaviour to a constructive partnership.

As a contribution to a general theory of co-evolution towards sustainable development, I try to identify the main *memes* of co-evolution in Chapter 5. Memes are the cultural counterpart of the biological concept of genes or simply the essentials of human artefacts. Ideas, technologies and infrastructures with memes that make them fit for their prevailing selection environment (that is, those tha solve perceived problems for their human environment) are most likely to produced. The foremost meme of co-evolution is the deliberately coordinate evolution of technology and behaviour in a way that makes socially desired behaviour attractive. Other crucial elements of co-evolutionary projects are also identified and systematically scrutinized against the existing body of literature. Among them are the role of public participation, the diplomacy of inventiveness, social embedding strategies of new technologies, the building of critical mass to overcome path dependencies and strategic alliances between designers and users of technologies. These memes are not meant as ready-made ingredients of co-evolution. They are rather a proposal for linguistic modules to use in descriptions of co-evolutionary cases. They might also serve as digestible units of inspiration instead of one bulky chunk of thick description. Lastly, they can be used to systematically construct a definition of co-evolution, which is presented in Chapter 5 (section 'Definition of co-evolution').

In Chapter 6, I anticipate and respond to a number of criticisms of the concept of co-evolution. Among the allegations that try to shake the foundation of co-evolution might be the argument that co-evolution is either too radical or not radical enough, that it is doomed because either professional interests or common sense will blind out co-evolutionary options, and that co-evolution can exacerbate unsustainable practices if people are given too much say in the design of new technologies. Representatives of other academic disciplines could assert that the concept of co-evolution is merely old wine in new bottles, while adherents of the Great Man theory of history could reply that co-evolution depends on mere chance because it only works if there happens to be a great leader around. These arguments are tackled with reference to empirical evidence and theoretical literature, thus enabling a specification of the conditions under which I claim validity for the concept of co-evolution.

One caveat seems appropriate for the claim with which I furnish my predication about co-evolution. It helps to make sense of and to linguistically grasp real world projects that pursue certain approaches to sustainability – probably without calling it co-evolution. At first, I was tempted to write 'without knowing that it is co-evolution', but I refrained because it would suggest that there is a pre-linguistic 'Truth' 'out there' that is co-evolution. Under such an assumption, the cases under scrutiny would have finally discovered it and successfully mirrored it, thus coming closer to the end of history. This is clearly not what I believe. To clarify this in philosophical terms: I am more concerned with the question 'what can we do?' than with the ontology of sustainability and with corresponding epistemological problems. My concern is much more humble and pragmatic, as in William James' conviction that 'the finch with the better adapted beak isn't smarter or nobler than the other finches' (James according to Menand, 2001, p145). Similarly, an idea carrying the meme of co-evolution is not closer to how the world was 'meant to be' than a low emission engine or a low consumption lifestyle. To my mind, it simply has the potential to solve some problems of a society that values the ideal of sustainability. In that regard, my proposal is not at all humble. It advocates what Spinosa et al call 'history making'. From this perspective, people who want to make history have to 'make choices instead of simply following the drift' (1997, p5). Sustainability strategists who put all their hopes into optimized technologies or into a large scale change of behaviour follow the drift of the prevailing sustainability discourse. Those who look up from their isolated efforts and discover options for synergies based on collaborations with the other camp, however, are on the best path to making history.

Notes

1   I do not subscribe to one ultimate definition of this concept. Rather, I argue that we are approaching sustainable development if we achieve improvements of at least one of its main three criteria without impairing any of them: integrity of local and global ecosystems, economic viability and social fairness (as determined in an undistorted public debate).

2   Online query at http://catalog.loc.gov/ on 19 January, 2005. Guided Search = (sustainable AND development) in keyword Anywhere (GKEY).

3   René Kemp during his presentation at the 4S/EASST Conference on 28 August, 2004 in Paris.

4   This expression builds upon Kenneth Boulding's term 'heroic decisions', which is cited in Lovins (1979, p7). I am grateful to Langdon Winner (via email, 17 December, 2002) for bringing this source to my attention.

5   It deserves mention that I do not put technology on a par with tools and machinery, which would be 'to substitute a part for the whole' as Mumford put it (cited in Pursell, 1994, p26).

2

The Nature of the Problem

The technical-fix approach

Advocates of the technology orientated approach to sustainable development usually do not put much trust in the likelihood that individuals will do what they should or refrain from doing what they should not do – with *should* being defined by sustainability experts or politicians. They rather trust in technology because it can, in the technophile's view, take care of many unsustainabilities, and because it is always obedient to its designer. Therefore, they argue that the solution lies in a large scale, qualitatively different industrial revolution focusing on ecoefficiency, high-tech ingenuity and market forces (L. Winner, personal communication, 7 March, 2002). This view is the sequel to the young Lewis Mumford's hope that technology would lead to 'improvements in environmental, social and economic spheres' (according to Ebersole, 1995). Concrete manifestations of this optimism range from incrementally improved resource efficiency of existing technologies such as high mileage cars and co-generation power plants, to radical technological innovations like hydrogen fuelled cars, nuclear fusion, genetic engineering or Supercritical Water Oxidation.[1] Rohracher and Ornetzeder explain that most 'architects, planners and energy experts' are among those for whom 'this technical strategy is the most favourable one' (2002, p73). According to Guy and Shove this approach follows the prevailing 'techno-economic paradigm' (2000, p55) and tries to optimize, but not to transform, the overall socio-technical regime, which consists of:

> *the whole complex of scientific knowledge, engineering practices, production process technologies, product characteristics, skills and procedures, established user needs, regulatory requirements, institutions and infrastructures.* Hoogma et al, 2002, p19

A closer look at the technology orientated spectrum reveals three main strands of thought. Representatives of the first recommend the installation of high efficiency technologies that perform their salutary work regardless of the attention or reaction of human beings. The efficacy of the second strand, in contrast, builds upon a supposedly automatic cooperation of people because technologies leave no non-cooperative alternatives. Activists of the third strand employ more subtle strategies, aiming to develop 'really' attractive technologies, which are then marketed to an intelligent public.

Tacit efficiency – Rendering cooperation irrelevant

Advocates of the first strand of the technology orientated approach purport that the right technologies will take care of what experts perceive as problems in an unobtrusive and tacit way, while they can 'leave the others to their erratic behaviour' (Latour, 1992, p230). Pfaffenberger (1992) mentions modern photocopy machines, which automatically reset themselves to make one copy after an interval of non-use, as a telling example of this strategy. Rohracher and Ornetzeder provide an example from their discipline, green architecture, to explicate the logic of this approach. The technical strategy, they expound, 'improves [the building's] environmental performance without. . . needing the cooperation of users after the technology has been implemented' (2002, p73). This account aptly presents the core idea of this strand of the technology orientated approach, that is, to change the supply side of the sustainability equation. Proponents of this idea believe that the 'right' technology and infrastructure has to be developed by engineers[2] and provided by the market so that people, that is, the demand side, can retain their normal behaviour and still avoid unsustainable outcomes. Their motto is 'pleasure without sorrow' (Steger, 1995), because a change in individuals' lifestyles would not only be impractical but also unnecessary. Wischermann argues along these lines that 'the reduction of resource use, as far as it is the result of the application of technologies, does not impose a certain way of living on humans' (2002). For most ecologically inclined engineers, this is the favoured ideal, which is why they develop ever more sophisticated technologies to eliminate any compromise to torque and horsepower as they design more fuel efficient cars (see Berlin Snell, 2002, p42). Von Weizsäcker, Lovins and Lovins aspire to push the envelope even further in their seminal book *Factor Four: Doubling Wealth, Halving Resource Use* (1997). The appeal of this slogan lies in its promise that reductions in consumption are not only avoidable but that additional amenities are possible on the path to sustainability. The technology orientated approach is, in other words, about 'having your cake and eating it'.

Sustainability experts who pursue this approach share a fascination with *delegation*, regardless of whether or not they use this expression. Latour defines this term as the 'transformation of a major effort into a minor one' (1992, p229). He uses a door closing device as a telling illustration of this phenomenon:

> *When people don't automatically close the door after they have used it, sometimes a human groom is hired who closes the door, or engineers invent technical solutions like mechanical grooms who close the door. In both cases, the closing of the door is displaced, translated, delegated, shifted to a groom.* Latour, 1992, p229

Delegation in Pfaffenberger's sense is 'a technical feature of an artifact [that] is deliberately designed to make up for presumed moral deficiencies in its users'

(1992, p293). This idea assumes that it is possible to arrange major technological improvements behind the scenes so that people do not have to change their habits and behaviour.

Many examples, some of which are presented below, demonstrate the limitations of this approach. One interpretation of Gourna, a small town in Egypt designed by architect Hassan Fathy more than 50 years ago, qualifies as such a case. The buildings in Gourna provided many canny amenities through their bioregionally adapted design. Some of the techniques applied by Fathy included 'vaulted roofs punctured by small openings to direct and cool the prevailing winds, courtyards to give each owner a "private piece of sky", crooked streets to emphasize the intimacy of houses, [and] communal wells to invite neighborly chats' (Sachs, 2000). However, the 'residents have plugged up the wind catches, drastically increasing the indoor temperature in summer and lowering it in winter. They have covered the courtyards, blocking out the sky. They have crammed concrete into the windows [explaining that] "We wanted something modern"' (Sachs, 2000). The above example shows how people willingly pay for the subversion of well intended technologies with reduced convenience because something else is more important to them.[3]

In other cases, individuals attempt to increase their comfort by modifying technology. A corresponding example has been conveyed to me by a student at the University of Texas at Austin who altered the air conditioning system in his research laboratory with pizza cartons and duct tape. He had moved his desk away from the place where it was anticipated to be by the designer of the air conditioning ducts. The new location was in the middle of the cold airflow so that our protagonist improvised a detour for the cold air ('A. Kuhn' [pseudonym], personal communication, 11 October 2002). The same logic of subversion explains how people who live in automatically ventilated high efficiency houses wish 'to have windows slightly open in the sleeping room even in winter [although] ventilation experts contend that such habits are irrational and the effect that would make people sleep well was the low CO_2 concentration and not cold air' (Rohracher and Ornetzeder, 2002, p79).

Cases like these may prompt the conclusion that 'humans are – to put it bluntly – too stupid, too selfish and too neurotic to make wise judgements' (Cornish, 1999, p11). I argue, however, that a major part of the problem rests with the impossibility of separating the main effect of a given technology from its side effects or side meanings, which often cannot be anticipated by the designer. Consider a scenario in which we wake up one day and find hydrogen fuelled engines under every car hood. We would still have to cannibalize our hard-acquired repair skills, change our fuelling routines and switch from our trusted car mechanic to a different repair shop. A telling example in this context is the failed attempt to replace traditional fireplaces in Africa with more wood efficient hearths that would direct heat better to cooking pots by encasing the fire. The main argument against this novelty was that the new fireplaces cooled and darkened the area around the hearth, which thus became unsuitable as gathering place and information hub. The creator of a technology usually focuses exclusively on one main purpose, whereas the users who are exposed to the technology over long periods must arrange their lives around all its effects in order to exploit the pleasant ones and to avoid those that are unpleasant. In light of the aforementioned accounts, I would argue that it is impossible to introduce new technologies that leave users completely unaffected. Hence, it is unrealistic to expect new technologies to perform the sustainability job behind the scenes while people continue doing whatever they did previous to the introduction of the innovation.

This phenomenon is part of the motivation of sustainability inclined technocrats to solve the problem in a remote 'machina sapiens' (Rybczynski [1983], cited in Ebersole, 1995), far away and unnoticed from the end user. A classic example is the installation of nuclear power plants that produce supposedly clean electricity for the oven of a cook who does not even notice, let alone care, where the power comes from. Unfortunately, any centralization of production activities always comes with a centralization of risks, which is rarely legitimized by democratic decisions. And as the level of sophistication of the production process increases, its perspicuity decreases. Risky and opaque technologies, however, are inherently uncanny. Even if some authors claim that this perception is irrational, it is nevertheless the public *perception* that determines the outcome of the next election. The 1998 victory of the German Social Democrat–Green government, for example, was largely due to their promise to phase out nuclear energy. Therefore, the issue of risk has not only a philosophical component, as concluded in Jonas' technology weary *Imperative of Responsibility* (1984), but also a very pragmatic one.

Prescription – Imposing social practices

Even a low-tech solution such as a mechanical door closer presupposes specific behaviour from its users in certain situations. Plumbers carrying a long pipe or travellers carting their luggage through a mechanically closed door probably experienced this implication if the door closed too quickly. In response, they might have learned to move more quickly through the door. This 'behaviour imposed *back* onto the human by non-human delegates' is what Latour (after Akrich) calls prescription (1992, p232). Some designers of technologies make deliberate use of this mechanism, encouraging specific changes of behaviour through prescriptive techniques. Their products make erratic behaviour impossible (domination) or make people want to do what they ought to do – in the designers' view of course (temptation). An example of the former category is the engine that does not ignite unless the driver is buckled up (see Latour, 1992, p232). The latter strategy is employed, for example, in the design of Victorian children's furniture that 'was specifically designed with rigidly straight backs to prevent children from "acquiring a habit of leaning forward, or stooping"' (Forty, cited in Pfaffenberger, 1992, p293). The same idea, translated to the design of buildings, is 'architectural determinism, the belief that architecture controls social relations or behaviour' (Ingersoll, 1996, p122). The most prominent example for this type of social engineering is Jeremy Bentham's panopticon, a circular prison building with the cells built into the curve of the circle facing inward so that the inmates could be observed from the guard tower located in the centre. The constant possibility of being watched was meant to coerce the prisoners to permanent compliant behaviour. Bentham's model has made a considerable career as some penitentiaries have actually been built according to this design.

Similarly, urban form determinism is what Thomas More (1478–1535) envisioned for Amaurot in Utopia, Gottfried Feder for the 'New City' in Nazi Germany,[4] Le Corbusier for Paris (see Figure 2.1) and Robert Moses for the beaches of Long Island.[5] Moses is said to have constructed the bridges from New York to Long Island intentionally low in order to keep public buses and their typical users, low-income blacks, away from the beaches (Winner, 1980). Although the intentionality of this design is subject to spirited debates in the STS community (e.g. Joerges, 1999a, b; Woolgar and Cooper, 1999; Latour, 2004), it serves well as an exemplar of a school of thought that considers architects and planners 'not as decorator but as organizer of life' (Ginsburg 1924, cited in Chan-Magomedow, 1983, p581). In this view of progress, only an elite, the experts, are endowed with knowledge about 'the one best way' (Postrel, 1998, p16) towards what they perceive as the ideal state; hence their disinclination to tedious democratic decision finding processes. This position may result from impatience, from a pragmatic interest in job security or from disciplinary solipsism.[6] Regardless of the motivation behind this expertocratic logic, it always has a 'totalitarian tendency of positivist utopianism' (Bisk, 2002, p24), which explains why Ingersoll rejects it as an 'anathema to the ideals of the liberal city' (1996, p122).[7] Sometimes, Benthamite utilitarians might argue, the means are legitimized by the end – for example, when the goal is sustainable development. Barber (1984) calls this disposition liberal realism, which is characterized by suppression of conflict for the benefit of the maximally effective provision of common goods. In this conceptual perspective, wise leaders skip the messy discourse of democracy in order to get those things done that have to be done. This position is actually not uncommon among 'environmentalists [who] expect enlightened dictators to bite the bullet of technological reform. . . if a greedy populace shirks its duty' (Feenberg, 1995b, p12). In this view, the authorship of artefacts comes with enormous power to infringe upon the freedom of choice.

Putting normative democratic qualms aside for the moment, the pragmatic question remains, whether such strategies succeed. In many, if not most, cases, the patronized human objects will find ways to regain their subjecthood by means of some creative or sullen form of subversion, disobedience, modification, sabotage, counterstatements (Pfaffenberger, 1992), antiprogrammes (Latour, 1992), on the election ballot or – to come back to the example of Victorian children's furniture – at the dinner table. A defiant child, for instance, could easily bear the inconvenience of sitting 'wrongly' on the 'right' chair, at least for the crucial hour when guests are visiting. This phenomenon of people voting with their feet is also known to many transportation planners:

After turning a two-way road into a one-way street . . . automobilists often display enormously innovative potentials in finding alternative routes through narrow backstreets. Traffic engineers might, of course, block this evasive reaction with additional measures but there is always a next move on the part of the citizen. Brand, 2005b

Source: Le Corbusier, from Urbanisme, Paris, 1922

Figure 2.1 *Le Corbusier's Plan Voisin for Paris*

In short, people can 'easily subvert the designer's agency inscribed into the artefact' (S. Moore, personal communication, 17 December, 2002). These arguments reveal that the prescriptive approach not only suffers from insufficient democratic legitimization but also from insufficient (long-term) success.

Win-win-win – Propagating attractive technologies

I have so far described two manifestations of the technology orientated approach to sustainability. First, the idea of installing efficient technologies behind people's backs, thus requiring neither changes of habits or behaviour nor abdication of convenience and fun. Second, the attempt to impose technologies that prescribe certain actions onto the users by leaving no other choice than to behave 'properly'. A third, and probably the prevailing, manifestation tries to avoid the subvertability and the lack of democracy of the preceding approaches by giving users the choice whether or not to use new technologies. Its proponents strive to design technologies that are presumably attractive enough – in terms of expense, convenience, pleasure and symbolic value – to be employed voluntarily by the average citizen while simultaneously yielding some common good and business opportunities. Solar collectors, for example, help preserve resources, reduce the energy bill for house owners and provide revenue for their producers; a classic win-win-win example. If the perceived individual benefit is too marginal, perhaps because of too long a payback period, the diffusion strategy is likely to fail because the number of people willing to make heroic choices for the sake of the common good is clearly limited. In market language, many 'good' technologies 'remain economically unrealistic on a large scale' (Ingersoll, 1996, p122). Ironically, this is the result of the deliberately built-in democratic touch within this third strategy: individuals retain a choice whether or not to make use of the technology.

Assuming that a given technological solution does serve the private interest better than its competitors, shouldn't it be taken for granted that people will discover this advantage and choose accordingly? Empirical evidence disenchants this expectation, thus supporting Guy and Shove's conclusion that 'the business of getting the "message" of science through to practice is far from easy' (2000, p52). This must be a blow to the optimism of idealistic modernists and to their belief in human ingenuity and the teleological nature of discoveries,[8] which they work to transform into universally applicable technologies. If their products fail on the market despite their 'objective' superiority and attractiveness, their explanation tends to be that 'some actors (i.e. scientists) know the truth about a problem, while other actors (i.e. non-scientists) do not and obstruct the solution in different ways' (Hillmo according to Guy and Shove, 2000, p63). A more blunt explanation for the turbulent path from the design workshop to the household states 'that end users' ignorance is at the root of the problem' (Guy and Shove, 2000, p61). How else can it be explained that something as simple as insulation, with its fantastic amortization performance, is so infrequently installed in homes in the UK? (Guy and Shove, 2000). Construction companies report that potential house buyers 'are not interested [in extra insulation] because they can't see it' (Guy and Shove, 2000, p106). A seemingly logical lesson from these examples suggests that 'individual decision makers [do not opt for] informed rational action' (Guy and Shove, 2000, p64).

The self-evident solution to this problem is to educate and to persuade people. This is the juncture where designers make 'appeals to social scientists to help lubricate the public acceptability of science and technological change' (Rip, 1994, footnote 9) that presumably will serve the common interest in environmental protection. This role is described by Guy and Shove as '"end-of-pipe" social science' (2000, p71). Those who accept this role tacitly subdue their professional role in hastening obedience to the reign of the technological paradigm, thus missing out on the opportunity to question its dominance in the first place.

But even if people are well informed, well persuaded and if they possess the (especially calculative) skills to recognize win-win-win potentials, they still need the willingness to leave beaten, but still good enough, paths, the time to organize change and the financial means to make an up-front investment. And even if all these conditions are met, further problems remain. One of them is the distortion of the free market through subsidies favouring unsustainable practices such as the burning of fossil fuels; an issue frequently overlooked by some apolitical techno-utopianists. This problem has long been unmasked, which is why most national sustainability plans aim at reducing these subsidies, at least on paper. Moreover, even if market distortions are not the problem, the market itself can emerge as an obstacle to the implementation of the 'best' technology. This is because the market, not the laboratory, is the place where the 'best' technology is determined. Schwartz Cowan provides a convincing example of this phenomenon in *How the Refrigerator Got its Hum* (1985). She demonstrates how, in the early 20th century, the electric refrigerator was pushed to market victory over its gas driven competitor despite its lack of compelling technical advantages. A major explanatory factor in this business success story is the alliance forged between the producers of electric refrigerators with the electricity utility companies, who had a vested interest in selling electricity. Their combined financial power permitted a more aggressive marketing campaign for the electric refrigerator than the producers of gas powered refrigerators could afford. In this holistic and more realistic view, the system around the humming, the electric refrigerator proved to be stronger in its socio-economic environment.

Further deliberations illuminate that neither people's ignorance nor market mechanisms alone should be held accountable for the insufficient success of the win-win-win approach. It is simply hard to provide technologies that are attractive enough with respect to the complex constellations of individuals' legitimate priorities. Most people dislike technologies that are noisy, aesthetically displeasing, difficult to operate, require initial training, frequent maintenance or a change of established routines – even if they save some money.[9] Ironically, if technologies are made cheap through economies of scale, many people do not like them either, because their design, targeted for the average user, does not account for the 'diversity of human practice' (Guy and Shove, 2000, p15). Why, then, should they buy something that would have undesired consequences for their social practice, something that implies 'perceived restrictions on user autonomy'? (Rohracher and Ornetzeder, 2002, p78). In other words, people usually have good reasons – however 'rational' – not to purchase technologies, not to use them or to modify them, often to the detriment of their efficiency performance.[10] Sometimes technology designers provide a deliberate option to modify the patronizing potential of their products such as my word processing software. with some tinkering in the *customize* tab, for example, it is possible to deactivate the auto-correction feature and thus to begin a sentence with a lower case letter. Designers of office buildings utilize the same logic when they allow users to control the room temperature with a moderately hidden knob, as is the case in a certain department of the University of Texas at Austin.[11] Yet, the room temperature is set too low for the skirt dressed administrative assistants because the dean is supposed to wear a jacket and he does not want to sweat. Consequently, the low-level employees find their remedy in individual space heaters, even while outside temperatures reach a sizzling 104 degrees Fahrenheit ('E. Johnson', personal communication, 10 October 2002). This example shows again how the legitimate complexity of priorities can obstruct the recommended application of seemingly attractive technologies.

Disenchantment I – Wrapping it up

Now we can put on record the following shortcomings of the three strands of the technology orientated approach. Attempts to secretly improve the gears in the black box usually do not go completely unnoticed or they change side effects of existing technologies, which individuals have learned to exploit. In reaction, people often look for ways to subvert or modify new technologies. A typical counter reaction of technology designers is to build prescriptions into their products, that is, mechanisms that leave no other choice for users but to behave in a certain way. As I have tried to demonstrate, this approach is not only undemocratic but often, at least in the long run, not very successful. Common reasons for failures of the prescription strategy lie in the capability of people to find even more sophisticated ways to alter technologies, in their willingness to put up with the negative consequences of 'improper' behaviour, or in the inability of static, imposed technologies to adapt to external changes. The third strand of the technology orientated approach tries to avoid the shortcomings of the other two but runs into the well-known problem of seeming user ignorance. Attempts to educate people and to market new technologies to them might alleviate this problem but the obstacles of market distortions and vested interests among established market players still must be overcome. In addition, such attempts fail to account for the complexity of people's priorities, which in many cases are absolutely legitimate.

The list of drawbacks of the technology orientated approach cannot be concluded without references to at least two more problems, shared by all three strands. One of them is the *rebound effect*, described by Radermacher as the 'subsequent erosion of the positive potential of technological innovation by increases in population size and overall activities and the concomitant increase in consumption of material and energy' (1999). In other words, efficiency gains are overcompensated by absolute growth. A well-known example of this phenomenon is the catalytic converter, whose positive effect per mile driven has already been nullified by the absolute increase in the number of cars (Roth and Altwegg, 2001, p13) and by the environmental problems caused by the platinum mining industry. The mathematics behind the rebound effect is governed by the logarithmic law of growth: an increase in efficiency by 100 per cent is consumed by a 3 per cent annual growth within 24 years.[12] Increased efficiency is sometimes even used – or abused – as financial or moral justification for consuming larger quantities of a given product that has just been made more resource efficient and as an excuse for deferring the improvement of '*system* efficiency' (Hoogma et al, 2002, p125, emphasis added). The strategy to make more efficient use of a scarce resource has another built-in problem that is common to all three strands of the technology orientated approach: it does not tackle problems that relate to other resources and health or equity issues. Hydrogen fuelled cars, for example, cannot prevent noise, accidents, sprawl, congestion, asphalt deserts, big box retail, low mobility for senior citizens, etc.

This critical but hopefully fair assessment of the technology orientated approach to sustainable development is rather disenchanting. In light of its serious problems, advocates of this approach are invited to acknowledge that their efforts to produce the right technologies have not brought us much closer to a sustainable society. Even the World Business Council for Sustainable Development states, 'technology enables change but cannot be the sole driver of innovation' (Brown et al, 2000, p11). With respect to urban planning, I share Pezzoli's conclusion that 'reaching an appropriate urban-ecological balance is not a purely technical issue'

(1998, p346) and Hoogma et al's finding that 'there are no technical fixes to the problem of sustainability. Behavioural changes are needed too' (2002, pp180–181).

The behavioural-fix approach[13]

Members of the second main camp of the sustainability discourse decidedly reject the idea of a 'technical fix' and argue instead for a 'cultural or social fix' (Hoogma et al, 2002, p2). They claim that the allure of efficient technologies implies beguiling but false promises that cloud from our view the obvious fact that human weaknesses are the prime cause of the unsustainable state of the world: lack of reflection or education in the eyes of the optimist and insatiability or laziness in a more misanthropic version. The self-suggesting remedy is thus a mix of education, rational reasoning, demonstration, incentives, persuasion and laws, intended to change people's behaviour toward more enlightened, more moral or even heroic choices and to a new lifestyle of sufficiency. This term implies a deliberate refutation of the technophilic dogma of efficiency. The latter is not trusted by behaviour orientated strategists as a successful means to keep our fast-paced society on the tracks toward sustainability. Most know by heart the litany of shortcomings of the technology orientated approach as expounded above. They are frustrated or even scared by what they call the Faustian nature of technology, which makes it necessary to devise ever new technical solutions for problems caused by earlier generations of technologies. Fear of technology is often called Neo-Luddism, with reference to Ned Ludd and his comrades, who chose violent modes of resistance to the encroachment of job-killing machines in the 19th century. Albery and Wienrich (1999) queue in these technophobic ranks with the title of their compendium of social innovations: *Social Dreams, Technological Nightmares*. Bisk paraphrases the same idea in only slightly less polemic language: 'The Postmodern critique identified the simplistic hubris of Modernism and showed how this hubris resulted in catastrophe in ecology, politics, economy, etc.' (2002, p22). The logical solutions for such antimodernists is to halt the technological arms race, to stop developing GMOs and nanotechnology and to start buying organically grown produce from small, local farmers. The cliché climax of this vision is a pre-industrial state in harmony with nature where we will reach almost Buddhist contentment and discover that we have simply liberated ourselves from the slavery of consumerism.

   Representatives of three main strands of thought can be identified under the behaviour orientated approach: those who pursue a carrot and stick strategy, those who are willing to manipulate people's desires, and those who try to convince people through rational discourse about the necessity or attractiveness of changing their behaviour.

Carrots and sticks – Pushing and pulling the societal cart

Adherents of the carrot and stick approach, also described as a push and pull approach, do not place much stock in the ability of people to be enlightened and/ or in the link between insight and voluntary action. Therefore, they conclude, it is necessary to intervene with a decisive helping hand. Attractive incentives in the form of financial or other rewards can be tied as carrots on the pull side of the cart named society. The stick on the push side corresponds to an absence of rewards at best and to various forms of punishment at worst.[14] The former version is promoted in Agenda 21: 'Some progress has begun in the use of appropriate economic instruments to influence consumer behaviour. These instruments include environmental charges and taxes, deposit/refund systems, etc. This process should be encouraged' (UNCED, 1992, chapter 4.25).

An inherent disadvantage to this approach is its systematic discrimination against the low-income sector of the population. This argument, rotated by 180 degrees, means that wealthy people can simply buy themselves out of the desired behaviour. Eventually, the economically underprivileged might suffer severe consequences such as losing their jobs because the daily commute by car becomes prohibitive if taxes on gasoline reach heights of effective leverage and if public transport is not an affordable and viable alternative.

Another problematic feature of this approach is the role of the coachman who determines the direction of the horse cart at his discretion. In analogous political settings, someone decides who gets punished and who gets rewarded and for what kind of behaviour. Here, the carrot and stick approach reveals an authoritarian flavour that is not usually embraced by its advocates but ultimately is exculpated as the only means to meet the end of escaping global collapse in a necessarily timely fashion. The stick version of this approach is more dangerous, as its extrapolation leads to a hypothetical culmination in what has been called eco-fascism:

> *A Postmodernist would meet this challenge [sustainability] by calling to lower the world's population from 6 billion to 2 billion . . . and to 'educate' the remaining 2 billion to adopt the way of life of a European village before Charlemangne . . . in the Rousseau/Robespierre tradition of 'forcing people to be free'– a chilling oxymoron that began with the guillotine and ended with the gulag.* Bisk, 2002, p24

Even though this scenario is vastly exaggerated, it makes clear that an aggressive carrot and stick approach can easily turn into an object of legitimate criticism. A moderate version in a democratic environment faces the reciprocal shortcoming of achieving only marginal results, because every democratically elected government knows that if it steers the cart into too sharp a curve, it is likely to lose support on election day. This almost happened to the German Red–Green government in 2002 after it implemented the first step of an ecological tax reform that increased the price of gasoline by approximately 3 per cent. The narrowness of the remaining corridor of choices that lies between ineffectiveness and the possibility of being voted out makes this approach a less than promising candidate for the 'silver bullet to sustainability' (S. Moore, personal communication, 23 January 2002). A loophole out of this dilemma could be an education programme that would make people want the government to make them want what they ought to want [sic]. This approach is described in more detail in the next two sections.

Truer pleasures – Making people want what they ought to want

A slight variation of the aforementioned approach still does not trust in people's intellectual and/or moral capacities and still is elitist but operates less openly. While the carrot and stick approach does not conceal the attempt to steer people towards actions that they do not genuinely prefer, the truer pleasures approach intends to make people want what they ought to want, that is, to change people's 'real' desires and to redefine what they perceive as pleasurable. For this purpose, it is mandatory to change people's value systems so they can better appreciate non-conventional and non-monetary things like health, autonomy over how they spend their time, tasty food, physical exercise, a feeling of unity with mother earth or a clear conscience.[15] Along the same lines Agenda 21 emphasizes the necessity of 'reinforcing values that support sustainable consumption' (UNCED, 1992, chapter 4.25). Both ethically and pragmatically motivated agents of this approach strive to act on this call by convincing people that they can and should redefine their self-interests. Most respective arguments contain the claim, at least implicitly, that the actual issue is about re-discovering and unearthing the true and pristine self-interest of human beings, which has been buried by our manipulative, consumerist culture. Accordingly, if we adopt this enlightened self-interest, then will we behave the way we ought to behave; we will find a new quality of life through which enjoyment and satisfaction is possible with less consumption. I found this stance, to my surprise, even in the responses of business representatives. Some members of the World Business Council for Sustainable Development from the Philippines are reported to 'believe in a need to revert back to "more simple living" and "real" pleasures' (Brown et al, 2000, p44).

Some authors back the feasibility of this approach with empirical evidence such as the Index for Sustainable Economic Welfare, which demonstrates the weak correlation between consumption and perceived happiness beyond a minimum level of consumption necessary to meet basic needs (Koeppl, 2001, p12). It fits into this logic that the suicide rate in Switzerland, one of the richest countries in the world, is almost ten times higher than in the Philippines, which is among the poorest nations.[16]

Strong, the initiator of the 1992 United Nations Conference for Environment and Development (UNCED) in Rio de Janeiro, provides anecdotal evidence as he promotes 'lifestyles of "sophisticated modesty" [as practised by] people in enclave groups, such as monastic communities' (2001, p25). Among the groups that include this approach in their strategic arsenal are many non-governmental organizations, as well as companies selling ecologically friendly products and research institutes exploring the benefits of switching from quantity to quality of consumption. The renowned Wuppertal Institute, for instance, not only has a research division for Factor Four efficiency but also for 'new models of prosperity'.[17] The common denominator of most sufficiency groups is that they:

fend vehemently. . . against the allegation of preaching asceticism. . . [They argue:] 'To live differently means to enjoy more consciously, it does not mean to renounce enjoyment. It is not true that only scratchy cloths and sandals are environmentally friendly. Sustainable lifestyles should not be associated with renunciation but with joy, not with grey but with all natural colours, not with prohibitions but with acceptance of life and with sensual pleasure'. Enquete Commission of the German Parliament cited in Steger, 1995, p26

But how to actually get there? Related techniques range from blunt brainwashing to advertisement attacks, from the attempt to parent the Soviet citizenry to 'new men' to the BBC project New Home, New Life, 'an entertaining and captivating radio soap opera [that] aims to impart educational messages. . . about self-help, self-reliance and sustainability' (United Nations Office for Project Services/ Afghanistan Rural Rehabilitation Programme, 2001). The former end of this spectrum clearly has the indigestible, antidemocratic flavour of manipulation, whereas the educational intent of the latter is more palatable – the border between them is, however, blurry. Even if one were willing to put aside the ideological half of these concerns, the pragmatic half would linger. The Soviet experiment, after all, has failed.

Steger is not a believer in this concept as effective strategy toward sustainability. He deliberately phrases his faithlessness polemically: 'Here, sustainable growth turns into a village idyll [with an] eschatological desire for harmony' (1995, p26). The truer pleasures advocates, however, have a typically missionary argument against such charges: 'you can't say that you won't like it until you've given it a serious try'. But who wants to jump first into such a commitment that is hard to undo if it is really serious? This severe first-mover disadvantage will reappear further below where it is analysed as a special version of the prisoners' dilemma.

Rational arguments – Trusting the enlightenable citizen

The third strand of the behaviour orientated approach relies on suasion to change people's behaviour through rational arguments about the necessity of change. Its radical adherents share an early critical theory position, where the infrastructure and technological regime in which people are located appear as the result of power structures that cannot be changed with the given means and in the necessary time frame. Therefore, change has to emanate from the bottom – from the enlightened people, even if they have to fight an uphill battle against the 'wrong' structures. A slogan of this process could be phrased 'if the powerful elite do not change the rules of the game, we simply play it differently'. Even some established elite entities support this idea of leaving the responsibility with the people. Thus, they hope, it might be possible to approach sustainability without changing the capitalistic rules. It is therefore not surprising that this attitude can be found in Agenda 21. Chapter 4 exhorts governments to:

> *encourage the emergence of an informed consumer public and [to] assist individuals and households to make environmentally informed choices [by] providing information on the consequences of consumption choices and behaviour so as to encourage demand for environmentally sound products and use of products.* UNCED, 1992, chapter 4.22

Clearly, an indispensable assumption of governmental and non-governmental adherents of this strand is that the masses *can* be enlightened, that their awareness can be raised through rational arguments. Correspondingly, 'many educational efforts and information strategies are targeting attitudes of users and aim at behavioural changes [such as] lowering temperature in rooms not often used. . . avoiding waste, using public transport' (Rohracher and Ornetzeder, 2002, p73). Some respond to such an appeal because they want to capitalize on monetary advantages like a reduced energy bill. Unfortunately, such potentials seem not to be pervasive; otherwise our unsustainabilities would be solved and you would not be wading through this book. But this was not the last card of those who put their hopes in rational arguments. They rather claim two more trumps: one is the idea of making people judge new social practices not on the basis of monetary criteria alone but through valuing the alternative pleasures they entail. I am afraid this card has already been played – *out*played in my view – above, but here is the second trump card: it acknowledges the impairment of conventional convenience but relies on ethical arguments for the sake of clean air, God's creation, future generations or the population of Bangladesh's low-lying coast.

As rational and valid as these arguments may be they rarely resonate with an individual's sensory perceptions; or *not yet* as in the case of future generations; or not any more because most industrialized countries have indeed succeeded in resolving many problems that stink, hurt and look ugly, while longer-term problems of sustainability have often not been alleviated. Some environmentalists perceive this as perfidious because 'the industry solved problems and thus cuts the ground from under the feet of further criticism' (Steger, 1995, p26). The author of this assessment underpins his argument with empirical findings from 'opinion polls [that] show repeatedly that most citizens perceive improvements in their personal environment and that deteriorations are seen more on the global level, further away and more in the long run. Perception is reality' (Steger, 1995, p26). With this phenomenon in mind, Beck asks the striking question 'what would happen if radioactivity itched?' (1997, p71). As long as it doesn't and as long as we can go fishing after watching a TV documentary about the truly or allegedly detrimental state of the earth it will be difficult to reach the kind of mass-enlightenment required to trigger voluntary pre-emptive action. Those who couple rational arguments with ethical imperatives should at least be aware that their claim has to include a positive resolution of this problem. They may then proceed to argue that heroic choices are plain necessary to stop our fatal trajectory towards global collapse. Waiving permanent and instant satisfaction appears then as no price for the survival of *Homo sapiens*. It is mostly environmental zealots who express this 'truth' of unavoidable asceticism and renunciation but even the *Brundtland Report* is not free of this doctrine: 'We do not pretend that the process [toward sustainability] is easy or straightforward. Painful choices have to be made' (World Commission on Environment and Development, 1987, p9). Therefore, everyone has to do his or her share. Only then, the argument goes, can we overcome the unsustainable 'ideology of comfort and the tyranny of custom' (O'Toole, 1995).[18]

A survey conducted in Germany gives advocates of heroic choices reason for hope; it reveals that about 50 per cent of interviewees believe that 'everybody should be willing to accept a lower standard of living for the sake of the environment' (Bundesumweltministerium, 1998, p81). Rohracher and Ornetzeder question the practical relevance of these findings in very diplomatic terms: 'As it often turns out, even if one manages to raise environmental consciousness, the links between attitude and behaviour are rather weak' (2002, p73). Gillwald in comparison states her scepticism more directly because she thinks it is 'not very likely that the majority of the population would practise strict ecological lifestyles' (1995, p36). Winner shares this assessment and warns 'you can't ask people to make heroic choices' (personal communication, 7 March 2002). The same argument is presented by Bisk in polemically exaggerated disguise: 'Frantic, self-righteous calls by neurotic dropouts to give up soap and hot water and live in teepees are not likely to have wide appeal' (2002, p25).

Another problem saps the effectiveness of the rational arguments approach because individuals tend to ask, 'why should I, of all people, make the first step?'. This is a legitimate and age-old concern, a manifestation of the so-called prisoners' dilemma (see Taylor, 1976) that effects a massive first-mover disadvantage. In the context of sustainability it leaves the majority of people hesitant to ride a bike to work, to buy fair trade coffee, to install solar collectors, because they have no guarantee that others will act accordingly. In fact, most people are willing to do their share if they are ensured that there will be no free riders who benefit from the cleaner air, pesticide free drinking water and so forth that they 'produced'. In addition, these public goods will not materialize unless a significant share of the population acts accordingly. This allows for the widely deployed excuse 'I alone won't make a difference anyway'. Not only every individual but also all organizations, governments and businesses are affected by this dilemma. I find it therefore improbable that the current tragedy of the commons, that is, 'the tendency of individuals to over-exploit publicly-owned assets' (Newcomb, 2001), will be resolved with the rational argument approach within a satisfactory time frame.

Disenchantment II – Wrapping it up

The issues expounded above pose serious questions to Mugerauer (1996), who subsumes the main ideas of the behaviour orientated approach to sustainability: 'If we take seriously that we may be able to actually transform current values, beliefs and practices into a new way of behaving, then sustainability may be possible'. The above discussion outlined specific shortcomings of the various strands and all of them share at least two crucial flaws. One is a top-down notion of varying severity and transparency, which places governments, leaders, organizations, preachers, zealots, ascetics, prophets or educators – depending on the school of thought – at the Olympus of enlightenment. The definition of enlightenment, however, is usually made at the clouded peak and unfortunately there is more than one summit. On each the masters defend their authority or, in secular terms, professorship, renown or simply their job. The resulting clutter leaves the people in yet more confusion. The other flaw stems from the plainly pragmatic economic dominance of the technological paradigm. Throngs of companies harness the power of their capital, advertising personnel and lobbyists for a non-behaviour orientated approach because it yields a chance for profit whereas renunciation, whether heroic or joyful, is sheer poison to the economy. Consumption and sustainability could nevertheless become bedfellows if the emphasis of modern consumption switched from material goods to personal services. There is hardly anything unsustainable in a massage from the therapist in the neighbourhood twice a week. It is an unfortunate feature of regular massages that they do not make as good a status symbol as a new car.

Ringing bells

The preceding elucidation of the technology and the behaviour orientated approach to sustainable development may not be untinged by my own interest. After all, my core argument rests on the premise that the mainstream sustainability discourse is indeed polarized with respect to these positions. If no one else shared this perception I could either claim a lone and ineffective genius status or rethink my position. In this regard I am grateful for comments that challenge the cogency of – and thus made me rethink – my perception of a divided sustainability debate. Glaser, for example mentions that the dichotomy I identify 'can be considered overcome in the field of technology research for at least 10 years', but he adds what I would have added: environmental 'policy has a predilection for simple solutions' (J. Glaser, via email, 9 December 2003), which presupposes the emergence and maintenance of simplified problem definitions. Therefore, it is difficult for holistic notions to trickle from scholarly journals to parliaments, newspapers and dinner tables.

I have also encountered the argument that typical policy measures such as regulation, taxes and market incentives transcend the simple black-and-white structure of technology versus behaviour. My point here is a little more complex and is presented in detail in Chapter 6 (section 'Established professions will undermine co-evolution'), but in order to avoid readers dropping the thread of the argument I decided to anticipate its core ideas. First, mainstream political measures can usually be boiled down to one of the two halves of the sustainability discourse: they intend to speed up the development and adoption of new technologies or they are designed to trigger a change of social practices. Second, many such measures are indeed crucial as *part* of the solution but they are insufficient as stand-alone programmes. Third, they are only at the disposal of national or international policy-making bodies whereas the focus of this book is the regional and local level. Fourth, many policy programmes do contain technical and social components but too often in an *additive* logic: technological improvements plus more prudent choices. What I will argue for in the remainder of this book, however, is a *synergistic* relationship of technical and social change. Fifth, I do not claim that nobody has ever overcome the dichotomy. On the contrary, there are cases of synergistically synchronized technical and social changes that inspired the genesis of this book in the first place.

Apart from these home-made thoughts there are also external sources providing corroboration for the perception of a discourse split. There are those colleagues who report that my description of the sustainability discourse rang their bells; and there are many others who have rang my bells as I was looking for orientation and structure in the babel of the debate. Among them is Hellman whose cartoon, presented in Chapter 1 (Figure 1.1), is the most instantly comprehensible illustration of the contemporary debate that I have come across. Hoogma et al put the same impression in words: 'We tend to call for either a technical or a social fix' but they are quick to add their scepticism 'whether we are indeed trapped within these two contending positions' (2002, p3). This dichotomy is expressed in more theoretical parlance by Ingersoll, who perceives two main strands of thought in the search for 'the reduction of entropy, [ranging] from nostalgic retreats to high-tech assertions' (1996, p122). He elucidates the former as a 'trend, which involves a righteous retreat from industrial and metropolitan civilization. . . [that] belongs to the world-weary tradition of monasticism' and the latter as a 'technological utopia [with] technocratic implications' (Ingersoll, 1996, p122). Of the same tenor is Winner's interpretation of the two favoured options to approaching sustainability: one makes use of 'eco-efficiency, technical ingenuity, market forces and high tech' whereas the other is rather a 'local, small scale democratic approach' (L. Winner, personal communication, 7 March 2002). And according to Feenberg, there is a similar split among environmentalists. One group:

> *argue[s] for technical changes that would . . . enhance efficiency in broad terms by reducing harmful and costly side effects of technology. [Members of the other group] hold out the pious hope that people will turn from economic to spiritual values in the face of the mounting problems of industrial society.* Feenberg, 1995b, pp12–13[19]

This dichotomy within the sustainability discourse is also perceived outside North America and outside the academic realm. Busse, for example, writes in a German newspaper about the debate over whether we have to practise renunciation or whether the ecological improvement of goods will suffice (2002, p45). Albery and Wienrich (1999) exploit this dichotomy even for the sloganistic title of their book *Social Dreams, Technological Nightmares*. This sort of polemics is unlikely to be welcomed by technophilic advocates within the discussion, which is why Steger attributes communication problems between industry and environmentalists to this divide in the discourse: 'One group talks about reduction of emissions, the other talks in effect about lifestyles and the society of the future'(1995, p26). Postrel, who herself stands firmly anchored at the technology end of the spectrum, implicitly confirms this dichotomy by pointing at the diametrical end of her world-view, what she refers to as the 'radical greens [with their] popular, semiserious slogan "Back to Pleistocene!"' (1998, p12). This charge is well known among sustainability activists, which is why Quinn defensively declares that the task of sustainability efforts 'is not to reach back but to reach forward' (1996, p250). However, he is weary of the technophilic notion of progress, which he denunciates as a philosophy of 'taker cultures'. What he advocates instead is the promotion of a 'leaver culture', an ecologically less intrusive society such as that which preceded the 'takers' (Quinn, 1996, p250).[20] By means of this binary classification of human cultures, Quinn describes the dichotomy within the sustainability literature only in new terms. Perhaps the strongest support for my perception of dichotomy of the sustainability discourse comes from Costanza, who talks about 'two basic world-views . . . [which] have been described in many ways . . . [whose] distinction has to do with one's degree of faith in technological progress' (2000). The main characteristics of these two world-views, as perceived by Costanza, are presented in Table 2.1. With these descriptions, Costanza develops compelling visions of how the world could look in the year 2100 if either of the two world-views succeeded. According to these scenarios, we will end up in a peaceful, 'Star Trek' world if the technological optimists are right and successful. If, however, the technological sceptics are correct in their assumptions and if they succeed with their political ideas, we will live in a harmonious 'Eco-topia' (Costanza, 2000).[21]

Table 2.1 *Characteristics of the basic world-views according to Costanza*

Technological optimist	Technological sceptic
Technical progress can deal with any future challenge	Technical progress is limited
Competition	Cooperation
Humans dominant over nature	Humans in partnership with nature
Everybody for themselves	Partnership with others
The market as guiding principle	The market as servant of larger goals

Source: Costanza, 2000, Table I

Guy and Shove (2000) make an especially interesting observation in this regard. They looked at the slogans used in British government campaigns to encourage citizens to conserve energy and found that their emphasis has varied over time between technophilic and behaviour orientated approaches, thus implicitly substantiating the perception of a dichotomy:

> The 'Save it' campaign of the 1970s . . . was about turning off lights, lowering thermostats and cutting back on demand. . . The next wave . . . 'Get more for your monergy', was about the promotion of efficiency, not conservation per se. Rather than cutting back, the goal was to maintain expected levels of service. . . The third phase. . . 'Saving the Earth Begins at Home'. Guy and Shove, 2000, p13

tended to target human behaviour again.

Latour's observation of a discursive dichotomy reaches far beyond the sustainability discourse to a general pattern of how people try to make the world a better place. He calls this the 'age-old Mumfordian choice . . . either to discipline the people or to substitute for the unreliable people a . . . groom' (Latour, 1992, p230). With his flair for felicitous phrases, Latour distinguishes between the adjectives intra-somatic and extra-somatic in this regard. The former signifies approaches that target innate human traits, morality and comprehension, as the agents of socially desirable results. Approaches of the latter kind, in contrast, 'never rely on undisciplined men, but always on safe, delegated non-humans' (Latour, 1992, p246). I take it from statements like these that not only mavericks share the perception of a dichotomous trait in the discourse about sustainable development. On the contrary, it seems that the distinction between smart technologies and heroic choices has already helped a number of authors find an orientation in this discourse. If the hitherto presented accounts ring a bell with some readers, it has proved its usefulness once more.

The seamless web

A linguistic tool that has proven useful to gauge a certain object in no way implies any statement about the usefulness of the object itself. For the matter at hand, the perception of dichotomous traits in the sustainability discourse does not say anything about the usefulness of the dichotomy itself. As indicated above, it seems that this polarity is rather unfortunate and that adamant advocates of either side are only 'watching half the court during a tennis game' (Latour, 1992, p247). This one-sided perception of the arena is usually accompanied by a biased perception of the dynamics taking place on it. In tennis lingo, some spectators only see balls flying from left to right while others pay attention only to balls travelling in the opposite direction. Those who pay undue attention to how the technical realm influences the social realm are usually referred to as technological determinists. The reciprocal position, which grants too much emphasis to how society shapes technology, is known as technological voluntarism. Many empirically informed studies have shown that neither position is able to describe fully what happened in the history of socio-technological development. Rather, it seems that society and technology are mutually linked and constantly interacting in a 'seamless web' (Hughes, 1988). Along these lines, Bijker declares 'the social shaping of a technical artifact and the social impact of that technical artifact' fundamentally inseparable (1992, p97). Guy and Shove describe on the same grounds 'the inter-dependence of socio-technical change' (2000, p7).

The following example, modified after Latour (1992), may provide a glimpse of an everyday life manifestation of this circular phenomenon. People do not like draughts, which is why they invented the door. Unfortunately, not everyone closes doors reliably, hence, engineers devise simple, mechanical door closers. However, these impede plumbers carrying long pipes, who wedge a cotter under the door. The now permanently open door causes draughts again. Therefore, engineers install motion detectors, which open the door for employees and strangers alike. A card reader could produce some relief from this problem but would not please the plumber and other legitimate visitors, etc. Similar games of action, re-action, re-re-action and so forth are played in every domain of human activity, including architecture, urban design and sustainable development.

The dynamics of this ineluctable and ceaseless interaction between designers and users of technology or infrastructure have been termed by Latour as the 'programs and antiprograms of action' (1992, p251). Pfaffenberger similarly describes these phenomena as 'technological drama. . .to emphasize the performative nature of technological "statements" and "counterstatements". . . and to emphasize that the discourse involved is not the argumentative and academic discourse of a text but the symbolic media of myth. . . and ritual' (1992, p286). See Figure 2.2 for an overview of the various terminologies within the general sustainability discourse.

Even though the process toward sustainable development is certainly not exempt from such recursive manoeuvres, it seems that they are not acknowledged by all sustainability activists. This explains why Rohracher and Ornetzeder lament that 'traditional strategies of optimizing *either* technology *or* behaviour are often "blind" about interactions between the spheres of the social and the technical' (2002, p74, emphasis added).

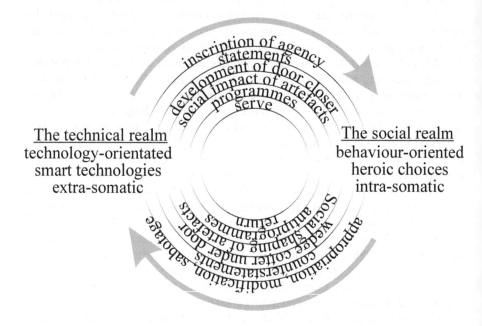

The technical realm
technology-orientated
smart technologies
extra-somatic

The social realm
behaviour-oriented
heroic choices
intra-somatic

Figure 2.2   *The 'Seamless Web' or 'Technological Drama'*

Technological voluntarism

Those who are unaware or in denial of 'anti-programmes' sail under the flag of technological determinism. Adherents of this stance therefore would bet that we would end up with cars, corkscrews and silicon chips again if we replayed world history with the exact same starting parameters. Science and technology studies have unmasked this Laplacian world-view in the last decades as fairly naïve. Seminal texts in this field have demonstrated how technology is socially shaped (MacKenzie and Wacjman, 1985) or socially constructed (Pinch and Bijker, 1984).

In this view, techno-logic is at best one of a myriad of factors that determine the direction of technological development.[22]

One of the most widely cited examples of this phenomenon is Schwartz Cowan's explanation of *How the Refrigerator Got its Hum* (1985). Her analysis shows that technical superiority is just one factor out of many that influence a society's decision whether or not to adopt a new technology. The introduction of the bicycle, for example, drew such non-technical criticism, even 'condemnation from religious leaders, moralists, physicians and members of the public frightened by such an unusual machine' (McGurn cited in Rosen, 2002, p1). While the bicycle as we know it today rose to a ubiquitous device, the recumbent bicycle did not because it stumbled over its own success. An early version of it outran every conventional bicycle in races organized by the Union Cycliste Internationale (UCI) whose officials 'banned it. . . because they felt it had an unfair aerodynamic advantage. . . [Consequently,] bicycle manufacturers would not make recumbents because all the money and prestige was in the UCI approved. . . bicycle' (Buttimore, 2001). Like the bicycle, the design of the now omnipresent automobile is subject to social, yet far more intricate factors. Among them are 'predictions about the stresses they will have to bear. . . which is itself the product of a complex compromise between engine performance, legislation, law enforcement and the values ascribed to different kinds of behaviour' (Akrich, 1992, p205). This set of factors is very different in every society, which substantiates that there can be no universally optimal car because what is considered optimal is culturally dependent. Decisions about urban infrastructure are not spared from such non-technical considerations. One of the best known examples in this regard is probably 'the streetcar conspiracy [describing] how General Motors deliberately destroyed public transit' (Snell, 2001; see also Szoboszlay, 1999).

Similarly, the so-called American Dream was one of the major driving forces behind suburbanization in the United States, despite its 'objective' disadvantages (Doss, 1998). A comparative look at Communist, Arabic, Chinese and other types of cities reveals the same, that urban form is not only determined by the logic of maximum efficiency, but by cultural preferences, attitudes, power, visions, religion, etc. A view beyond technical rationality is therefore a necessity for the true realist. Bijker and Law summarize this insight as follows:

> *Politics, economics, theories of the strength of materials, notions about what is beautiful or worthwhile, professional references, prejudices and skills, design tools, available raw materials, theories about the behaviour of the natural environment – all of these are thrown into the melting pot whenever an artifact is designed or built.* Bijker and Law, 1992b, p3

Many other authors identify similar factors in the development of technologies, including the influence of 'the technical culture, social values, aesthetic ethos and political agendas of the designer' (Pfaffenberger, 1992, p282). Guy and Shove similarly mention the importance of 'design conventions, forms of investment analysis, theories of space utilization, concepts of the normal "home" – [and] the networks of power at play' (2000, p66). The latter point is also stressed by

Rohracher and Ornetzeder, who talk about 'power relations . . .between users, planners/architects and producers' (2002, p80).

In the light of these arguments, technological determinists are invited to share Pfaffenberger's conclusion that 'technology . . .is at least partly a political phenomenon' (1992, p282) and to see that 'there is no inherent and compelling logic of technical development' (Rohracher, 1999, p3. See also Bijker and Law, 1992b, p8). Among the first authors who made this argument are Winner (1977), Pinch and Bijker (1984) and MacKenzie and Wajcman (1985). To turn the tables, this also means that 'there are potential choices – not necessarily conscious and manifest ones – inherent in the design of artifacts and technical systems' (Rohracher, 1999, p3). In the voluntarist view, societies may, then, use these choices to evolve as they desire.

Technological determinism

The conviction that society is the master yoking technology for its needs – or at least for the desires of the powerful – is seen as a wish driven illusion in the eyes of technological determinists. They hold that the aforementioned optimists tend to overlook empirical evidence of how technological developments provide the first step to which society, voluntarily or involuntarily, reacts in its wake.

The development of sunscreens with high sun protection factors, for example, protected people during their normal outdoor activities, but not only that. In addition, people reacted to the ready availability of this technology-in-a-bottle with more excessive sunbathing (British Columbia Cancer Agency, 2002). An even more notorious example of the deterministic technology push is the Tamagotchi, an electronic toy that took the world by storm during the 1990s. I cannot see what pre-existing social demand this gadget might have met. Rather, it seems that it was pushed into every teenager's hand because someone had developed it. A saying related to this strategy is cherished in the business world: 'if there is no market, create one' (Clarke, 2001). Consumer desires are forged in a similar fashion by the entertainment industry, which develops ever more demanding software, which requires ever faster computer processors.[23] But electronic media not only influence our purchase decisions, they also 'radically alter the way people think, feel, act' (McLuhan according to Whittenburg and Shedletsky, undated). The culmination of this trend, the ultimate determination of human behaviour through technology, has been formulated in Sloterdijk's vision of artificially designed morality genes (Sloterdijk, 1999).

The effect of the automobile on settlement patterns and lifestyles is another example of how we have surrendered part of our range of options to technology. Cars made it possible to spatially separate working, shopping and living locations, which created suburbs, which in turn increased the need for individual transport. Such a highly mobile society triggers the consequential emergence of big box retail, which perpetuates the need for cars because big box retail erodes small retailers and impacts negatively on the decentralized availability of goods.[24] Thus, we are constrained by 'path dependencies for which no one has really opted' (Hoogma et al, 2002, p180) and we find ourselves not infrequently in circumstances that force us to do what we don't really want to do.[25] I found one of my colleagues, who drives an sport utility vehicle (SUV) despite her environmental convictions, in such a predicament. She asserted that she used to drive a compact car, until SUVs became so prevalent that she was afraid of being overlooked in traffic with her little car: 'eventually I had to upgrade' ('J. Smith', personal communication, 7 March 2002). The same mechanism lingers behind the 'technological treadmill' (Cochrane, 1978) that forces farmers to choose between the two equally galling alternatives of intensification and abandonment. Pippin summarizes these manifestations of technological determinism in the analogy 'that the "technological tail" was beginning to wag the "human dog"' (1995, p44).

The mechanisms sketched above might be slightly simplified, but they exemplify cases in which 'technologies organize or "configure" their users' (Guy and Shove, 2000, p7). In reciprocal terms: men are objects in the 'drift [of] autonomous technology' (Winner, 1977, p88; see also Ellul, 1964), which follows its idiosyncratic and predetermined trajectory along the discovery of ultimate physical truths. Those who accept or embrace this view of progress also negate the historical effectiveness of free will because there is only one workable path of history, that of obedience to the laws of nature. It would therefore be simply stubborn or utterly stupid not to walk this path, and it would be the best strategy toward sustainability to help along those who have not yet advanced to the state-of-the-art technology.[26]

From repudiated to strategic co-evolution

Notwithstanding the arguments of technological determinists, it has to be acknowledged that often people do not succumb to technological prescriptions. Examples in preceding chapters demonstrated exactly this: Victorian children refused to sit as the designer of their chairs wanted them to sit. Users modified Hassan Fathy's smart vernacular buildings. 'One household might be using between two or even ten times as much energy as a neighboring family' (Guy and Shove, 2000, p15) in a technically identical dwelling. They all engage in what Pfaffenberger calls 'resistance to technological domination . . . [such as] user modification, sabotage, . . . revolutionary alterations . . . [and] the fabrication of counterartifacts' (1992, pp285–286). This partial rehabilitation of technological voluntarists could easily be followed by another round in favour of technological determinists and so on. Hughes (1994) incorporates this observation that technology and society drive each other in his theory of 'technological momentum', which is a chronologically mediated blend of voluntarism and determinism. In this view, social forces have a great deal of influence in the early stages of the life cycle of a technological system. However, according to Hughes, the possibility of shaping technology decreases as it matures into a mass produced entity with strong self-momentum and vested interests driving it. This theory matches McLuhan's (1964) famous statement that 'we shape our tools and they in turn shape us' (cited in Lapham, 1994, pxxi).[27] Eventually every technology reaches its climax and gives way to a new generation of technology, which again is shaped by society, which in turn has been shaped by previous technologies. From a historical perspective, I suggest that this process is a ceaseless loop characterized by an ongoing dynamic of mutual shaping and being shaped. It is clear then that neither the technical nor the social is an unmoved mover or, in vintage terminology, a *movens immotum*. Rather, both are moving and moved, hence *movens motumque*.

The acknowledgement that technology and society are contingent upon each other despite our efforts to insulate them from each other[28] opens up a new option – at least a theoretical one: what if we gave up our futile attempts to contain these contingencies and rather harnessed them strategically? What if we accepted that 'social and technical change come together, as a package' (Bijker and Law, 1992b, p11) and that they in fact co-evolve? (see Guy and Shove, 2000, p6). What if we embraced co-evolution? This concept and terminology was first suggested to me by Guy and Shove in the context of energy efficient architecture: 'Rather than viewing energy-saving technology as a stream of potential that is variously blocked by confounding features of the social world, we . . . highlight the co-evolution of social and technical systems of energy efficiency' (2000, p131). Rohracher and Ornetzeder argue in the same tenor for a 'fruitful co-evolution of technology design and use' (2002, p74). This resonates with Hoogma et al's postulate: 'What we need is technical change *and* social change. . . [by] *aligning* the technical and the social' (2002, p181, emphasis original). This path is, in their words, a 'co-evolutionary process' (p21).

After this theoretical derivation of a call for co-evolution it remains to be seen whether this idea passes the reality check. As decision criterion for this test, I suggest the capability of co-evolutionary concepts to gauge and describe cases that managed to draw nearer to the ideal of sustainability. For this purpose, the following chapter contains detailed accounts of such cases that achieved remarkable steps toward sustainability. The question whether the concept of co-evolution proves to be a useful conceptual and linguistic tool for their description will re-emerge thereafter.

Notes

1 'An ingenious process that uses high temperature and high pressure to turn hazardous wastes into harmless substances (water and carbon dioxide)' (Center for Energy and Environmental Resources, 2002).

2 US President George W. Bush also pursues this approach, as can be extrapolated from a statement in his State of the Union Address on January 28, 2003. In this speech Bush expressed his belief that 'in this century, the greatest environmental progress will come about . . . through technology and innovation'.

3 I am grateful to B. Parmenter who suggested an alternative interpretation of this case. In her view, Gourna fell victim to a patronizing and politically motivated resettlement campaign. The effect was that the tenants 'would not [have been] be very amenable to the project no matter what the architectural approach was' (B. Parmenter, personal communication, 18 April 2003). I therefore limit the purpose of my interpretation to a mere demonstration of

what delegation could be and especially of how users can subvert a designer's brilliant ideas.

4　Feder was Nazi commissioner for settlements and designed 'Die Neue Stadt' (The New City) of 20,000 inhabitants as a blueprint for the ideal German settlement (Feder, 1939). One of his arguments was that people in non-metropolitan areas tend to have more children, which was crucial for the growth of the German race. I am grateful to Bromley and Schenk (2002), who brought this manifestation of urban form determinism to my attention.

5　For more information on these and other examples of the prescription approach to urban planning see Brand (2005a).

6　This is not to say that advocates of the behaviour orientated approach are immune to such interest laden rationalizations or disciplinary chauvinism.

7　Lovins calls such a system 'friendly fascism – a managed society which rules by a faceless and widely dispersed complex of warfare-welfare-industrial-communications-police-bureaucracies with a technocratic ideology' (1979, p58).

8　Teleological in the sense of completing the proper path of science (see Moore, 2001, p13).

9　The aforementioned case of wood efficient hearths in African communities highlights the important compliance of technologies with habits.

10　At the level of urban infrastructures people do not have the choice of not buying them or of modifying them, but they can choose not to use them, or not to use them in the way they were intended.

11　The University of Texas employees, in fact, are lucky if a manipulation of the thermostat actually changes the office climate. After all, it seems more common than one would fear that technicians who are 'fed up with complaints from sweaty men and shivering women. . . install dummy thermostats to give workers the illusion of control' (Sandberg, 2003).

12　X = Resources used per unit of service
D = Services performed per year (e.g. miles driven)
t = Years
Scenario A: non-growth and non-efficiency:
Total resources used = $X \cdot D \cdot t$
Scenario B: one-time 100 per cent efficiency gain and 3 per cent growth:
Total resources used = $X/2 \cdot D(1.03)^t \cdot t$
When is $X \cdot D \cdot t = X/2 \cdot D(1.03)^t \cdot t$?
Answer: $t = 23.45$
(Calculation by L. Omberg)

13　Because a change of behaviour is often attempted through prescriptive technologies, the full title of the behaviour orientated approach to sustainable development should carry the addendum 'without technology'. The proponents of the approach described in the following, however, pursue a change of behaviour per se.

14　Carrots are also often used to speed up the adoption of new technologies and sticks to quicken the phase-out of old ones. This demonstrates the linkages and affinities between some of these approaches but it does not void the general distinction between technology and behaviour orientated approaches.

15 The campaign against sport utility vehicles, 'What Would Jesus Drive', is an example of such a hybrid between rational and moral arguments in support of reducing consumption. The campaign pledge contains the statement 'I believe He [Jesus] wants me to travel in ways that reduce pollution and consumption of gasoline' (Evangelical Environmental Network, 2002).

16 The actual suicide rates in Switzerland and the Philippines are 20.2 and 2.1 per 100,000 people, respectively (World Health Organization, 2001).

17 See www.wupperinst.org/FaktorVier and www.wupperinst.org/Seiten/ Abteilungen/ agnwm_projekte.html

18 While O'Toole does not use this expression in the context of sustainability, it poignantly mirrors the position of advocates of heroic choices.

19 In a later publication, Feenberg (1999) presents this divide as the sequel of 'the early debate between Paul Ehrlich and Barry Commoner. The still current issue dividing them is whether modern technology can evolve in environmentally sound directions, or whether we must return to more primitive conditions to save the planet' (p19).

20 The combination of Quinn's view that leavers preceded takers with his assertion 'to reach forward' results in a slogan like 'forward to the roots'. Technophiles see this stance as reactionary in comparison to their ideal of moving forward.

21 Costanza's matrix of 'Real State of the World' and 'World View' includes two more cells. One is labelled 'Mad Max' to describe a world governed by technological optimists, although their assumptions about the state of the world are incorrect. The other is 'Big Government', the consequence of technological sceptics designing policy even though their scepticism is not warranted by reality (2000).

22 For technological voluntarists, it is very likely that we would end up with a completely different technological regime if we replayed world history with the exact same starting parameters. When they look back at history they claim that artefacts and technologies 'might have been otherwise' (Bijker and Law, 1992b, p3).

23 In this context, Vitaliano inveighs: 'Your PC has been completely buried by DVD overload. Not a pretty sight on your computer screen, except for Intel, who will be glad to sell you ever faster, more expensive CPU's' (1998, p16).

24 Lovins casts this observation in a single sentence: 'Much of our prized personal mobility is really involuntary traffic made necessary by the settlement patterns that cars create' (1979, pp57–58).

25 I heard the most insightful thoughts on this mechanism in a lecture by Franz Josef Radermacher in 1998 at the Catholic University of Eichstätt, Germany. I therefore suggest referring to this problem as the Radermacher dilemma.

26 This view is the natural sciences' extrapolation of Hegel's deterministic view of history as moving humankind toward its inevitable end in accordance to a divine plan. Ironically, Marx's adaptation of this idea almost ignored the role of technology, while the rationale behind technological determinism and Hegelian/Marxist determinism is virtually identical.

27 Winston Churchill made the same point with a more direct relevance to the built environment: 'We shape our dwellings and afterwards our dwellings shape us' (cited in The Churchill Center, 2002). I was unable to find out which of the two men inspired the other.

28 For an example of a failed attempt to insulate the development of a fighter air plane from social influences, see Bijker and Law (1992a).

3

Co-evolution in Action

This chapter contains a rich description of two cases that made remarkable progress toward sustainability with strategies that qualify, in my view, as co-evolutionary. The analytical and interpretive content of this section is deliberately kept to a minimum to avoid colonizing the readers' perceptions. They should rather have the chance to develop their own unfettered interpretation of the raw data presented therein. My own angle on this material is presented in subsequent chapters. This strategy, along with rigorous naturalistic methods as described in Box 3.1, is intended to make my argument as transparent as possible, to enable the reader to comprehend what I see and why I see it, and lastly to support the trustworthiness of the conclusions drawn.

Box 3.1 Methodology in a box

The conclusion's credibility, transferability, dependability and confirmability also depend on the suitability of the methods employed. A thorough description of the methodology and methods of the study that led to this book is available at www.coevolution.info. For readers who cannot take this long route, however, it is necessary to present at least the main ideas and techniques that governed the research process.

In adopting a constructivist position à la Lincoln and Guba (1985), I subscribe to the notion that what appears as fact always has interpretive slack that needs to be narrowed in a dialogue between researchers and the people of the setting they study. The statements in this dialogue, however, must not be blindly taken at their face value because they might be purposefully or unconsciously distorted. This is why I call my approach with Kincheloe 'critical constructivism' (1993). This calls for a systematic and reiterative confrontation, also known as triangulation, of interview data with the literature and archival data. This approach allows researchers to learn and to adjust their *working* hypothesis as well as their research design as they go – in comparison with positivist investigations that can only furnish support or falsification for a preconceived and fixed hypothesis through a static procedure. A constructivist, naturalistic or hermeneutic enquiry is therefore much more flexible but takes on the burden of making the choices that guided the selection, analysis and interpretation of data as transparent as possible.

Literature: The study of relevant literature, combined with my personal experience, can be seen as the entry point into a hermeneutic spiral. I explored the existing body of knowledge in a variety of academic fields such as sustainable communities, learning organizations, radical innovation, social innovation, creative cities, alternative dispute resolution, participation techniques, pragmatism, the history and theory of urban planning, science and technology studies and others.

Archives: The electronic archive of the provincial newspaper *Het Belang van Limburg* and the personal archive of an employee of the Flemish Department of Transportation provided the majority of archival data for Hasselt. In Fürstenfeld-bruck, I studied materials from the archive of the newspaper *Fürstenfeldbrucker Tagblatt* and from Brucker Land's own archive. Access to the latter, however, was slightly constrained as proprietary and financial data were off limits.

Interviews: Existing contacts in both cases helped me to start a snowball sampling process. The total number of suggested interviewees climbed asymptotically to roughly 30 people in each case, which gave me the liberty to pursue a more and more purposive sampling method (Erlandson et al, 1993). Overall, I conducted 15 interviews in Hasselt and 11 in Fürstenfeldbruck, averaging 52 minutes each. Besides these official interviews, I also conducted numerous informal conversations with citizens, bus drivers, shopkeepers, etc.

All interviews were transcribed verbatim, which resulted in roughly 104,000 words of written text. This information, as well as the archival data and literature excerpts, was 'unitized [into] the smallest pieces of information that may stand alone' (Erlandson et al, 1993, p117), which ranged from 10 to 200 words. Each unit was printed on a separate index card, making a total of 2800 cards at the end of this process. The content analysis was performed through several rounds of sorting and re-sorting of all index cards. The purpose of this process was not to check whether the data fit into a preconceived pattern but to find out what pattern the data themselves suggested.

A cornerstone in the attempt to preserve transparency throughout the research process was a 'reflexive journal' (Erlandson et al, 1993, pp143–145) where I recorded all current findings, tentative interpretations, strategic decisions and so forth. I wrote 18 entries in this journal, each between one and two pages long, during the fieldwork phase, which helped me to trace the path of my deliberations, detect detours, shortcuts, gaps and unexplored territories, to 'park' ideas and to account for any adjustment of the emergent research design. The reflexive journal is available upon request and thus allows me to forestall any potential allegation of arbitrariness.

Hasselt

The city of Hasselt, located in the northeastern part of Belgium, owes its existence to the traffic along the route of commerce between Cologne and Bruges. During its almost 800 year old history, it grew to its current central function as the capital, commercial core and education centre of the Belgian province of Limburg. It currently serves 800,000 people in this capacity. The population has grown with the city to over 68,000, which makes Hasselt the twelfth largest city in Belgium. 38,000 students attend the many schools within the city limits, 46,000 employees work in Hasselt and 164,000 customers visit Hasselt's shops every week. Due to this strong retail function, Hasselt ranks fourth among Belgian cities in terms of commercial importance. The downside of this strength is the city's heavy dependence on outside customers, which proved detrimental when several local coal mines closed during the 1980s. Attempts to attract new customers were not exactly fostered by the traffic problems in and around Hasselt, which were generated by the large number of students, commuters and – still – shoppers. The public transport system was extremely underdeveloped and the car density was the highest in all of Flanders at 467 cars per every 1000 inhabitants (Lambrechts, 2000a).

In addition, the inner ring road (city map available at www.coevolution.info) was not only 'a physical barrier, very hard to cross' ('Luc Lieben-Claes',[1] interview 29 June 2000), but also the most dangerous road in the province, with over 30 accidents per kilometre annually (Stuurgroep Hasselt Levendig Stadscentrum [SHLS], 1994, p15). This inner ring (2.7km) encloses the city centre (7.4km^2) and 80 per cent of Hasselt's shops and service providers. Since the 1960s, Hasselt also has an outer ring (11km) that serves as major arterial for through traffic as well as distributor for traffic with a destination in Hasselt. Such was the situation in the early 1990s when several proposals were developed to solve Hasselt's traffic problems. Eventually, a socialist/green city government,[2] elected in 1994, tackled the issue with a comprehensive transport policy.

Actions taken

The overarching goals of this transport policy are to make trips to and within Hasselt as easy and safe as possible, and at the same time to ensure that staying and living in Hasselt is as pleasant as possible. These goals in official terms are 'accessibility, safety and traffic-related quality-of-life'[3] (Jacobs, 1996e, p16). The political strategy marshalled toward this goal is known by the phrase *Samen Anders Mobiel*, which can roughly be translated as 'Together, Differently Mobile' and has an intentional double meaning of 'everybody together' or 'all means of transportation together'. City officials claim that both meanings are given equal weight, that their 'integrated policy' (Lambrechts, 2001, p1) is indeed about people *and* about infrastructure.

The city officially distinguishes between a 'big' and a 'small' traffic policy. The former encompasses ambitious long-term projects such as the Mobility Plan, the Green Boulevard, the public-transport policy, spatial planning strategies and separate plans for bicycle use, parking, through traffic, the remodelling of the train station's forecourt, and the adaptation of the outer ring road. The small traffic policy, in contrast, is intended to provide quick relief for citizens through anti-parking bollards, speed-bumps, elevated intersections, the narrowing of streets, and so forth. In addition to these two policy levels, the city also engages in promotional activities such as car-free days and shopping by bus.

One of the main spatial planning strategies intends to densify land use around junctions of public transport in order to improve the availability of daily supplies at the neighbourhood level (Lambrechts, 2001). Another strategy is to reduce the number of empty houses in the inner city through negative tax incentives, with the goal of creating attractive living space. Future investments should not be made along the outer ring road, which would induce more traffic and conflict with the city's green-space plan. This objective did not find unanimous support, especially not among potential investors such as Colruyt and Toys R Us. Both wanted to build there and referred to building permits issued by the previous, conservative city government, which were not upheld by the new socialist–green government. The city, however, did not veer from its policy and declared through its alderman for spatial planning, Herman Reynders: 'We will defend our position all the way through the legal system. . . Colruyt and Toys R Us are welcome in Hasselt but not at this location' (Jacobs, 1996b, p1). Effects of this policy on the local business climate are presented further below.

Radial access roads

A traffic count in Hasselt in October 1995 revealed that 45 per cent of all vehicles on the inner ring road 'should not be there' (Guido Moerkerk, via email, 16 June 2002). Five per cent of the cars were just passing through the city without a single stop (Vandenreyt, 1995, p1) and another 40 per cent could have used the outer ring road even though either their origin or their destination was somewhere in Hasselt (Guido Moerkerk, via email, 20 July 2002). In order to divert through traffic from the inner ring road and to guide 'legitimate' traffic to the least vulnerable roads, the city now employs a combination of informational and infrastructural strategies. New traffic signs help inter-regional traffic find its way along the outer ring road. For visitors, three main access roads are promoted as the main routes to parking facilities near the city centre. Few houses line these roads whereas housing along the other radial roads was intensified after a thorough reconstruction: 'Car lanes were narrowed and the available free space added to sidewalks, cycle tracks and green areas' (Ministerie van de Vlaamse Gemeenschap, Afdeling Wegen en Verkeer Limburg [MVGWV], 2001, p13). In addition, the speed limit on most of these roads was reduced to 30km/h. The intended effect of this policy is to attract motorists along the three main access roads to parking places near the city centre, from which they can take the free and convenient buses to their final destination. Eventually, a solar-powered traffic guide system will provide real-time information about the availability of parking places to motorists on the outer ring road. The Department for Industrial Science and Technology of the University of Limburg at Hasselt has already completed a feasibility study of this project (Jacobs, 1996e).

Green space and living space

The general green-space plan intends to preserve natural areas around Hasselt and to extend them into the core of the city. In the early 1990s, there were still major green spaces along the outer ring road, while green spaces in the inner city and green belts linking these two were scarce. The reconstruction and greening of the radial approach roads as mentioned above is thus an important link between the transportation- and green-space policy.

The most spectacular green-space project in Hasselt, however, is certainly the Green Boulevard, designed as space for plants, animals and human beings alike; its technical details are described further below. It provides the inner ring road with approximately 450 trees and 'thousands of bushes' (Quintiens, undated, p3; *Hasselt: Stadt*, 1998, p4) that were planted for this purpose. Most of the trees are located on both sides of an eight metre wide strolling lane, which is also equipped with sculptures, statues, 'street lights, benches and other urban features [that] were specially designed to achieve a sense of integrated quality' (MVGWV, 2001, p21). Also deserving of mention are 420 *Verkeerspaaltjes* (anti-parking bollards), which are custom-made for Hasselt so that pedestrians can sit on them – unlike their conventional counterparts, which are constructed to discourage sitting. 'This is not a coincidence but well thought through' (Quintiens, undated, p4), because the Green Boulevard is meant as space for human beings and not for cars. The same reasoning led to a re-dedication of former car lanes to a number of new public squares along the Green Boulevard, some of them resuscitated versions of historic public places. The result is an 'enjoyable, spacious, green and car-free environment' (MVGWV, 2001, p13).

Remodelling the train station's forecourt into a transport hub

The remodelling of the area around the train station into a modern public transport hub links several elements of Hasselt's transport policy: train users need parking spaces or good bus connections, visitors arriving by train need information about bus lines and schedules, and users of the public transport system waiting for connections need restrooms and food, just to highlight a few connections between infrastructure and behaviour. Therefore, the train station's forecourt has been made optimally accessible to public transportation, pedestrians, bicycles, wheelchair users and the visually impaired. Taxis and private automobiles can access the station square to drop off or pick up passengers ('kiss and ride lane'). All bus lines converge at the station square, where displays at all 17 bus bays provide real-time information about the expected arrivals. A well-staffed information centre of the bus company, De Lijn, is located in the middle of the square and provides a heated shelter, maps of the bus network and bus schedules. A number of restaurants, pubs and concession stands have been renovated or opened around the area as a result of its steeply increased use. The city of Hasselt decided to change the plans of the former city government concerning the location of the Vlaams Huis, an administrative centre of the Flemish community that was to be built somewhere in Hasselt. It is currently under construction only 50 metres from the station square because it was argued that a public transportation hub would be most efficient if it was nested within an area of a high density of jobs and public services (all information from my own observations or from Verdee, undated).

The Green Boulevard

The Green Boulevard (Figure 3.1) is certainly the most visible element of Hasselt's transport policy. It is the result of a fundamental reconstruction of the inner ring road, which used to serve as major traffic artery with two lanes in each direction. The two lanes in the clockwise direction were completely rededicated to other purposes. The outermost section is now a wide sidewalk, beside a differently coloured bicycle track. This is separated by a curb from two car lanes, which allow only counter-clockwise traffic at a maximum speed of 50km/h and 30km/h along cobblestone stretches. Differently coloured bus lanes along the southwestern stretch of the Green Boulevard and at major intersections and bus stops ensure a smooth flow for public transportation (MVGWV, 2001). Another curb marks the outer edge of an eight metre wide strolling lane, which is lined with newly planted trees and street lights and furnished with benches and statues. It also hosts seven out of the nine bus stations along the Green Boulevard; the other two are strategically located at the Leopoldsplein and the Kolonel Dusartplein (city map available at www.coevolution.info). The strolling lane is followed by a cobblestone lane, which allows slow traffic in a clockwise direction over short stretches to destinations in the core of the city; it is also dedicated as a bicycle track. Immediately adjacent to the inner edge of the boulevard is a cobbled parking lane, which can be used by short-term visitors using meters and free by residents whose car has a sticker that authenticates their resident status. Finally, another sidewalk completes the Green Boulevard.

Public transport policy

Public transport was a stepchild in Hasselt for many decades. 'We had a bad bus system, only few buses and most buses drove only once an hour,' explains an employee of the public transport company De Lijn (Buntinx, interview, 26 November 2001). Since then, however, Hasselt's public transport policy has gained international attention because it is currently the only city in the world providing public transportation completely free of charge.[4] Its public transportation policy, however, encompasses much more than just this monetary aspect. The number of buses has tripled ('Odine Bormans', interview, 26 November 2001) up to nine bus lines, the catchment area of which encompasses 96 per cent of Hasselt's population. All lines converge at the train station, where easy transfer to other routes or to trains is ensured. Two bus lines are shuttle buses, one along the inner ring road, running at five minute intervals, the other connecting the station and market square six times per hour. Three other bus lines are served every 15 minutes during peak hours (7–9 am and 4–6 pm) and every 30 minutes at other times. Four more bus lines also run at half hour intervals throughout the day. All buses operate between 6 am and 7 pm Monday to Friday and between 8:30 am and 7 pm on Saturdays. A special evening line ensures that 'everyone gets home Saturdays until 11 pm' (s' Heeren, director of De Lijn in Limburg, cited in Jacobs, 1997d, p9). On Sundays, two bus lines run from 10 am to 6 pm, with extended hours of operation during the summer. The new bus routes and schedules have been developed in consultation with Hasselt's companies to ensure that their employees

Source: City of Hasselt, J. Jorissen

Figure 3.1 *Section of the Green Boulevard*

can use the buses to commute to work (MVGWV, 2001). All bus routes combined are furnished with 270 bus stops, which is double the amount of the old bus system. Many stops are protected with shelters; the three most frequented have 'pleasant, heated waiting rooms. . . equipped with telephones, washroom facilities and a dynamic real-time information system' (MVGWV, 2001, p27). This massive increase in service required a potent bus fleet, which was upgraded with 27 new buses. All of them are equipped with a kneeling system that makes them easily accessible by elderly and disabled persons. In short, they are 'the best available on the market right now' (unnamed bus driver cited in Jacobs, 1997f, p9.) The buses have built-in 'electronic equipment [that] allows [them] to operate the traffic lights' (MVGWV, 2001, p21) in addition to a permanent right-of-way over cars at intersections without traffic lights (MVGWV, 2001, p27). Fifty-seven bus drivers, 34 of them newly hired (Stad trekt, 1997), operate the bus fleet. They all 'received special training in public relations so that they could take care of the passengers instead of worrying about collecting fares' (MVGWV, 2001, p29).

Bicycle policy

Cyclists are either motivated by their environmental consciousness or by the real advantages of this means of transportation. The city of Hasselt worked to ensure the latter through a number of measures, most prominently through a steep increase in bicycle lanes. All of the remodelled radial approach roads got a bicycle lane, the entire Green Boulevard is now lined with one bicycle lane on each side and major intersections were remodelled with an underpass for cyclists and pedestrians. In order to make the whole day of a cyclist hassle-free, the city installed many additional bike racks and established three secure bicycle sheds. Public services and some companies grant a 'bicycle bonus of BEF6 [€0.15] per kilometre and [they] provide showers and cloak rooms next to the cycle sheds for their employees and workers who cycle to work' (MVGWV, 2001, p37). School children are also encouraged and helped to use their bikes through so-called *Fietspools* (bicycle pools), in which adults volunteer to guide children from their neighbourhood safely to their school. The city provides safety jackets, promotional pennants, stickers and logistical and marketing support for this programme. Even for visitors it is now easy to use a bicycle in Hasselt, as 20 white bicycles and some scooters can be borrowed free of charge for one day at the bicycle shed behind the city hall. Some of these bicycles are equipped with a child seat or with a transport trailer. The social dimension of this project is that it 'created jobs for some of the unemployed to recycle and repair bicycles' (MVGWV, 2001, p45).

Pedestrian policy

The remodelling of the radial approach roads allowed the sidewalks to be widened. This, in combination with efforts to improve the availability of daily goods at the neighbourhood level, encouraged people to run their errands on foot (Lambrechts, 2001). The aforementioned tunnels under major roads also supported this goal. The main focus for pedestrians, however, is dedicated to the shopping streets in the centre of the city, where access for cars is limited[5] and where even cyclists and bus users usually become pedestrians. Most people come there to shop, which is made less arduous through two parcel storage sites set up during special shopping seasons; local retailers co-sponsor this project for obvious reasons. Pedestrians with children can borrow strollers free behind the city hall (MVGWV, 2001) and plans are under way to provide shopping trolleys that can be taken anywhere in the shopping district (Jacobs, 1996h).

Parking policy

The primary objective of the parking policy is for people to be persuaded to leave their cars outside the inner city and find their way to their final destination by bus, bicycle or on foot. This presupposes not only good bus connections and bicycle sheds but also affordable and accessible parking facilities. Consequently, a number of parking sites were built 'next to the inner ring road so as not to interfere with the attractive city centre' (MVGWV, 2001, p13). The biggest of these is a parking garage with 800 spaces underneath the Kolonel Dusartplein, where one of the three main access roads meets the Green Boulevard (city map available at www.coevolution.info). And because the mere availability of space is not the only factor that matters, the parking lot at the Slachthuiskaai (500 spaces) – another of the three main access roads – has security guards (Jacobs, 1997e).

In addition to these incentives, the parking policy includes measures to discourage parking in the inner city. For this reason, the initial plans determined that 'the number of surface (paid) parking places [would be] halved in the city centre' (*Mobility with*, 1999, p5). Mayor Stevaert explains this seemingly radical move: 'Because the traffic that doesn't have to be on the inner ring will be diverted through our traffic guide system, we will effectively have more parking possibilities' (cited in Cloostermans, 1995, p14). This is of course a relative rationale because what matters is the ratio of parking spaces to people who need a parking space – a decrease in the latter improves the overall situation. In addition, Stevaert continues, 'we re-dedicate parts of the street [of the old inner ring] to new parking spaces' (Cloostermans, 1995, p14). This measure led to the aforementioned cobbled parking lane, which is reserved for 'resident-parking and for quite expensive short-term parking' (MVGWV, 2001, p19). Another element of the parking policy is the parking guidance system, which leads visitors to strategically located parking facilities. Plans exist to upgrade this system to a remote-controlled, real-time information system. A more low-tech part of the parking policy is a simple map showing the locations of all parking facilities, which is available free and distributed in particular to parking offenders (Jacobs, 1996c).

Campaigns

The technological/infrastructural changes described above were, in the vocabulary I suggest, intended to facilitate behavioural changes. The direction of these desired changes was explicitly articulated through campaigns as integral elements of Hasselt's transport policy. *Hasselt graag traag* (Slowly through Hasselt please) for example encourages motorists to drive slowly. The annual, Europe-wide Car-free Day is also promoted by the City of Hasselt with support from businesses, the chamber of commerce and schools (MVGWV, 2001). On this day, schools compete for the highest bicycle usage rate, people who cycle to work get a free breakfast and a chance to win a prize drawn during a special event in the city centre (MVGWV, 2001). Another contest, with bicycles as the main prizes, also takes place among the participants in the campaign *Met Belgerinkel Naar De Winkel* (Shopping with bicycle bells) (MVGWV, 2001). 'Winners use alternative modes of transportation' – this is the message communicated widely in Hasselt. To support this claim, a race was arranged during the 1996 Week of Mobility between a car driver, pedestrian, bus user, skater and cyclist. The goal was to travel 3 kilometres through the city and to pick up the newly released brochure *Mondig Mobiel* (Mobile as a true adult[6]) at the city hall. The results were widely communicated in the local media: the skater arrived first, followed shortly by the cyclist, who happened to be Mayor Stevaert. The driver came third but lamented paying €2.23 for parking. The bus user, who was the penultimate finisher, also had to pay €1.56 because the competition took place before the introduction of the free buses (see Meuris, 1996). At that time, the inner ring was perceived as a road – full stop. Nowadays, it is made appealing as the Green Boulevard and personified through a friendly logo: a G-shaped arrow consisting of green leaves pointing in a counter-clockwise direction, with a smiley in the middle.

Integration

It is important to emphasize the deliberate integration of all these measures because infrastructure and social practices are seen and treated as part of a larger system. The public relations officer of the City of Hasselt presents an example of the integration of traffic guidance, street design, parking policy and public transport: 'We would like people to drive to designated parking garages via the main access roads. . . From there they should be able to reach their destination hassle-free with the bus' (cited in Jacobs, 1997a, p13). To ensure the attractiveness of this desired behaviour, pull factors are combined with push factors: the designated parking garages have security and are optimally connected to the bus system, whereas parking spaces in central residential areas are relatively pricey. Another thread that runs through the web of measures is the combination of bicycle lanes, bonuses for commuting by bicycle, secure bicycle shelters and showers for employees who cycle to work. In a similar fashion, visitors coming to Hasselt by train are not only provided with clean, free and frequent buses but also with the possibility of renting bicycles, of storing their shopping at a safe place and of strolling under shaded parkways undisturbed by cars. The awareness campaigns also fit smoothly into this interpretation because new technologies need to be nested within a welcoming public discourse.[7] In other words, social acceptance of the behaviour facilitated by any new technology is a precondition for it to become mainstream.

Results

Comments on the effect of Hasselt's transport policy range from enthusiastic ('Following the obvious success of the project the scepticism disappeared' [*Mobility with*, 1999, p8]) to very contained ('Not everything the city does is wrong'

['Hendrik Lieshout', interview, 27 November 2001]). It should be kept in mind that the decisions made in Hasselt never were apolitical; neither are their effects and their perception. After all, there are elections to win in Hasselt and 'Steve Stevaert. . . won the last election [in 2000] with the Green Boulevard clearly' (Guido Moerkerk, interview, 27 November 2001). Therefore, appraising statements should be contextualized in the political interests of their authors: the enthusiastic quote above was made by an unnamed city hall insider; the latter resonates the discontent with the marginalization of its author's right-wing party (Flemish Blok) in the current city parliament. A former city employee emphasizes the fact that assessments of the transport policy are always politically charged: 'There is also a great deal of peptalk and public relations' (Frans Peperman, via email, 21 June 2001). I received what I consider a balanced appraisal from Guido Moerkerk, an employee of the Flemish Department of Transportation, who was personally involved in all stages of the process in Hasselt. Even though he is '100 per cent in favour of this project' he cautions that 'it shouldn't be only a good news show' (Guido Moerkerk, interview, 27 November 2001). Mr Moerkerk adds that a conclusive evaluation cannot yet be made, two years after the Green Boulevard was completed. Werner Mulders, a professional traffic expert who would have preferred even more radical measures, points in the same direction by asking for more time: 'At least it is a step in the right direction. . . and you can see that a city can become more beautiful, more pleasant and healthier. . . [and now,] let the buses drive for a while' (Werner Mulders, interview, 30 June 2000). The following pages take a closer look at these effects, as far as they can reliably be detected at this point in time.

Effects on individual motorized traffic

Sabin 's Heeren, director of the De Lijn public transportation company in Limburg, ascertained one month after the introduction of the free buses, 'the traffic pressure in Hasselt is already somewhat lower' (cited in Jacobs, 1997h, p1). A quantitative analysis supports this claim to some extent. Calculations for January 1998 reveal that the new bus system alone helped avoid 28,529 trips through the city centre per month; this corresponds to 920 trips per day or to almost 1 car per minute during the day.[8] 'The number of cars on the Boulevard has not decreased [as] dramatically [as] the number of bus passengers has increased' is how Moerkerk (via email, 10 February 2003) describes this moderate effect. Mulders' evaluation sounds fair, too: 'We have not at all reached a point where the car comes at the second place' (interview, 30 June 2000). People who did not switch from car travel to other means of transportation often changed their preferred driving routes, however. This shifted a large share of traffic – and the related problems – from the inner to the outer ring road. This effect was reported by many different sources, among them staff members of Stevaert's office, as well as his political opponents and authors generally benevolent toward the project (see Verdee, undated; Jacobs, 1996g; Lieben-Claes and 'Constantin Duverger', interview 29 June 2000; Moerkerk, interview, 27 November 2001; 'Eric Schonk', interview 7 December 2001). They proffer, however, differing assessments of this phenomenon. Some shopkeepers complain that the worsened traffic situation on the outer ring road keeps customers away from Hasselt (Moerkerk, interview, 27 November 2001). Others remark that these problems could have been anticipated (Verdee, undated) or even avoided by taking on the infrastructural measures in a different order: 'We preferred to do the reorganization of the second ring first. They [the socialist–green city government] did it otherwise' (Schonk, representative of the previous, conservative city government, interview, 7 December 2001). The Association of Train, Tramway and Bus Users (BTTB) demands synchronized traffic lights[9] on the outer ring road (Meukens cited in Jacobs, 1996g), which city officials have already promised for the future (Reynders cited in Jacobs, 1996g).

The massively reorganized inner ring road, that is, the Green Boulevard, is also not spared from criticism. Representatives of the current opposition in the city parliament, the Flemish Blok, scold the one-way rule on the inner ring. They argue that a whole circulation of 3.8 kilometres is necessary to reach or to leave the city. The result, by their account, is that 'some people try to sneak 200 metres against the one-way direction during off-peak hours' ('Robert Meulendijk' and Lieshout, interview, 27 November 2001). The conservative party is not completely happy with the one-way solution either, but they present constructive criticism for specific problematic spots. For Mulders, traffic expert at a Limburg college, the Green Boulevard is 'still a merry-go-round for cars. . . They could have gone much further with something like this:' drawing a one-way arrow on the inner ring to be used just by buses (interview, 30 June 2000). In Mulders' design, cars would only be allowed on the inner ring on segments between major radial access roads.

My interlocutors were more unanimous on the importance of reducing accidents, which was one of the major arguments for the new transport policy. One author reports that 'collisions on the short ring road have been virtually reduced to nil' (*Mobility with*, 1999, p8). Statistical data unmask this claim as slightly exaggerated (see Table 3.1), but the drop in the number of accidents is still impressive. Mr Moerkerk comments on these figures that 'we have another type [of accident]. Not these strong accidents any more, but we have a lot of accidents between pedestrians and cyclists' (interview, 27 November 2001).

Table 3.1 *Number of accidents on the inner ring road, 1994–1997*

	1994	1995	1996	1997
Injuries and damage to vehicles	33	29	39	10
Injuries – total	27	30	28	–
– per km	14	12	16	–
Total	65	72	67	18

Note: the free public transport system was introduced in July 1997.
Source: Planning Group, undated

Usage of public transport

'An absolute boom' is how Sabin 's Heeren, director of De Lijn in Limburg, describes the effect of the free bus system (cited in Jacobs, 1997h, p1). Immediately after the buses were made free on 1 July 1997, 12,000 people per day used them compared to the previous average of 1,000 people (Jacobs, 2001); a daily peak of 14,000 was reached during the annual parish fair (Snoeckx, 1997). Five months after the introduction of the new bus system, the one-millionth bus rider led the local newspaper to conclude that 'the first euphoria did not recede' (Jacobs, 1997j, p14). One year after the establishment of the new system, 2.7 million people have made use of it, an increase by a factor of nine compared to the previous annual average (Bormans, interview, 26 November 2001); in 2001 this number has reached 3.9 million (Stad Hasselt, 2001). Figure 3.2 charts the number of bus users on a monthly basis.

As impressive as these absolute numbers may be, their contextualization provides necessary deeper meaning. Traffic expert Mulders, for example, relates the steep increase to the initial situation: 'It's not that hard to get eight times better if you start out from very little' (Mulders, interview, 30 June 2000). This comparative view is shared by Lambrechts, who concludes that 'public transport in Hasselt is still not at the same level as in other cities where buses run every 20 minutes. In Hasselt it is still 30 minutes' (Lambrechts, 2001, p16). The same author draws attention to the ratio of passengers per kilometre driven by the buses. This indicator only rose from 0.6 to 1.6, because the number of annual bus-kilometres increased from 540,777 to 1,675,139 (Lambrechts, 2001).

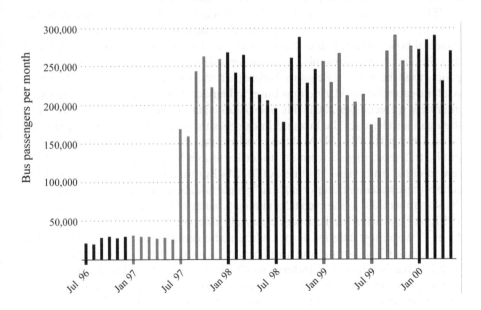

Source: Lambrechts, 2000b

Figure 3.2 *Histogram of bus users per month from July 1996 to May 2000*

But these data still leave interpretive slack concerning the reduction of individual motorized traffic. Such assessment requires information about the means of transportation new bus users would have used under the former public transport system. A qualitative answer is provided by a bus driver in a letter to a newspaper editor: 'Hasselters who didn't bother at all about public transport for years are now very loyal users of De Lijn' (Peuskens, 1997, p37). A college for traffic studies conducted a related survey among 2342 respondents in November 1997 (Hogeschool voor Verkeerskunde Diepenbeek, 1998). Of all bus users, this study concludes, 16 per cent switched from their car and 12 per cent from their bicycle to the bus. Another 9 per cent would have walked under the previous system. Visitors to the weekly market and the two local hospitals especially were found to have transferred from individual motorized transportation to the bus (Jacobs, 2001); the easy accessibility of these locations by bus certainly has a large explanatory value for this finding. No information could be obtained regarding how many people switched from car to bicycle use. Given the massive expansion of the bike lane system, it is reasonable to expect significant effects. The aforementioned survey also tried to ascertain why people in general were using the new buses. It revealed that 34.7 per cent of all bus users cannot use or do not have access to a car or bicycle.[10] Other reasons mentioned for the use of the bus system were: no fare (17.9 per cent), the new public transport system in general (14.1 per cent), the number of buses (9.1 per cent), the weather (8.9 per cent) and other reasons (15.3 per cent). The three main reasons for making the trip in the first place were school, work and shopping. Together these reasons accounted for 70.8 per cent of all trips by bus (*Hasselt: Stadt*, 1998).

The steep increase in bus use in Hasselt seems to be one of two elements that form a positive feedback loop. The second element is the vastly improved public image of buses, which makes bus use more socially accepted. It is not surprising that Stevaert emphasizes this phenomenon: 'We saw that within a few years more people took the buses in Belgium. Before that, the bus was something for Russians, not for a capitalist world. And now buses in Flanders have become sexy'[11] (Stevaert, interview, 6 December 2001). He is also quoted as saying that even 'the mother of the main jeweler uses the bus and finds this simply [excellent]' (cited in *Hasselt: Stadt*, 1998, p21). Also Mr Mulders confirms this effect: 'The lucky shot is that. . . public transport turned from an underdog into a landmark in Hasselt within a few months' (interview, 30 June 2000). Ms Buntinx, representative of De Lijn, echoes these statements, reporting that 'people talk about our buses now' (interview, 26 November 2001). She even talks about a 'change of mentality' (cited in Snoeckx, 1997, p11), which Moerkerk sees especially among school children: 'When I was 12 or 13 we almost laughed at the children who came by bus. . . Now all children take the bus. It's so normal and it will become a part of their life, they will grow up with it. That is important' (interview, 27 November 2001). Many interviewees and authors mention not only a new relationship between people and buses but also among people, caused by new social encounters on the bus. The author of a letter to a newspaper editor mentions the 'sedulous politeness of bus drivers [and the] animated conversations with previously unapproached denizens or even with strangers, the positive discoveries of so called "ghetto neighbourhoods", the daily sightseeing pleasure of a few elderly ladies, the polishing of a number of etiquette rules among all ages' (Oeyen, 1997, p37). Bormans, a frequent bus rider herself, noticed 'people started talking together in the bus' (interview, 26 November 2001) and Moerkerk elaborates:

> *Especially elderly people say to the driver, 'Hello, good morning; how are you doing?'. They smile; they say something. In another town: [Deepens his voice] you have to pay, you step on the bus, you put your ticket in there and devaluate it. But here, they have more pleasure in their life again.* Interview, 27 November 2001

All in all, the new public transport system 'strengthened the social fabric in Hasselt' as Stevaert claims (cited in Jacobs, 1997h, p1). An article in the local newspaper confirms that 'the social life has changed' (Jacobs, 1997i, p1) with respect to increased visits to Hasselt's hospitals. It is mostly elderly people who contribute to this increase. They 'used to sit in front of their television before because they couldn't get to town. Now we bring them to town' explains Moerkerk (interview, 27 November 2001). Even a representative of the right-wing opposition in the city parliament confirms – upon inquiry – that the free buses help the elderly and financially disadvantaged citizens (Lieshout, interview, 27 November 2001). Stevaert refers to the latter social group by stressing that 'the times of fare dodging are gone and I don't have to come up with measures to help our poor people – which would stigmatize them' (cited in *Hasselt: Stadt*, 1998, p20).

The only explicitly negative response to the new bus system is reported from citizens who now have to walk farther to the next bus stop due to a re-routing of some bus lines (Jacobs, 1997g). The BTTB, although strongly in favour of the project in general, provided some constructive criticism in regard to the itineraries and location of bus stops. Only after the implementation of these recommendations, the BTTB concluded, shall we call this project 'truly successful' (Meukens cited in Jacobs, 1996g, p12). By early 2003, the success of the free buses was beginning to become widespread because:

> *more and more we realize that the free public transport has some negative side effects from a traffic management point of view. . . During peak hours, the buses are full with school children and during the day, many pensioners take public transport to travel around. Some people, like me, are more and more inclined to change the system: keep the buses free outside peak hours, but let the passengers pay a small fee, say €0.5, during the peak hour.* Moerkerk via email, 10 February 2003

Parking

Criticism of Hasselt's parking policy comes from two opposing camps. One claims that there are still too many parking spaces in Hasselt to optimally support public transportation. The large parking garage under the Kolonel Dusartplein with 800 parking spaces in particular is the object of the BTTB's criticism because it 'will certainly attract car traffic' (Meukens cited in Jacobs, 1996g, p12). This and the new parking regulations throughout the city make Mulders conclude: 'No, no, his [Stevaert's] parking policy is not that far-reaching and not revolutionary at all. . . It lacks an overall concept and it doesn't hurt cars as much as I would perhaps wish it' (interview, 30 June 2000). The other critique, raised by members of the Flemish Blok, complains that 'people can't park their cars in the city any more' (Lieshout, interview, 27 November 2001). At least 'not free' should be added, because the same interviewee reports that 'the parking garage under the Kolonel Dusartplein is empty most of the time because it is too expensive' (Lieshout, interview, 27 November 2001). Based on my own observations, the former claim cannot be dismissed as vastly exaggerated, whereas the latter requires some context: one hour in said parking garage costs about €1.24, roughly as much as one cup of coffee. Therefore, it is comprehensible that people try to park on every possible side road, which are then 'crammed with parked cars' (Lieshout, interview, 27 November 2001). Ironically, this behaviour is facilitated by the free buses, because people now take every free parking space within 1 kilometre of bus stops near the city centre and take the bus from there to their final destination. The city reacted to this problem by reserving a certain number of parking spaces in every neighbourhood for its residents, who must display a special parking permit behind their windshield.

There are other free parking facilities at equally convenient locations, that is, within walking distance of the inner ring road, but they are overcrowded too. 'These parking spaces shouldn't be free,' explains Moerkerk (interview, 27 November 2001), who was personally involved in the planning of the new parking policy. 'But as you know, Hasselt lives from shoppers and employees. The city is afraid that they will not come to Hasselt any more if they make it too difficult, or expensive, for them to come to the town' (Moerkerk, interview, 27 November 2001). Especially for people who commute to work in Hasselt, a large Park and Ride facility near the outer ring road was constructed, which can be used free. However, 'there is never anybody there. The system of Park & Ride only works partly, at times of big events. . . But even then, the success is limited' (Moerkerk, interview, 27 November 2001). Instead, customers, workers and residents still compete for the free parking spaces near the city centre. In other words, the parking policy does not – or not yet – completely work as it was meant to. Interestingly, even Lieshout from the car-friendly Flemish Block, eschews this final judgement: 'This brings me back to the issue of mentality. Maybe it takes years for people to grasp that there is no other way; that it is necessary; that we have to pay. A parking spot simply cannot be free' (interview, 27 November 2001). The two opposing critical voices find reconciliation in this long-term perspective, because Mulders also amends his criticism with the words, 'but I understand that it takes time' (interview, 30 June 2000).

Green space and real estate effects

The BTTB and 78 per cent of 453 Hasselters surveyed (Jacobs, 1996i) applauded the plans for the Green Boulevard. Also the conservative party, who opposed it during the planning phase, now approves of its green dimension. Even the Flemish

Blok points to positive aspects: 'The absence of cars is nice for pedestrians. You feel free' (Lieshout, interview, 27 November 2001). The Flemish Blok's overall assessment of the socialist policy in Hasselt, however, is rather critical. Even though it sometimes sounds overly generalizing, it sheds light on some real problems of the Green Boulevard, in particular its tree-lined strolling lane: 'People just don't use it' (Lieshout, interview, 27 November 2001). Moerkerk also admits this phenomenon. He explains that the cobblestone parking lane between the inner sidewalk of the Boulevard and the strolling lane effectively functions as a barrier, even though there is very little and very slow traffic on it. The lower than expected frequency of pedestrians along most stretches of the Green Boulevard has also hampered the realization of another hope, the springing up of bars, cafés and restaurants with decks and porches. This effect was anticipated but 'it simply doesn't work', as Lieshout (interview, 27 November 2001) puts it. Moerkerk shares this disenchantment but mixes it with optimism: 'Maybe it's too short a period since it [the Green Boulevard] provided that possibility' (interview, 27 November 2001). In hindsight, city planners learned that small things like slightly elevated terraces near the sidewalk could have made the strolling lane more accessible and could have served as space for gastronomic enterprises. The case of the Hotel Century is an example of how this was meant to happen. The hotel is located at one of the major intersections on the inner ring road (Sint-Truidersteenweg and Luikersteenweg), which is why there was almost no decking before the reconstruction. In addition:

> *they were in the middle of the exhaust fumes of the cars. . . It was not pleasant to come there to drink something. [But] if you come there nowadays, they have such a beautiful place. The terrace is overcrowded every weekend in the summer.*
> Moerkerk, interview, 27 November 2001

This creation of 'spatial value added' (Verdee, undated, p18) also affected the housing market because:

> *living on the boulevard is interesting now. Before, living on the ring road was really not pleasant. If you had a house on the ring road, you didn't want to live there. . . But what is important, maybe the last three or four years, really many many houses along the ring road have renovated their façade. So they painted them new or they cleaned them or they put new windows in it and this process is still going on. That's very nice. That made the public space more valuable.*
> Moerkerk, interview, 27 November 2001

The disadvantage for tenants, however, is a significant increase in rents. With reference to this mixed effect of increased property value, Moerkerk shrugs and smiles: 'Some people benefited very strongly from public money. . . Well, maybe that's not such a positive point of our project' (interview, 27 November 2001). People moving to Hasselt confirm this ambiguous effect on the real estate market through their choice of location for their houses. 'They still move to the outskirts of Hasselt. . . They come to the inner city to work or to shop at best, [which leaves it] still dead after 6 pm' ('Lieben-Claes', interview, 29 June 2000).

City marketing and local pride

'This project was Hasselt's best ever city marketing project' is how an official publication of the Flemish Department of Transportation subsumes the external effects of the Green Boulevard (MVGWV, 2001, p29). The free bus system inspired a great deal of attention – a 'direct hit' as Mulders calls it (interview, 30 June 2000). Ninety-eight articles were published in the Belgian press and at least 28 articles in foreign publications (*Hasselt: Stadt*, 1998), while a range of television stations, from the local broadcasting company to CNN (MVGWV, 2001) disseminated information about the 'miracle of Hasselt' (*Hasselt: Stadt*, 1998, p22). Approximately 120 visits by foreign media, representatives of other cities, educational associations and study groups (*Mobility with*, 1999) were made to the city in the year after the free buses were launched. In response, 'even the people outside our province know the concept of the Green Boulevard' (Moerkerk, interview, 27 November 2001), which has triggered curiosity and fostered tourism in Hasselt. That much attention in turn makes the citizens of Hasselt 'very proud of their buses' (Mulders, interview, 30 June 2000). One respondent sensed 'a will to live, a dynamic and a strongly improved image of the city compared to 10 years ago, when Hasselt was a dead city' ('Lieben-Claes', interview, 29 June 2000). This revival of Hasselt also attracts 'many new citizens' (Duverger, interview, 29 June 2000) and in their wake, a number of new businesses.

Business climate

Hasselt is traditionally a city of traders and retailers, whose well-being the authors of the new transport policy claim to have kept strongly in mind. Initially, however, Hasselt's shopkeepers articulated their scepticism, especially about the new parking policy, with the slogan 'No parking – no business' (Peperman, interview, 26 June 2000; Moerkerk, interview, 27 November 2001). But 50 days after the introduction of the free buses, Dirk Jacobs (1997i, p1), reporter on the local newspaper, quoted only enthusiastic responses from shopkeepers: 'No, we can't complain at all,' said the owner of a sandwich bar, who noticed that 'many more curious people come to discover Hasselt – precisely because of the free buses'. A shoe retailer has 'many more customers because of the free buses. . . We had some concerns initially but now we are totally convinced of the positive effect of the free buses for the image of Hasselt as a shopping city' (Jacobs, 1997i, p1). Ady Franssen, chairman of the local retailers' association, praises the free buses as a 'direct hit for the publicity of our city' (cited in Jacobs, 1997i). This experience convinced the retailers' association to pay for a substantial expansion of bus services on two Sundays during the Christmas shopping period in 1997 (Jacobs, 1997j).

Other elements of Hasselt's transport policy, for example the Green Boulevard and the one-way traffic on it, are not equally popular among shopkeepers. Meulendijk (Flemish Blok) even reports that 'all the retailers in the city are against it' (interview, 27 November 2001). My own informal conversations with several shopkeepers met with only sporadic complaints; an impression not shared by Moerkerk: 'Shopkeepers say there is not enough parking space . . . and there are too many traffic jams around the ring road so people don't come to Hasselt' (interview, 27 November 2001). After a short pause he adds: 'But shopkeepers always complain. You will not find a shopkeeper who is happy with things.' Nevertheless, he admits that some complaints are quite legitimate, especially for shopkeepers on the west side of Hasselt's centre. They report that the bus that runs every ten minutes between the train station and the central market place keeps people from walking this stretch. Retailers along this bus route thus have fewer people strolling by their windows and allegedly fewer customers and they are lobbying for less frequent services (Moerkerk, interview, 27 November 2001). An indication of the overall situation for retailers is provided by Lieshout, who claims that more shops in the centre of the city are vacant than ten years ago (interview, 27 November 2001). Moerkerk corroborates this appraisal but underlines that the new transport policy cannot be made accountable for every problem. He instead points at the unfortunate economic situation in general, at the natural turnover of shop-ownership, at a lack of resourcefulness on the part of store proprietors and especially at other cities' efforts to revamp themselves: 'In more and more cities [it] is interesting to shop and to walk around. So there is more competition. Hasselt is not the only city in the province any more where it is pleasant to shop' (Moerkerk, interview, 27 November 2001).

A newspaper article from mid-2002 paints a more promising picture, citing the result of a survey among chain merchants. Fifty-two of them expressed an interest in opening a store in Hasselt, which makes it the second most attractive investment destination in all of Belgium. The organizer of this survey, Geert De Ras, elaborates: 'It is remarkable that the renovation of the city centre and the mobility enhancements clearly play a role' (cited in Jacobs, 2002). A report for an EU-sponsored project draws similar conclusions:

> *Hasselt is since five years an expanding city. . . People, business companies and investors are attracted by the local dynamism. Infrastructural works (Groene Boulevard), construction works and investment by government, local authorities and the private sector, the growth of the trade and service business are signs of this qualitative growth. . . The unemployment rate is lowering since the last five years [and] the economic situation in Hasselt is evolving in a positive direction.*
> Educatieve Wegwijzer, 1999

Budgetary effects

The city of Hasselt paid €2.92 million, that is 24.7 per cent of the total costs for the remodelling of the inner ring road. The free buses cost the city €992 thousand annually in its municipal budget, or €14.38 per citizen (Jacobs, 2001). An assessment of the financial implications of the project, however, must transgress the city limits because 'everything works here because of state subsidies' (Moerkerk, interview, 27 November 2001). (For more details on and a discussion of the financial construction of Hasselt's transport policy, refer to www.coevolution.info). The other side of the balance sheet shows savings due to reduced maintenance costs for 'parking [spaces], roads, traffic signs' (MVGWV, 2001, p29). The Flemish community also avoided major expenditures, namely an estimated €37 million for the construction of a previously planned third ring road (Kindhäuser, 2000). 'This does not even include the costs of devaluation of space, noise, the pollution of air and water, accidents, global warming', which Kindhäuser (2000, p66) mentions as the projected inevitable consequences of a third loop.

Despite these advantages, not everybody endorses the economic aspects of Hasselt's mobility policy. Lieshout affirms that 'ever since Hasselt has its free buses, public transport got debased everywhere else in Limburg' (interview, 27 November 2001). Moerkerk, an employee of the Flemish Department of Transportation disagrees:

> *Each year the bus system in six to eight towns in the province is re-modelled. . .*
> *Of course, many towns are still unhappy because they are at the end of the list*
> *(there are 44 towns in Limburg), but . . . De Lijn is certainly improving services*
> *all over the province, not only in Hasselt.* Via email, 10 February 2003

Lieshout finds more reasons to grumble, stating that 'the community pays. . . Everybody has to pay' (interview, 27 November 2001) even if one does not use the bus. The ideology behind this concept is put plainly by Moerkerk: 'That's where Steve [Stevaert's] socialist part comes in' (interview, 27 November 2001). The author of a letter to the newspaper editor explains in this context: 'Isn't it the actual goal of taxes . . . to reach a socially fair redistribution? I have no problem that my tax money is used to finance someone else's street or to subsidize someone else's association' (Oeyen, 1997, p37). I take the publication of several letters to the editors on this issue as an indication that the financial construction of Hasselt's transport policy stimulated a healthy discourse about solidarity, the role of government and the purpose of public spending. Its most spectacular manifestation was the proposal of Jos Geuens, chairman of De Lijn in Flanders and member of the Flemish parliament, to introduce a public transportation tax of about €57 (*Hasselt:Stadt*, 1998) per family each year to be used to fund free public transport for everyone. Apparently, this idea was too bold for most Flemings because it received 'a lot of negative reactions' (Peuskens, 1997, p37) and little praise. Nevertheless, it indicates a certain niche in the public discourse, which has certainly gained momentum from the Hasselt experience.

Legacy and inspiration

It seems that Hasselt's transport policy inspired other cities to 'adopt parts of it. And many mayors take Hasselt as the ideal' (Lieshout, interview, 27 November 2001), whereas 'six, seven years ago, they saw public transport as something annoying, making too much noise, hindering circulation and so on' (Duverger, interview, 6 December 2001). Nowadays, Duverger continues, 'the thing is spreading out [he smiles] and almost every mayor in Flanders is demanding . . . what you can call the basic system' (interview, 6 December 2001). This has led to a variety of new public transport strategies in a number of cities aimed at increasing bus services and making them free or more affordable for otherwise immobile citizens – children and/or senior citizens – 'to let them become part of the community', as Duverger explains (interview, 6 December 2001). Less than one year after the free buses were introduced in Hasselt, eight other communities were negotiating with De Lijn regarding how bus fares could be either reduced or abolished (*Hasselt: Stadt*, 1998). For example, every teenager between the age of 12 and 14 from Gent can now use any means of public transport in Flanders free of charge (Jongeling, 2001). All these initiatives make use of the Mobiliteits-convenant, a Flemish covenant of 1996 to support the self-help efforts of cities with Flemish subsidies. This external support must not only be invested in public transport but also in infrastructural and other systemic measures; an idea that stems largely from the experiment carried out in Hasselt. Moerkerk reports happily about this diffusion because other cities 'know the concept of the Green Boulevard. . . [and that] it is about city building' (interview, 27 November 2001). The neighbouring city of Genk (circa 60,000 inhabitants) also initiated a reconstruction of its city centre to make it more enjoyable to live in and pedestrian-friendly, 'the same kind of thing' (Moerkerk, interview, 27 November 2001).

Fürstenfeldbruck

Almost 191,000 people live on 435 km^2 in the German county of Fürstenfeldbruck, west of Munich. This makes it the most densely populated county in Bavaria even though it includes more remote rural areas on its western side. However, 80 per cent of the population live in the eastern urban municipalities close to Greater Munich. These communities account for the steep increase in the county's population, which rose by 11 per cent from 1987 to 1997[12] (Landwirtschaftsamt Dachau, Fürstenfeldbruck, Landsberg, 2002). In the same period, the percentage of people employed in the agricultural sector decreased from 5.4 to 3.1 per cent. The total number of farms also declined, from 3204 in 1949, to 1246 in 1980 and 815 in 1999. While the number of farms with more than 75 hectares rose from 18 to 45 in this period, the number of farms with under 20 hectares dropped from 782 to 395. This divergence is known as the 'Wachsen oder Weichen' (grow or perish) dilemma, also described by Cochrane as the 'technological treadmill' (1978). It is caused by a steady decrease in revenues for agricultural products due to technological advances, intensified use of agro-chemicals and the globalization of agricultural markets. In 1982, a farmer earned €24.0 per 100 kilograms of wheat; 12 years later, this figure has fallen to €12.8 (Brand, 1997). The result of these trends is that for every Euro spent in a bakery, only 3 per cent trickles down to a farmer (Bürgerstiftung Zukunftsfähiges München, 2002). While some farmers, especially in the eastern part of the county, have found alternative sources of income by selling farmland for real estate development, many face additional problems as the younger generation is less and less willing to take over their parents' farms. This problem is causally linked to the low social status of farmers, which is related in turn to their image as environmental evil-doers.

Brucker Land: Actions taken

The county of Fürstenfeldbruck is home to BRUCKER LAND[13] (www.brucker-land.info). This organization was established in 1994 by citizens who shared the conviction that the ever-more industrialized and globalized system for the production and distribution of agricultural products was partly responsible for the deterioration of certain economic, social and ecological parameters in their county and beyond. Employing a reciprocal logic, they were convinced that the strategy, 'From the County, For the County', would cure or at least mitigate those ills. In order to put this slogan into action, they built a strategic alliance of 'five columns': farmers, food producers (mostly bakers and butchers), environmentalists, representatives of the Catholic and Protestant churches and consumers. Together they founded the Brucker Land Community of Solidarity e.V. ('e.V.' is the most common legal form of non-profit organizations in Germany), whose objectives are expressed in its statute, and include support for family-size farms that maintain the cultural landscape; reduction of pesticide and fertilizer residues in the environment; preservation of the decentral and regional food processing infrastructure such as mills, dairies, bakeries and butchers; area-wide availability of healthy, regionally grown foodstuffs of the highest quality and superior freshness; reduction of emissions and energy consumption in the distribution of agricultural goods; transparency in the food production chain from producer to consumer; and a heightened public awareness of the many interconnections of these elements.

In order to create a legal foundation for their plans, a limited liability corporation, Brucker Land GmbH, was established in 1995. This entity serves as a broker between the farmers and food producers (bakers and butchers) of Fürstenfeldbruck County.[14] It provides a set of legally binding production and processing criteria (see below) and controls their compliance. Products that meet these criteria receive the legally protected Brucker Land logo and are sold in most food retail stores, bakeries and supermarkets – 140 outlets altogether – exclusively in Fürstenfeldbruck County. But Brucker Land is much more than a commercial food wholesaler because the pursuit of the aforementioned public goods is hardwired into its corporate structure. The board of trustees, for example, has a built-in majority of non-commercial interests, as represented by environmentalists, church representatives and consumers over farmers and tradesmen. This structure ensures that the rigorous production stipulations, which are the result of intense negotiations, cannot be watered down. The required 'controlled cultivation', for instance, is a compromise between conventional and orthodox ecological methods.[15] For grain, this means that no pesticides, stem shortener, sewage sludge or growth regulators may be applied in the actual cultivation year. Mineral fertilizers can be deployed after thorough soil surveys but their necessity is minimized by mandatory crop rotation. As for livestock husbandry, the farmers do without growth-enhancing drugs. They are only allowed to feed regionally grown fodder, which has to be free of pesticide residues and genetically altered components. The original directives are much more detailed than can be presented here and they exist for each product respectively. They are accessible to the public, as are the inspection reports, conducted by regional agencies and private laboratories that audit compliance with these rules. Similar rules regulate the post-harvest processes to ensure uncompromised freshness and quality.

Compliance with these directives causes a reduction of yield per acre or per animal. In return, the Brucker Land farmers are paid roughly double that of farmers producing conventionally produced goods. This extra expense is handed on to the consumer, who has to pay between 12 and 35 per cent more for Brucker Land products than for standard groceries. Table 3.2 shows the average prices for selected conventional, ecologically grown and Brucker Land products.

Table 3.2 *Prices of conventional, organic and Brucker Land products in 2001*

	Conventional German average[a]	Conventional high-quality[b]	Orthodox organically grown	Brucker Land recommended retail price[d]
Eggs	€0.15/egg	€0.20/egg	€0.28/egg[c]	€0.27/egg
Rye bread	€2.25/kg	€2.50/kg	€3.40/kg[e]	€3.27/kg
Whole milk	€0.66/l	€0.82/l	€0.97/l[c]	€0.92/l
Potatoes	€0.73/kg	€0.85/kg	€1.12/kg[c]	€0.90/kg
Wheat flour	€0.54/kg	€0.91/kg	€1.36/kg[b]	€1.29/kg

Sources:
a Hannappel, 2002
b Prices on 12 February 2003 in various supermarkets in Peissenberg, Germany, inflation adjusted O.-M. Brand, via email, 14 February 2003
c Based on prices from 1999, inflation adjusted, Fleissner, 2000
d Seiltz, via email 9, September 2002
e Ludwig Stocker Hofpfisterei GmbH, 2003, inflation adjusted

The participation of supermarkets deserves special mention for several reasons. First, it was a pioneer achievement for a German regionalization initiative to have their products sold in supermarkets. Previous attempts had failed due to supermarkets' increased efforts to deal with low-volume suppliers, which Brucker Land managed to minimize through its highly professional management and logistics. Second, the decision to include supermarkets has been criticized as catering to the faceless food industry and as missing the opportunity to re-establish village stores throughout the county ('Gerhard Krömeke', interview, 22 January 2002). Most Brucker Land representatives, however, defend this retail strategy as the only way to achieve a critical mass of turnover and as a deliberate strategy to utilize existing structures and avoid the huge overhead costs of maintaining retail outlets of their own. Third, the incorporation of supermarkets is a striking example of the attempt to make it easy for people to 'do the right thing'. They do not have to visit five different (eco-)farmers in order to get fresh, eco-friendly, locally grown groceries. Smaller towns in the rural, western part of the county do not have supermarkets, but most have at least a bakery and/or butcher's. These stores, too, sell most Brucker Land products, which not only provides them with an additional source of income but also makes it convenient for people living in these areas to avoid heroic choices and still buy locally grown food.

An integral characteristic of Brucker Land is its extensive marketing strategy. A number of informational brochures have been distributed to all households in Fürstenfeldbruck County; a billboard is placed in every field under contract; over 100 posters are permanently mounted in the various retail outlets; and many other promotional items are available, such as balloons, stickers and cotton bags. Brucker Land has also received very supportive press coverage, leading to over 1000 articles in the first four years of operation (Brand, 1997). 'Action marketing' is seen as a very important aspect of the public relations strategy, which includes the appearance of traditional brass bands when introducing new products or so-called *Regaleinsätze* (shelf missions). The latter term refers to personal product promotion by one or two volunteers in front of the Brucker Land shelves in supermarkets. This marketing technique originated from the lack of a large marketing budget and resulted in an effect that no money can buy. The shelf missions gave Brucker Land a face and a human touch, which is confirmed by the manager of a large local supermarket: 'Brucker Land makes credible advertisement with a heart' (Adalbert Schnitzer, cited in Brand, 1997, p91). Around 2000 of these missions have been conducted since the foundation of Brucker Land (Seiltz, via email, 2 March 2003).

Brucker Land: results

'It did not turn out as well as [the head of Brucker Land] wants us to believe.' This is the assessment of one of my interviewees, who is not affiliated to Brucker Land and who clearly prefers the good old times. Those who are personally involved in the project, however, see its effects in a much more positive light. Of 24 interlocutors, 23 selected one of the two highest ratings on a six-point scale that ranged from 'Brucker Land is a failure' to 'Brucker Land is a success' (Brand, 1997). An unbiased evaluation of Brucker Land requires, but is not limited to, a look at factual information, such as its array of products. It includes by now 40 different types of bread and a great variety of other baked products, wheat flour, rye flour, spelt flour, durum semolina, potatoes, two types of milk, one type of cheese, eggs, honey, four types of pasta, apple juice, sunflower oil, onions, beetroot, pork, beef (both also as convenience meals) and numerous types of sausages, tomatoes, carrots, gherkins, celery, cabbage, mayonnaise, a dill sauce and three types of mustard. A growing number of these products is available from organically grown ingredients, best-sellers among them are nine types of bread. Brucker Land asparagus, courgette and cucumber may be eaten in seven participating restaurants. Low-volume specialties include two types of mead and two herbal teas. Some non-food products are also produced and marketed by Brucker Land, including sheep's wool, hay, straw, rapeseed oil and wood, for further processing into furniture.

Table 3.3 *Brucker Land production volume for selected years*

		1994	1995	1996	1997	2001	2004
Wheat	Participating farmers	11	13	18	11	12	9
	Cultivated area[a]	86.7	61.8	164.3	126.8	148.3	98.8
	Volume sold	100	100	330	330	300	240
Rye	Participating farmers	9	24	32	20	23	16
	Cultivated area[a]	81.8	123.6	432.2	196.9	469.5	160.6
	Volume sold	200	200	660	660	500	390
Spelt	Participating farmers	–	–	–	–	–	12
	Cultivated area[a]	–	–	–	–	–	148.3
	Volume sold	–	–	–	–	–	150
Potatoes	Participating farmers	–	–	8	6	5	5
	Cultivated area[a]	–	–	27.7	18.3	19.8	–
	Volume sold	–	–	70	90	104	65
Milk	Participating farmers	–	34	34	34	25	–

Sources: data from various files provided by Seiltz and from the author's diploma thesis: Brand, 1997. Some numbers were derived through calculations from these data.
Unit of cultivated area: acres; unit of volume sold: tonnes.
[a] It is not useful to calculate the yield per acre from these data because farmers usually cultivate more land than they can sell from in a good harvest year. They err on the safe side in case of plant diseases and because some products can be stored for a long time (grain for up to three years, for example).

The volume of production of the Brucker Land venture is shown in Table 3.3. It also indicates that the demand for Brucker Land products in Fürstenfeldbruck County is reaching its saturation point. The amount of some products sold has actually declined in the last few years. For Elsbeth Seiltz, managing director of Brucker Land, this is no reason to lament but a normal process in what she calls the 'consolidation phase' (interview, 15 January 2002). After all, some products have attained a market share of 15 (milk) to 30 per cent (bread) in certain stores (Brand, 1997), thus exceeding the Brucker Land coalition's initial ambitions, which ranged from a 5 to 25 per cent market share, depending on the product (Reginet.de,

2002). The total area covered by crops cultivated for Brucker Land in 1996 was 300 hectares. After adding the estimated grazing and feeding area for cattle and chickens, plus the land used by bees producing honey, Brucker Land utilizes a land area around the size of New York City's Central Park, which is 340 hectares. This amounts to 1.8 per cent of the 18,695 hectares of arable farmland in Fürstenfeldbruck County.[16] The annual turnover has levelled off at approximately €1.35 million. Transactions with bakeries account for roughly one third of this amount, one quarter is the result of transactions with butchers and the rest of the turnover is generated at supermarkets. Among the expenses of the Brucker Land GmbH are salaries for 30 part-time employees, who telecommute from their homes when possible. The partners of the Brucker Land GmbH opted not to disclose information regarding its profits. One of my interviewees, however, related that 'of course we are operating cost-covering' ('Arnulf Langer', interview, 5 February 2002). Another inner circle person even calls the economic results of the Brucker Land abattoir 'magnificent' ('Fritz Herrwig', interview, 30 January 2002). Brucker Land was able to attract some quantity buyers like the county hospital and ten restaurants that serve seasonally adapted meals. The main clientèle, however, are individual customers in Fürstenfeldbruck, 92 per cent of whom are able to recognize the Brucker Land logo (GALB, 2001), and they can shop for Brucker Land products in 140 stores throughout the county (GALB, 2001), among them 70 supermarkets (Seiltz, via email, 9 September 2002).

One of Brucker Land's largest problems is the absence of post-harvest facilities in the region. The intense concentration process in the food sector has left only a few small mills and no dairy in the county. Due to its rigid processing regulations, Brucker Land cannot utilize just any facility. It was finally able to find a cooperative dairy 29km from Fürstenfeldbruck in the neighbouring county, which creates not only additional expenses and emissions but also dependence. When management problems and financial pressures brought this dairy to the brink of insolvency in 2001, Brucker Land milk almost toppled with it (Seiltz, interview, 15 January 2002).

A synopsis of the above evidence still documents the development of Brucker Land as an impressive success story, but it does so as if this were an end in itself. What is at least equally important is the assessment of whether Brucker Land has met its own goals and how it affected its 'five columns'.

Impact on the farmers

Approximately 120 farms, or 14 per cent of all farms in the county, are official partners of Brucker Land (Reginet.de, 2002; GALB, 2001). A map showing the location of all farmers and all retail outlets is available on www.coevolution.info. According to the Bavarian Minister of Agriculture, they get 'fair prices and planning reliability' (Miller, 2001). Nevertheless, 'Leopold Klein' believes that 'economically it doesn't make a huge difference [for the farmers]' (interview, 25 January 2002). This statement was made with explicit reference to the additional work accruing for the farmers: 'They have to grapple with it, they have to go to meetings, they have to equip themselves' ('Klein', interview, 25 January 2002). My own calculations reveal that the net additional income for a farmer ranges between €2000 and €4000 per year.[17] Farmer 'Jakob Kellermann' puts this sum in context: 'We have to face it that we can't save our farms with this programme. Well, but why shouldn't I participate? At least I have a few hundred Marks or two- or three-thousand Euros extra. That's better than nothing. And it gives me the feeling that I've tried something' (interview, 25 January 2002). After all, the Brucker Land programme is attractive enough to make some farmers willing to produce exclusively for the coalition. This would, however, contradict a crucial element of its philosophy, which states that as many farmers as possible should get the chance to participate – for an optimal diversification of risks and of benefits. Therefore, no farmer is allowed to till more than 12.4 hectares per crop for Brucker Land. Despite these measures, there are still more farmers who would like to produce for Brucker Land than the finite demand allows the coalition to accept. This stirs up envy among those farmers who cannot participate ('Kellermann', interview, 25 January 2002). A balanced assessment of Brucker Land's impact on the farmers in Fürstenfeldbruck County must conclude that it has not brought about a sweeping improvement of their economic situation. It does, however, supplement their finances and – not least importantly – it improves their reputation and provides them with a sense of self-determination

Impact on the food processing tradesmen

Almost all bakeries in the county, 14 independent enterprises with 50 subsidiary branches, sell bread and pastries made from Brucker Land flour (Seiltz, via email, 2 March 3002). Six large bakeries have even switched their complete bread range to Brucker Land. Three butchers also have completely converted their operations according to Brucker Land guidelines. Nineteen butcher's branches participate in the retail programme and sell other Brucker Land products such as milk and cheese. The participation of these food trade enterprises 'contributes to secure their existence', as the Bavarian Minister for Agriculture declares (Miller, 2001). 'Manfred Dengler', who is intimately involved in Brucker Land, corroborates this appraisal. He claims that there are 'clear economic stabilization effects' (interview, 28 January 2002) for bakeries and butchers involved with Brucker Land. Unfortunately, quantitative financial data is hard to come by. What can be said, however, is that 'the substantial fear of failure among bakeries in the mid-90s has not materialized. Whether or not this is due to Brucker Land has yet to be proven' ('Klein', interview, 25 January 2002). Mr Herrwig, a baker, would not go so far as to say that particular bakeries have been saved by Brucker Land. When I rephrased the question to, 'Would you do it again for economic reasons?', he sidestepped the question, saying that he would 'do it again for all reasons' (interview, 30 January 2002). Among those other reasons is the fact that 'our trade has been pushed to the foreground of the public awareness again. People realized that it is not a matter of course that they have a bakery near them' (Herrwig, interview, 30 January 2002). 'Klein' stresses such non-monetary rewards as the most important effects for the participating craftsmen: 'They might say, "I don't earn much more – but I enjoy my trade much more"' (interview, 25 January 2002).

Impact on consumers, environmentalists and church representatives

The environmentalists on board with Brucker Land were realistic enough not to expect vast improvements in environmental indicators from this initiative. The trend, however, points in a positive direction, as computations by Mr Dengler reveal. He calculated that at least 5000 litres of gasoline are saved per year, which corresponds to 11.6 tonnes of carbon dioxide and 1.1 tonnes of nitrogen oxides avoided. A more local impact can be expected from the annual avoidance of 1700 litres of pesticide use that is credited to Brucker Land (Dippold, cited in Brand, 1997). The jury of the European Nature Conservation Year 1995 considered these effects worthy of the title 'German National Contribution', which was awarded to Brucker Land and 49 other projects in Germany.

The benefit for customers is impossible to measure, especially because different people value different aspects of food. Those who care most about fresh and regionally grown groceries from farmers they can trust would probably get better products if they did not mind the extra effort of buying from farmers directly. Those who eat only organically grown products are better advised to shop at specialized eco-stores – for up to 230 per cent higher prices (Fleissner, 2000). Both scenarios require a form of heroic choice: time commitment and/or financial renunciation. Those who value the aforementioned characteristics to the extent of affordability indeed find the *pareto optimum* of quality, price and convenience with Brucker Land products. Dengler mentions an additional advantage for consumers: 'realization of what consumers have always demanded: more involvement or access and more contact with the production and with the processing of their food' (interview, 28 January 2002).

The goal for religiously motivated actors is the 'preservation of God's creation', as Elsbeth Seiltz noted on several occasions, which overlaps widely with the aims of environmentalists. Some representatives of the former group have, in addition, a specific idea of how this objective can be approached, namely through a change in people's mindset. This is what one of the slogans frequently cited by Seiltz, who assigns herself to the church 'column', suggests: 'through the stomach into the brain'[18] (interview, 15 January 2002). Has Brucker Land managed to affect people's attitudes? Any change of this parameter eludes quantitative grasp, but anecdotal evidence does actually affirm this question. Dengler talks about a 'widening of one's horizon', which results mostly from the personal encounter of consumers with farmers during shelf missions (interview, 28 January 2002). Almost all other interviewees reported similar observations. One of the most often used expressions in this context was 'sensitization' to the situation of the respective partners (see also Miller, 2001).

Maybe the most unmistakable assessment of Brucker Land is the fact that people 'vote for it with their feet' ('Klein', interview, 25 January 2002) because its concept has been adopted by eight other counties around Munich. The clarity of this evidence outshines all other attempts to examine whether the five interest groups are content with the experience made in Fürstenfeldbruck. They are.

Unser Land: actions taken and results

The propagation of the Brucker Land idea has materialized in eight other counties around Munich in the form of eight other LÄNDER (the German plural of Land). The population in these counties – including Fürstenfeldbruck and the city of Munich – is shown in Table 3.4. Together, they represent a gigantic market for groceries produced on the 2973km² of agricultural area in these counties.

Table 3.4 *Population and agricultural area in the counties around Munich*

Name of LAND[19]	Name of county	Population	Agricultural area in miles²
Dachauer Land	Dachau	124,886	383
Ebersberger Land	Ebersberg	112,949	271
Unser Land	München Land	282,735	213
Starnberger Land	Starnberg	120,696	150
Brucker Land	Fürstenfeldbruck	187,703	237
Landsberger Land	Landsberg am Lech	101,684	399
Weilheim-Schongauer Land	Weilheim-Schongau	123,363	491
Tölzer Land	Bad-Tölz Wolfratshausen	112,683	325
Werdenfelser Land	Garmisch-Partenkirchen	85,841	160
Miesbacher Land	Miesbach	89,442	288
Unser Land	Kreisfreie Stadt München	1,205,923	55
Total		2,547,905	2972

Sources: Bayerisches Landesamt für Statistik und Datenverarbeitung, 1999, 2002

Most of these new Länder were founded in 2000, with bread and meat products being available in most counties after autumn 2001; many more products were launched throughout 2002. The long-term ideal is to offer the same product range as in Fürstenfeldbruck County. The Länder are united under the umbrella organization UNSER LAND e.V. (Our Land) (see www.unserland.info), which was officially founded in February 2000 with the help of the Bavarian Farmers' Association (Bauernverband) and the Offices of Agriculture (Landwirtschaftsämter) in the respective counties. The commercial arm UNSER LAND GmbH was founded shortly afterwards, in May 2000. Its goal is for a significant share of the food supply for Munich to be supplied by its own hinterland. It is still in the set-up phase as more farmers, tradesmen and supermarkets are joining in and as an increasingly sophisticated system for the delivery logistics into Munich is being developed. As of mid-2005 the inhabitants of Munich could purchase Unser Land products in 136 retail outlets, of which were 91 supermarkets and 45 bakeries.

Unser Land has managed to establish partnerships with 18 crop farmers, 10 apiarists, 60 apple farmers, 84 bakeries (not including their separate branches), 5 butchers, 9 restaurants and 118 supermarkets. In the first year of operation, 500 tonnes of grain, 3500 pigs and 320 cattle were sold. The projected sales volume for exemplary products for 2005 is 4.1 million eggs, 800,000 litres of milk, 320 tonnes of potatoes and 106,670 litres of apple juice. The total turnover of Unser Land in 2002 was around €1.26 million (these data do *not* include numbers from Brucker Land. Data source: various files provided by Elsbeth Seiltz). These operations are supported by a staff of 20 part-time employees who are mostly affiliated with small farms, thereby contributing to the farms' financial viability. A further increase in turnover is expected in the coming years. Among the driving factors is likely to be Manfred Vollmer, one of the largest gastronomes of Munich. His restaurant chain serves 10,000 traditional Bavarian meals per day, some of which are already available with Unser Land ingredients (Kellermann, interview, 25 January 2002). The same holds for food served in his large tent at the world-famous Oktoberfest in Munich.

The protagonists of Unser Land are not settling for these results. Two grant applications have been filed that would help strengthen Unser Land's presence in the city of Munich and assist in developing a similar model in a number of counties in the Allgäu-Region in southern Germany. Regardless of the decisions on these applications, the visionaries behind the coalition are thinking even further ahead:

> *Well, Brucker Land grew to Unser Land, which comprises half of Upper-Bavaria. And now we discuss this issue with more adjacent counties and one day we might have a 'Länder' structure encompassing the whole of Bavaria. And if this runs rampant it might grow all over Germany . . . and with further development turn into a global structure.* 'Klein', interview, 25 January 2002

Mr 'Klein' acknowledges the fanciful character of this scenario, but emphasizes the need to answer the question, 'do we want to go this way?' (interview, 25 January 2002). At the level of the day-to-day operations of Unser Land, it can be seen as a process of catching up with what has been accomplished in Fürstenfeldbruck. Meanwhile, the leaders of Brucker Land are pursuing new ambitions in the energy sector, which has always been Ms Seiltz's original concern (Seiltz, interview, 15 January 2002). The first step on this path was the launching of 'Brucker Land – Sun Land'. This project establishes a strategic alliance of local plumbers, a credit union and other partners. Together they were able to offer very affordable solar thermal collectors, which were immediately in great demand. This project was honoured with the German and the European Solar Award in 1999. Currently, over 500 of these solar collectors have been installed on private roofs (Landratsamt Fürstenfeldbruck, 2002). The results of Brucker Land – Sun Land encouraged decision-makers in Fürstenfeldbruck to make far-ranging choices. In April 2000, a Brucker Land Energy Forum adopted a resolution that calls for complete energy autarchy by the year 2030[20] (Umweltinstitut München e.V., 2002), which is also endorsed by the county chief executive (Karmasin, 2002). The Centre for Innovative Energies in the County was founded in 2001 to provide institutional support for the pursuit of this goal. It is a cooperative effort between Brucker Land, the aforementioned credit union and the County of Fürstenfeldbruck. The range of its operations covers solar collectors, photovoltaic panels, insulation measures, the refitting of cars for the use of rapeseed oil and co-generation of power and heat in micro-power plants fuelled by wood chips, rapeseed oil and manure-generated methane. Evaluations of its activities to date range from 'beautiful success' (Langer, interview, 5 February 2002) to 'stunning success' (Seiltz, interview, 15 January 2002).

This proactive stance by the county is seen by many as a legacy of Brucker Land. It has received such enormous praise from politicians of the Bavarian state that the local conservative government could not afford to lag behind. Consequently, the county chief executive has pledged support for Brucker Land and talks about cooperation between environmentalists and farmers and about sustainability in his campaign brochures (CSU im Landkreis Fürstenfeldbruck, 2002) in what sounds very much like Brucker Land language.

Notes

1   Every time I introduce respondents whose identity is protected, I present their full pseudonym name in quotation marks.
2   To be precise: the governing coalition consisted of the Socialist Party (SP), the Green Party (AGALEV), the People's Union-Flemish Free Democrats (VU) and the Flemish Liberals and Democrats (VLD).
3   Flemish original: *verkeersleefbarheid*. This and all following translations from Flemish and German to English are my own unless stated otherwise.
4   To be precise, all 11 city lines are free to everyone. Regional buses are free only to citizens of Hasselt within the city limits.
5   Only delivery vehicles are allowed on these streets during shopping hours. Users of private cars can access these streets only after working hours and on Sundays.
6   The Flemish word *mondig* is used here because it suggests several meanings: 'Adult, mature, independent, emancipated. So it means that you are mobile in all these ways' (Moerkerk, via email, 10 February 2003).
7   See Pfaffenberger, 1992 and Chapter 5 (section entitled 'New technologies require social embedding') on this issue.
8   This calculation is based on the following measurements and assumptions: Total number of bus users in January 1998: 269,146. Percentage of bus users who would have used their car for the same trip before the new bus system came into effect: 10.6 per cent, based on a survey of the Hogeschool voor Verkeerskunde Diepenbeek (1998). Daily distribution of traffic: 75 per cent from 6 am to 6 pm, 25 per cent from 6 pm to 6 am (data from *Hasselt: Stadt*, 1998).
9   The Flemish expression for such a system is *groene golf*. It signifies a way of electronically linking sequential traffic lights that allows car drivers to have a green light at every traffic light if they maintain a certain speed. This ideal speed, which varies over time, is indicated on a dynamic display system. The overall purpose is to smooth the traffic flow.

10   The study does not indicate whether out-of-town students who arrive by train and transfer to their educational institution by bus fall under this category. However, a closer look reveals that this category is chosen three times more often by non-Hasselt citizens than by Hasselters.

11   In this and some later instances, I corrected Mr Stevaert's English to make it more readable while I made every attempt to preserve the original meaning.

12   This may not sound steep for US American readers who witness 3 to 4 times steeper growth rates in certain regions. For German standards, however, 11 per cent growth in one decade is uncommon.

13   The term BRUCKER LAND – all in capital letters – is a registered brand name. For improved readability, however, I use the spelling Brucker Land henceforth.

14   This mechanism applies to the majority of Brucker Land products. For some others, such as milk, the Brucker Land GmbH functions as wholesaler which actually buys the raw products, organizes post-harvesting processes and resells them to food retailers.

15   It deserves mention that 18 out of 23 key personalities of Brucker Land expressed a general preference for purely organic farming by choosing either of the two categories closest to 'I support organic farming very much' on a six-point scale that ended with 'I strictly deprecate organic farming' (Brand, 1997). The most widely shared stance among representatives of Brucker Land is quite pragmatic: the consumers have the final say with their purchase decisions. Nevertheless, organic farming made it into official documents of UNSER LAND, the extended version of Brucker Land, as a long-term goal (Brückmann, 2002b).

16   Data for 1999. Source: Landwirtschaftsamt Dachau, Fürstenfeldbruck, Landsberg (2002).

17   A sample calculation for wheat farmers in 2001: 12 Brucker Land farmers produced 310 tonnes of wheat. They were reimbursed €204.5 for each tonne, amounting to €63,395 in total. This sum was apportioned to 12 farmers so that each farmer received €5283 on average. The revenues for conventionally grown and marketed products would have been approximately €3302. The bottom line is a difference of €1981 between conventional and Brucker Land cultivation. A number of farmers, however, produce more than one crop for Brucker Land, which is why I assume the range of net gains as €2000 to €4000 per year (data compiled from various files provided by Seiltz).

18   As Brucker Land shows, this motto does not trigger sermons for reversal and renunciation.

19   All LÄNDER – all in capital letters – are registered brand names. For improved readability, however, I use a lower case spelling henceforth.

20   It should be noted that Brucker Land has never and still does not intend to reach autarchy with respect to the food supply of the county.

4

Towards a Theory of Co-evolution

Limits to describe are limits to imagine

My main argument for a vocabulary of co-evolution is that the conventional vocabularies of either technology orientation or behaviour orientation cannot adequately describe certain cases of significant achievement toward sustainability, such as Hasselt or Fürstenfeldbruck. If this claim can be supported, it follows that either approach alone is also limited in describing and therefore proposing future cases. Feenberg makes exactly this point in regard to any deterministic philosophy; and both the technology and the behaviour orientated approach are deterministic in some respect. 'Determinism . . . makes it seem as though the end of the story was inevitable from the very beginning. . . That approach confuses our under-standing of the past and stifles the imagination of a different future' (Feenberg, 1995b, p7). A planning-related thought experiment illustrates this point. Imagine someone who has never heard of mixed-use zoning. If this person encounters a mixed-use area in the real world, she will have difficulty finding an appropriate word to categorize her perception, much in the same way a child cannot fit a triangular wooden shape into a sorting block that only has a rectangular and a circular hole. The resolution (as in screen resolution) of her perception-space is limited to two drawers – one is labelled *residential*, the other *industrial*. These two elements also constitute her decision-space because if such a person is asked to devise a plan for a new development, she can only assemble the components she has available into a split-use proposal. Someone who is familiar with the concept of mixed-use would probably recommend rethinking the binary question 'should we put residential or industrial here?' In the same way, I recommend rephrasing the question 'do we need better technology or more moral behaviour?' to 'would it help if technology and behaviour co-evolved?' I make this suggestion because the concept of co-evolution seems better suited to accommodate certain shapes of reality – such as those just described in Belgium and Germany – than traditional linguistic templates.

The two respective halves of the prevailing sustainability discourse would have been at their best to describe strategies as the following. An exclusively extrasomatic/ technology orientated approach in Fürstenfeldbruck might have translated to a strong focus on heavily intensified agriculture with genetically modified organisms, thus increasing some farmers' income and reducing the use of pesticides at the same time. In contrast, an intrasomatic/behaviour orientated approach might have included an awareness campaign targeting consumers regarding their responsibility to buy their groceries only from organic farmers and to use bicycles or public transportation to shop. An analogous strategy in Hasselt might have included attempts to talk people into switching from their cars to bikes or the few buses, whereas an extrasomatic approach might have involved the construction of a third ring road or more meticulously engineered traffic flow management, including tunnels to conceal the traffic noise along the inner ring road.

These imaginative proposals are not as exaggerated as they might initially appear. A field trial with GMOs was indeed carried out in Fürstenfeldbruck County in 1992–1993. It stirred a passionate debate about the pros and cons of utilizing this technology, with arguments ranging from 'many small and medium-sized farms . . . can be saved from insolvency' (Andreä, cited in M. L., 1993, pFFB8) to 'genetic engineering cannot halt the disappearance of farms'.[1] A predominantly intrasomatic approach was and still is advocated by Krömeke, who favours a 'culture of scarcity' (interview, 22 January 2002) and who opposes the distribution of regional products through supermarkets. In Hasselt, the regional plan had space reserved for a third ring road and the former city government's overall traffic concept 'wanted to prove in particular that the mobility problem can be made subject to "engineering"' (*Mobility with*, 1999, p9). Moerkerk explicitly distinguishes the strategy that was chosen against this previous proposal, whose authors, he said, 'made the mistake of only looking at the "engineering" side of it. . .[For him] the success of the Hasselt project is all about a combination of measures, definitely not only by engineers: engineering, mentality, environment, city building, social issues, communication' (Moerkerk, via email, 16 July 2002). Even Krömeke, who is not fond of every aspect of Brucker Land, describes it as 'a third way. . . between industrial agriculture and [orthodox] ecological farming' (interview, 22 January 2002). The challenge proper for any vocabulary is not to describe what has *not* been done but to describe what *has* been done. Table 4.1 depicts the respective highlights of the cases of Hasselt and Fürstenfeldbruck. These mark the essence of the solutions found in each case, as will be described in further detail in Chapter 5.

It might be helpful to revisit Table 4.1 during the reading of the remaining chapters, especially when additional case studies are being presented. Some triple 'X's in columns 5 and 6 indicate that the respective core elements – represented by rows – can be well described in either of the prevailing vocabularies. Neither, however, is capable of consistently describing all rows, especially not the combination of a change of behaviour and technological/infrastructural measures. The concept of co-evolution as I will present it below *does* have this capability. This will hardly surprise, given that this concept has been developed for exactly the purpose of describing cases like Hasselt and Fürstenfeldbruck. I therefore claim that co-evolution is a useful conceptual and linguistic device, an expedient 'LogIcon' (Joerges, 1999b). This is itself a linguistic device to describe 'pictures to think with' (Joerges, 1999b, p427) or a 'piece of ready-made-discourse – a "discoursette"' (Joerges, 1999b, p414). Rip argues along the very same lines that

Table 4.1 *Core elements of the two cases and discourse-specific strengths to describe them*

	Column 2	Column 3	Column 4	Column 5	Column 6	Column 7
Row 2				Strength to describe		
Row 3		Hasselt	Fürstenfeldbruck	Extra-somatic	Intra-somatic	Co-evolution
Row 4	New technologies new range of choices	Green Boulevard . . . New buses. . . Extra lanes for buses, strollers and bicycles. . . Public transport hub. . . Reduced parking spaces	New brand with easily identifiable logo. . . New production and processing standards. . . New regional distribution system	XXX		XXX
Row 5	New technologies make socially desired behaviours attractive	Buses are free and run frequently, thus providing unprecedented convenience. . . Cycling is safer and faster on new bike lanes	Regional products are fresh, safe, healthy, tasty, easy to identify and ubiquitously available at affordable prices	X	X	XXX
Row 6	Participation facilitates synchronic preadaptation	Participatory inventory of the most problematic traffic points. . . Stakeholder participation. . . Widely communicated plans. . . Info-Bus . . . Stevaert is 'an expert in people'	Initial survey about the needs of the people. . . Participation of five major social groups; one of them is 'consumers'. . . 'The consumers are involved in all affairs'		XX	XX
Row 7	New technologies require social embedding	Buses are 'sexy' and even the local elites find them 'excellent' . . . 'Samen anders mobiel' and other campaigns	Traditional term used as brand name. . . 'There's something going on here'. . . 'Shelf missions' for face-to-face advertisement. . . 'Light from outside'	X	XXX	XXX
Row 8	Strategic	Retailers	Alliance includes		X	XXX

Table 4.1 *Core elements of the two cases and discourse-specific strengths to describe them (continued)*

	Column 2	Column 3	Column 4	Column 5	Column 6	Column 7
	alliances are more productive than ideological purity	cooperate with city government ...'Working together is the key'...'We could speak openly'	traditional adversaries... 'Solidarity is cohesion'... 'Everybody benefits'... Compromise of controlled cultivation			
Row 9	Inventiveness enables a departure from the prevailing discourse	'Lots of creativity' in Stevaert's policy plan... External inspiration... Input of experts... 'Steve Stunt'... Collective deliberations	'Built upon people's creativity' ...'It pays to bring forward creative ideas'... External inspiration...'All the ideas came from here'... Collective deliberations	XXX	X	XXX
Row 10	Critical mass is crucial to overcome path dependencies	Do not 'fight only symptoms' ...'No patch-work'...'You have to do it 100%'...'Three steps at a time' ...'Break vicious circle'	'Think big'...'In ten years, this must be known all over the world'...'A global network of thriving sustainable regions'	XXX	XXX	XXX

Note: the number of 'X's in Table 4.1 correlates with the ability of a specific vocabulary to describe what happened in either case in its respective row. The 'X's do not signify a quantitative measurement; they merely represent my impression of relative significance. This impression is certainly open for discussion and interpretation but I assume that it is comprehensible for most readers who are familiar with the content and outcomes of the two case studies (columns 3 and 4), with the technology and behaviour orientated approach (columns 5 and 6) and with the concept of co-evolution (column 7) as described in the remainder of this chapter.

one of the most important contribution STS scholars can make to solving societal problems is that of:

> *naming, i.e. using a name (a concept, a label) to mobilise one's own and others' experience and items from the literature to understand one's own situation better*

and derive action strategies... [because] 'naming' locates situations, problems, options in the landscape of our society. Rip, 1994

Names are, to use Paul Carter's words, 'lighthouses for getting on' (1988, p9), just as new analytical frames are 'new strategies for thinking' (Jacobs, cited in Mehaffy, 2004). It should become clear then that sustainability agents whose LogIcon only contains words such as engineering, optimization, high-tech and efficiency have not only a limited ability to describe but also a limited ability to imagine. The same holds for those who work with a LogIcon built around heroic choices. The reverse logic suggests that because the vocabulary of co-evolution is well suited to describe cases like Hasselt and Fürstenfeldbruck, it is also suitable to describe new cases and therefore, to imagine future ones. The venture to elaborate this vocabulary therefore appears truly worthwhile and is undertaken in Chapter 5.

Co-evolution as deliberate symbiosis

Based on the earlier description of the projects undertaken in Hasselt and Fürstenfeldbruck, I conclude that both indeed evaded the dichotomy trap or, to put it more positively, harnessed the 'interplay of design and use' (Rohracher, 2001, p224). With reference to the circular and iterative relationship between technology and behaviour as illustrated in Figure 2.2, I suggest the authors of these two projects kept this dynamic and iterative cycle in focus rather than only one of the two arrows. Converting this description into a prescription, I argue that it should be possible to enter into this circuit with a pinch of technological voluntarism and to devise technologies or infrastructures (the arrow from right to left) that make it easy for users to behave in a certain way (the arrow from left to right). With inspiration from authors in the field of sustainable architecture, I propose to call this process a 'fruitful co-evolution between technology design and use' (Rohracher and Ornetzeder, 2002, p74) or 'co-evolution of social and technical systems' (Guy and Shove, 2000, p131).

The term co-evolution is borrowed from biology, where it became prominent with Ehrlich and Raven's work on *Butterflies and Plants* (1965). The mere term, however, was apparently used long before that 'and the idea was very present in *On the Origin of Species*' as Rand (1999) explains. He offers the following definition of co-evolution: 'A change in the genetic composition of one species . . . in response to a genetic change in another' (Rand, 1999). Geiger (2002) adds that this change has to be reciprocal. He distinguishes between two types of co-evolution: an antagonistic version that leads to an arms race, typically a sequential escalation of prey defences and predator resistance. In contrast, cooperative co-evolution, also called symbiosis, can result in mutually beneficial consequences for the partners involved. My concept of co-evolution of technology and behaviour clearly has the cooperative version of change in mind. It does, however, not completely meet Rand's definition, which sees change on either side as the 'response' to a change on the other side. This would not be much different from Pfaffenberger's 'technological drama' (1992), which is a sequence of action and re-action and re-re-action and so on. What my notion of co-evolution implies – and where the term cannot do full justice to its biological prequel – is an explicit agreement between co-evolving partners to take a simultaneous and concerted step forward. Plants and animals simply do not have this capability to conduct a conscious and discursive exchange of ideas and interests.

A palpable need for co-evolution in this sense has been conveyed to me by Stappen: a perfect public transport system is of not much good if people do not make use of it – for whatever rational or irrational reasons. Vice versa, it is of no avail if people are willing to use public transport if there aren't any buses to ride (see Stappen, 1995). This mechanism amounts to a prisoners' dilemma centred on the question 'who takes the first step, the users or the providers?' In the logic of co-evolution, this is a false alternative. What we should look for instead is a holistic 'improvement of the socio-technical product' (Rohracher and Ornetzeder, 2002, p78). The first step in this process must be to bring providers and users together so they can jointly shed light on the situation. What they could then realize is that the explanation of this situation rests neither exclusively with individual failings nor with wrong structures alone but with their unfortunate stalemate. At this point, it should become evident to the participants of such a dialogue that progress requires concerted action between the supply and demand sides.

In what follows in Chapter 5, I have developed a more analytical account of the concept of co-evolution by taking a closer look at its disaggregated building blocks as introduced in Table 4.1. Four different expectations are attached to this step. First, the set of memes can serve as heuristic for a systematic comparison of different cases. Second, the concept of co-evolution can be systematically checked element by element against empirical evidence. Third, these pieces can – if they pass the empirical test – serve as digestible units of inspiration[2] instead of one bulky chunk of thick description. Fourth, empirically supported building blocks of co-evolution can be used to systematically construct a definition of co-evolution.

The memetics of co-evolution

Before I continue with this step, I suggest a brief detour to introduce the term *meme*. This move permits further helpful analogies in the language of evolution and clarification of the nature of co-evolution. The concept of memes is a LogIcon whose introduction is commonly credited to Dawkins in his 1976 book *The Selfish Gene*.[3] A meme is the cultural equivalent of a gene, the elementary building block of living beings. Organisms whose genes make them well adapted to their environment have a higher likelihood of survival. Similarly, those artefacts – 'tunes, ideas, catch-phrases, clothes fashion, ways of making pots or of building arches' (Dawkins, 1989, p192) – are most likely to be reproduced when their memes are fit for their cultural environment; where 'perceived usefulness' is the main criterion of fitness. The concept of memes, for example, has proven its usefulness as a linguistic tool, which is why it is still around in the academic environment. This observation is exactly what Menand (2001) puts in the collective mouths of the fathers of American pragmatism, Dewey, James, Holmes Jr and Peirce: 'Ideas are not "out there" waiting to be discovered, but are tools – like forks and knives and microchips – that people devise to cope with the world in which they find themselves' (Menand, 2001, pxi). If memes are never ultimately true but rather a contingent product of human creativity, then they are malleable, which alludes to an important common point between memes and genes: mutation and variation.

Genes mutate by random variation and the result is either retained or discarded by their environment. The plants and animals we see today are, by definition, the result of variations that have proven their fitness and continue to do so in the process of evolution; this does not, however, guarantee that they will survive until the end of time. The same holds for memes. The automobile, for example, has extremely successful memes that have 'found a medium of replication in the consciousness of humans'[4] (Csikszentmihalyi, 1997, p46). Examples of these memes are the linking of automobiles with social status, the public belief in the auto-industry as a job creator and especially the generation of their own indispensability through the facilitation of urban sprawl. If the environment changes for automobile-related memes – that is, legislation, taste, rituals, cultural attitudes, and so forth – it is quite possible that these memes will become relatively less successful. It is important to see that laws, fashion and preferences are also memes and thus subject to mutation. The big question then is whether their mutation should happen by chance only or by deliberate intervention.

An extrapolation of this question into the policy realm leads to the confrontation between free market and centrally planned economies. The first approach is favoured by economist, neuroscientist and Nobel-winner Friedrich Hayek, who pleads for 'the party of life, the party that favours free growth and spontaneous evolution' (cited in Postrel, 1998, p30). Among his like-minded comrades is Postrel, who 'shows how and why unplanned change and open ended trial and error are the keys to human betterment' (Dynamist.com, 2002). This laissez-faire stance is diametrically opposed to Brulle's argument, according to which 'ecological problems must be dealt with in much shorter time frames than can be anticipated for slow, gradual, or unintended social change. . .We cannot leave this up to vague, indeterminate, undirected social change' (Brulle, 2000, p6). Csikszentmihalyi supports this interventionist approach and argues that 'we have to take things in hand and shape the artefacts that will determine our future' (1997, p47). From his analysis of the self-momentum of the memes of weapons and automobiles, he derives a call for 'eumemics', the attempt to ensure that 'the memes that are going to colonize. . . the minds of our descendants are not going to be too detrimental to human survival' (Csikszentmihalyi, 1997, p47).

With my endorsement of the concept of co-evolution as a simultaneous and concerted step forward I tend toward the interventionist approach (however not to its culmination in a centrally planned economy). This decision is grounded in the unique human capacity to anticipate the consequences of their actions, at least to some degree.[5] Not using this capability would be utterly non-human. Some planning is therefore a necessary, yet not sufficient, condition of what I present as the concept of co-evolution. Two further human traits are at least as important: creativity and communication. The role of the former is undisputed among laissez-faire and interventionist strategists alike, but the latter seems to be undervalued in both camps. I argue that only through communication is it possible for the potential partners[6] of a potentially symbiotic relationship to discover the potential for mutual benefit and thus to deliberately design artefacts with respective memes. This contractual element makes the simultaneous and concerted step forward possible and liberates us from waiting for the one lucky shot in the blind play of trial and error.

The memes we devise through creative, deliberate and communicative planning efforts might prove unfit or even disastrous, however. This is what Schwartz Cowan means by 'today's mistakes may have been yesterday's "rational choice"' (cited in MacKenzie and Wajcman, 1985, p261). From this insight stems the awareness that deliberately designed memes have to prove their fitness in their particular environment over the course of time. If they cannot be declared successful, we have to adapt the memes of our mental creation. For example, the city of Hasselt initially decided to make their bus system free only until a major evaluation in 2001. As we know today, the system passed this test and the city council decided to continue the free buses until at least 2006. No one knows how this evaluation will go, but[7] it is quite possible that Hasselt's mobility plan might have to be adapted to new societal, legal, political, technological or environmental contexts. After all, 'human institutions are nothing more than sets of agreements which must be either confirmed from time to time (often by rituals when new members enter the society) or consciously altered, as in our perpetual law-making' (S. Moore, personal communication, 21 December 2002). I therefore do not claim that co-evolution leads to ultimate solutions, but I argue that it helps to find smart adaptations when adaptations are necessary. Concretely, I hope that when Hasselt has to revise its mobility policy that it will not dogmatically retain the solution of free buses but again will take a co-evolutionary stance and hopefully find a consistent solution.

In this evolutionary view of progress there can be no such thing as the ultimately best meme, just like there can be no ultimately best gene. Living beings as well as 'ideas are provisional responses to particular and unreproducible circumstances, their survival depends not on their immutability but on their adaptability' (Menand, 2002, pxi). This notion is very close to William James' (one of the founders of the school of thought known as Pragmatism) procedural model of truth where everything is in permanent transition toward something new, but never toward a predetermined truth, never toward the end of history. Taking this logic of mutability seriously means that we should not implement plans with potentially irreversible consequences. Jonas (1984) would support this as an ethical position, whereas in pragmatist terms it would simply result from a will to succeed, because irreversible and unintended consequences are simply a non-success for any memitor (analogous to genitor).[8] In this view, the terms 'sustainable' and 'long-term successful' become undistinguishable.

If I take my own call for adaptability seriously, I have to accept that it also applies to the concept of co-evolution proper. Consequently, I have to acknowledge that the idea that I advertise might one day lose its usefulness. But in the current cultural environment I think co-evolution has some potential yet untapped.

Notes

1   Several articles in the local newspaper Fürstenfeldbrucker Tagblatt in March and April 1993 report this or similar statements made by the Regional Ecological Farmers, the State Association for the Protection of Birds (LBV), the Green Party, the Social-democratic Party and the regional direct marketing association, Bauernquelle.

2   I use the term 'units of inspiration' here instead of 'elements of a blueprint' because the portability of the building blocks has to be examined by those who may appropriate them.

3   Laurent (1999) questions the role of Dawkins as the progenitor of memes with compelling arguments. According to Laurent, the term had predecessors in ancient Greece and was used by Richard Semon as early as 1899 with almost the identical denotation as in Dawkins' usage. Maurice Maaeterlinck is also said to have used the word 'mneme' in 1927 in a sense very close to Dawkins' meme.

4   Csikszentmihalyi (1997) made this point originally with reference to weapons, but from what follows in his text it becomes clear that he would not hesitate to apply this expression to the automobile as well. A similar statement was made by McLuhan, who observed that 'technology has reduced us to the "sex organs of machines"' (cited in Feenberg, 1995b, p5).

5   Dawkins derives major hope from this:

> *unique feature of man . . . his capacity for conscious foresight. . . Even if we look on the dark side and assume that individual man is fundamentally selfish, our conscious foresight – our capacity to simulate the future in imagination – could save us from the worst selfish excesses of the blind replicators. We have at least the mental equipment to foster our long-term selfish interests rather than merely our short-term selfish interests. . . We, alone on earth, can rebel against the tyranny of the selfish replicators.*
> Dawkins, 1989, pp200–201

6   For example, the providers and users of urban technologies.

7   Besides the fact that the transport plan of Hasselt does not fall or stand with the free buses alone.

8   Whether this position is 'truly' ethical or pragmatic does not matter in my view, which is, again, a pragmatist's position.

Notes

5

Memes of Co-evolution

This chapter presents each meme of co-evolution as identified in Table 4.1 one by one. Like all attempts to disaggregate a heap of empirical evidence into meaningful sub-units, this approach is vulnerable to criticism from people who would have analyzed the data at a different angle into different pieces. I agree that my choice is just one of several feasible ones – but I trust that readers whose motivation to understand the clockwork of co-evolution is fuelled by an intent to facilitate co-evolutionary projects themselves may find the angle of analysis employed here useful.

New technologies provide a new range of choices

An immediate lesson to be drawn from the arguments of the STS community is that preferences, needs and the social practices they generate are not immutable, genetically hardwired or, in any other way, eternally fixed. They might appear innate and just plain normal because in our personal memory they have always already been there. But if we look closer, we can unmask most of them as a function of historically grown circumstances, primarily of prevailing technological regimes, that is, the densely knitted networks of artefacts, ingrained habits, power structures, legal frameworks, support institutions and social expectations. The concept of technological regime was introduced by Nelson and Winter (1977) and is still useful for a conceptual grasp of our modern situation. A prime example of a technological regime is the transport system in its widest sense and its effects on, say, typical US suburban dwellers:

> *They do not tarry in their car for one hour per day because they have an innate preference for that place but because a complex set of factors causes enormous traffic jams: dispersed settlement forms, a spatial separation of work and home. . . caused in part by the frontier ideology of the early settlers, the value of private property for the founding fathers, the urban planning paradigm of the Athens Charter, home construction subsidies to WWII veterans, lobbyism by the automobile industry and a host of others.* Brand, 2005b, p4

The resulting social practices lead to further technical adaptations like traffic management systems, living room-size cars with particle filters in their ventilation ducts, audio-books for the bored commuter and many more, which cement the transport infrastructure that has spawned them. Cases like these suggest that in a mature (transport) regime the technical and behavioural side stabilize each other or as Kemp and Rotmans formulate it, 'supply and demand not only interact but also interlock' (2001, p1).

Analogously, the inhabitants of Fürstenfeldbruck County did not buy apples from New Zealand because they wanted to support antipodean farmers but because a complex set of political, technological and logistical factors made them more easily available (i.e. in every supermarket) than locally produced apples. I am convinced that this demand, in turn, has lead to improvements in apple transportation containers and so forth, thus consolidating the global apple regime and the range of choices for Fürstenfeldbruckian shoppers.

It is crucial to emphasize that the prevailing range of transport or shopping choices resulted from a host of previous decisions and not from an inevitable, natural logic. This is essentially behind Guy and Shove's observation that 'choices and options are. . . socially constructed' (2000, p68) and behind Hoogma et al's claim that 'technological options, user preferences and . . . institution[s] are not given ex ante, but created and shaped' (2002, p21). They are influenced by a huge array of circumstances including laws, habits, social obligations, conceptions of morality, risk perceptions and also technological options and infrastructural conditions.

A case in point is the introduction of the cast iron oven, which was shaped by the interests of producers, traders and fuel suppliers. Upon mutual agreement, these groups excluded certain alternative designs so that the customers simply could not choose them (Guy and Shove, 2000). The same lesson can be learned from a study by Morland, who questions the widely held assumption that 'when people aren't eating healthily, it's because they choose not to' (cited in Duenwald, 2002, pD5). She offers an alternative explanation by showing that access to grocery stores is a crucial explanatory variable with respect to the consumption of fruits and vegetables. In this context, it is especially notable that access to supermarkets in predominantly white neighbourhoods in the US is, on average, five times better than in black neighbourhoods (Morland, cited in Duenwald, 2002). As a conclusion we should probably ease from individual decision-makers the burden of their moral responsibility to choose wisely, simply because they do not have all possible choices. Rather, we should ask what structures incite certain practices. Guy and Shove even go so far as to state that 'we should abandon individualist explanations of technical change, including those that rely upon rational consumer action' (2000, p66).

The good news, then, is this: if regimes are not God-given and consequently alterable, so must be the preferences and social practices that evolved with them. Hunt and Wynne emphasize in this regard that 'public opinion, or even individual standpoints, are not fixed and immutable, but change in relation to a number of factors' (2000, p17). Almost identical comments are made by Haus and Klausen who argue that 'motivations . . . are not fixed once and for all' (2004, p3) and by Fainstein who supports Healey's claim that 'people do not have fixed interests' (2000, p458). Shove joins this tenor and maintains that preferences and needs are not 'stable and taken for granted [but rather] socio-technically configured [and] immensely malleable' (2002, p9). Most readers will have experienced an interesting manifestation of this phenomenon themselves: the advent of affordable inkjet printers has steeply increased the social expectation for and consequent the production of colourful reports, sophisticated transparencies and student papers with fancy graphics.

Box 5.1 Car sharing

The remarkable success of car-sharing initiatives (also known as car clubs in the UK) throughout Europe and especially in Switzerland underlines the importance of generating new choices. In a car-sharing system, multiple households have access to a cooperatively or commercially managed pool of automobiles in their neighbourhood that they can use for as short a period as one hour. For the participants, this means a car is available whenever they really need it, for example to transport heavy shopping goods or to get to a place that is impossible to reach by public transport. This new choice has attracted more than 100,000 people in Germany, Austria, the Netherlands and Switzerland to sign up as member of a car-sharing organization. Switzerland alone, where this idea mainly originated, is home to nearly 50,000 car-sharers who have access to close to 2000 cars in around 1000 locations across the country (Ledbury, 2004, p19).

Renting a car on an hourly basis simply did not exist as an option prior to the establishment of car-sharing initiatives. This triggered many people to rethink and to redefine their preferences and interests. Thousands of people concluded, upon careful scrutiny of their genuine transport needs, that individual car ownership becomes dispensable and so does the rationale – or pretext – to make even unnecessary trips by car because it reduces the cost per mile due to sunk costs embodied in one's own car. As several studies have shown, membership of car-sharing organizations indeed leads to an 'unlearning and abandoning of . . . habitual mobility patterns' (Hoogma et al, 2002, p172). It has been observed that:

> *after becoming car-sharing members, annual kilometres travelled dropped. . . Some used public transport, bicycle, or motorbike . . . to make trips that would formerly have been made by car, but a considerable number of trips were simply not made. Also, formerly car-free households, who used occasionally to borrow or rent a car, did not drive more after joining a car-sharing organization. . . Despite the car-sharers' reduction in total mobility, they did not feel restricted. In fact, they reported an improved quality of life. . . In some cases, giving up 'unnecessary' car trips was accompanied by a change in other activities as users reported seeking out shopping and leisure-time opportunities closer to home.* Hoogma et al, 2002, p157–158

The decision of many people in Hasselt to use public transport or to cycle to work co-emerged in a similar way, together with the improved bus system and the more attractive cycling infrastructure. The previous range of transport choices was defined by four car lanes along the inner ring road, an unattractive public transportation system, dangerous and unpleasant walking routes, and so forth. To go to work by bus or by bike was, under these circumstances, not a realistic alternative. To live on locally and ecologically grown food was also an unreasonable option in pre-Brucker Land times because '70 to 80 per cent of all bio-groceries available in supermarkets are merely dried products' (Nehls, cited in Trotz Agrarwende, 2001). Because eating muesli three times a day is neither healthy nor palatable, I conclude that when people do not buy pesticide-free and regionally produced groceries, it is not only because they choose not to. This observation is the foundation of Brucker Land's underlying philosophy: it is necessary 'to reopen the possibility for consumers buying regionally produced groceries where they usually shop' (Reginet.de, 2002) or, in other words, 'to present [the consumers with] something they cannot escape because they get it really well prepared' (Seiltz, interview, 15 January 2002).

Another project in Hasselt follows the same logic: the city helps finance neighbourhood parties in order to stimulate the desired effect of civic cohesion (Stevaert, interview, 6 December 2001). Clean streets, too, are desired, which is why the city donates official city flags to social organizations that can sell them to the public. These organizations thus gain some revenue and flags trickle into many households. Then, on certain occasions, 'we can ask the people. . . to fly the flag at their house. And I think that people. . . don't fly a flag at their house and let the garbage stand outside their door' (Stevaert, interview, 6 December 2001). Although I have never heard or read a statement by Stevaert that sounded like 'make people want what they ought to want', he appears to act according to that motto. Similarly, 'Ulrike Haberkorn', a member of Brucker Land, described her new shopping behaviour quite bluntly in this jargon: 'I do what I ought to do' (interview, 22 January 2002).

Figure 5.1 provides supportive evidence for this mechanism. It shows children of Las Gaviotas, Colombia, playing on a see-saw, which is constructed to function as a water pump as well. I assume that most readers find it easy to imagine that these children enjoy pumping water, or in other words, that they want to do what they ought to do. From my non-authoritarian perspective I prefer the expression 'that they want to do what has been defined as socially desirable in a participatory debate'.

The bottom line is that social practices can change. After all, Hasselt's 'sustainable mobility policy . . . intended to result in different traffic behaviour'[1] (Lambrechts, 2001, p11). Brucker Land, too, declared as one of its goals 'to change people's behaviour' (eNorm, 2002; and many other sources) in a non-manipulative way through the co-emergence of circumstances and social practices. Hence no one should give up the attempt to influence people's behaviour just because a moralistic approach has not proven particularly successful or because its manipulative cousin is unacceptable for normative and/or pragmatic reasons. These two strategies are not the only options. The belief in a legitimate and effective alternative is what fuels not only my hope but also Landry's rhetorical question: 'Can we imagine an approach to transport and land use which encourages us to

Source: Luis Guillermo Camacho, copyright ZERI

Figure 5.1 *Children playing and pumping water in Gaviotas, Colombia*

reduce car travel willingly? One that makes us want to return to walking or cycling for enjoyment?' (2000, p72). Co-evolution as implemented in Hasselt provides an optimistic answer, as does Brucker Land in regard to purchase decisions. A definition of co-evolution must therefore include a statement about the possibility of changing people's social practices through changed circumstances.

A synopsis of the above arguments suggests that any strategy to create fortunate relationships between technical options and social practices should start out by questioning the prevailing corridor of choices. We usually do not reflect upon it because it has been internalized as second nature. Winner has coined the expression 'technological somnambulism' (1977, p315) for this phenomenon. Being fully awake would entail a clear understanding of the gravitational pull that technological and regulatory circumstances exert on our social practices; a clear grasp of what makes socio-technical everyday life tick. STS scholars call this important step a regime analysis consisting of first and second order learning effects, as Schot and Rip (1996) would refer to it. The former signifies the accrual of knowledge about technical options; the latter goes further in its attempt to 'encourag[e] users and other actors . . . to rethink their perceived needs and basic assumptions' (Hoogma et al, 2002, p203). This process, if conducted in 'a meaningful dialogue can help its participants to discover that many of our preferences and attitudes are contingent upon the current but historically grown technological, political and infrastructural circumstances' (Brand, 2005b, p4). The discovery of their constructedness, then, can lead to the discovery of their malleability and eventually to 'co-evolutionary dynamics, that is, mutual articulation and interaction of technological choices, demand and possible regulatory options' (Hoogma et al, 2002, p28). A concrete implication for practitioners is thus to design innovation processes not with an exclusive focus on technical performance (first order learning) but with built-in arenas for dialogic second order learning. In epistemological parlance: to move from technical knowledge to experiential knowledge that helps us to see where and how the prevailing corridor of choices needs to be altered.

New technologies make socially desired behaviours attractive

The new corridor of choices should, of course, contain options that make the socially desired behaviour attractive. Taking into account what has been said before, this meme may sound obvious or even banal; I maintain, however, that the notion of *attractive* has yet to be scrutinized because upon closer inspection it will become clear that the cases described in this publication do not exclusively cater to conventional and static notions of attractiveness.

Related statements from Hasselt and Fürstenfeldbruck include mention of the following: comfort (A, B, C, D, E; see Table 5.1 for references); mobility (B, C, F); information (B, G); time savings (B, C); pleasure, quality of life, joie de vivre, clear conscience and taste (A); cleanliness, aesthetics and freedom of mobility (I); self-determination, affordability and happiness (H); safety (B); quality (D) and convenience (J).

Table 5.1 *References for multiple quotes*

A	Seiltz, interview, 15 January 2002
B	SHLS, 1994, pp3 and 9
C	Stevaert, 2000b
D	Hugo van Wesemael, cited in Jacobs, 1997d, p9
E	Stevaert, cited in Meuris, 1996, p1
F	Bormans, interview, 26 November 2002
G	Haberkorn, interview, 22 January 2002
H	Stevaert, interview, 6 December 2001
I	Moerkerk, interview, 27 November 2001
J	Reynders, cited in Rutten, 1995b, p13

The ideals mentioned show that what mattered in Hasselt and Fürstenfeldbruck is *perceived* attractiveness and that its cumulative definition can be quite broad. It includes standard characteristics of attractiveness, such as convenience and cost, but it also borders on 'truer pleasures' as critically described in Chapter 2. Before turning to the latter notions of attractivenesses, I suggest a brief look at the more conventional ideals.

In Hasselt, the most widely communicated aspect of its transport concept is attractive in a very conventional sense: free buses. This factor is, according to Stevaert, 'psychologically very very important' (interview, 6 December 2001) but it is only one of many measures taken to make buses, bicycling and walking more attractive. All of them are based on the observation that the prospect of reduced convenience makes it very unlikely for environmental behaviour to become mainstream. Stevaert explicates this rationale in a booklet about his energy policy: 'The transformation of awareness to actual behaviour is almost non-existent if environmentally friendly behaviour requires more effort or more time, if it means a forfeit of comfort, or if we are confined in our freedom of mobility' (2000a, p24). The designers of Brucker Land share this position to a large extent, which is why they built a number of conventional attractions into their project. The wide availability of Brucker Land products is certainly among those attractions with the highest relevance for people's purchasing decisions. Others are the unrivalled freshness of groceries, their professional presentation, easy identifiability and – given the many food scandals in Europe in the past decade – the degree of safety Brucker Land products stand for. Seiltz expands the range of conventional advantages by arguing that people whose car is fuelled by Brucker Land rapeseed oil 'can drive more and with a clear conscience . . . [because] their carbon dioxide balance remains neutral' (interview, 15 January 2002). This argument is in fact atypical for Brucker Land because it implies a surprising technophilic tinge. It also overlooks car-related problems unsolvable by alternative fuels such as noise, sprawl and accidents. To do justice to Seiltz, however, I should contextualize her statement as a refutation of my provocative question of whether Brucker Land capitalizes on people's willingness to make heroic choices.

The epitome of a conventional motivation, monetary gain, prompts thousands of Bangladeshis every day to make use of a technical infrastructure and at the same time to practice socially desired behaviour. They efficiently conduct their small agricultural enterprises for the benefit Bangladesh's growing population. This presupposes knowledge about current prices at the nearest market. The acquisition of this knowledge, however, used to consume unreasonable amounts of time and resources because of the necessary physical trip to the market. This impaired the effectiveness of the entire agro-economy in Bangladesh and hence the food situation of its population. This problem inspired the crew around Muhammad Yunus, the founder of the internationally renowned Grameen Bank, to establish Grameen Telecom, a non-profit 'company dedicated to bringing the information revolution to the rural people of Bangladesh' (Grameen Communications, 2005). The now almost ubiquitous access to so-called Village Phones made, in co-evolutionary parlance, the socially desired behaviour attractive. Further information about this project is provided in Box 5.2.

Box 5.2 Grameen's village phone

The idea of the Village Phone Programme in Bangladesh rests on Muhammad Yunus' conviction that 'technology must be designed with poor people in mind as users' (personal communication, 10 April 2003). For a variety of reasons a system of mobile phones suits many vital needs of the rural population in Bangladesh much better than a wired network, and can therefore play an important role in implementing GrameenPhone's rationale that ease of communication is a basic requirement for a flourishing business – regardless of its size – and that good business is a prerequisite of good development. In other words, the Village Phone Programme uses the telephone as a weapon against poverty.

In 1997, GrameenPhone launched its service in cooperation with Grameen Bank, probably the most well-known micro-credit lending institution worldwide. The general idea is that a Grameen Bank member obtains ownership of a mobile phone under the lease-financing programme of the bank and provides the services to the people in the adjoining area, covering both outgoing and incoming calls. As of December 2004, there were more than 95,000 Village Phone subscribers who provide access to telecommunication for the rural poor in almost every village of Bangladesh, 60 million people in total.

The operator's income is derived from the difference between the air-time charges paid by customers and the billed amount required to be paid by the Village Phone operator along with a flat charge for each incoming call. Most operators of these 'mobile public call offices' are women who gain exciting income-generating opportunities and benefit from their enhanced social status. According to some studies, the introduction of Village Phones has made a tremendous social and economic impact in the rural areas. One of the studies was conducted by the TeleCommons Development Group for the Canadian International Development Agency. It concluded:

> *The Village Phone Program yields significant positive social and economic impacts, including relatively large consumer surplus and immeasurable quality of life benefits. The consumer surplus from a single phone call to Dhaka, a call that replaces the physical trip to the city, ranges from 264 per cent to 9.8 per cent of the mean monthly household income. The cost of a trip to the city ranges from 2 to 8 times the cost of a single phone call, meaning real savings for poor rural people.* GrameenPhone, 2005b

The Village Phone Programme has gained widespread global recognition and has been featured extensively in international media as 'one of the greatest success stories in international development' (GFUSA, 2004). The idea has spread to other countries, even to other continents and meanwhile GrameenPhone has become the largest cellular phone company in all of South Asia with almost 2,000,000 subscribers.

Sources: Grameen Telecom, 2001; GFUSA, 2004; GrameenPhone, 2005a

As pointed out earlier, there are sustainability activists who try to promote new preferences and needs[2] to make certain things and social practices appear as 'more truly attractive' and it seems worthy of some lines to examine whether the success of Hasselt or of Brucker Land is based upon such tactics. For Hasselt I could not, for example, detect any attempt to advertise slowness as a new ideal. On the contrary, I could only identify strategies to meet needs and desires that were already mainstream before the implementation of the new infrastructures, most notably the desire for safe, cheap, fast and reliable transport. Even the desires of citizens who want to drive their cars into the city are still being met.

A corresponding assessment of Brucker Land, however, is more ambiguous, because the widely advertised quality of these products is clearly meant to supersede the desire for food quantity or food bargains. Klein explicates this rationale by suggesting that reducing a meat serving from 150 to 120 grams will save money that can be reallocated to pay for the more expensive Brucker Land meat (interview, 25 January 2002). His reasoning becomes almost contrived as he elaborates that 'if you eat meat every day, you cannot really enjoy it any more... Therefore, if renunciation, then renunciation is a gain in your quality of life'. Seiltz, too, emphasizes 'joy of life' but has to admit that this argument 'is not yet as apparent with groceries' (interview, 15 January 2002), as in the aforementioned example of cruising with rapeseed fuel. Her baseline, however, is unshaken: 'it tastes good and it is all natural'. Similar statements were made by Haberkorn,[3] Dengler[4] and other interviewees. Whether or not these arguments endorse truer pleasures is hard to say. If the citizens of Fürstenfeldbruck County had already wanted to buy fresher and tastier products, then Brucker Land simply facilitated the satisfaction of pre-existing desires. The same conclusion would hold if consumers wanted to 'make sure that I'll still have a bakery in my town in five years' (Dengler, interview, 28 January 2002) or if they genuinely wanted to 'do something' for the environment or even for the farmers in their county. Brucker Land made it much easier for all of these motivations to be put into action because it is not necessary to cycle seven extra miles to the potato farmer or to wait for the farmer's market on Saturday. In short, the purchase of Brucker Land products in the supermarket can satisfy existing internal motivations.

But did Brucker Land in fact address such pre-existing desires or did it simply succeed in reprogramming consumers with new desires or a willingness for heroic choices? I do not know of empirical data that would answer this question, but I claim thorough knowledge of the cultural environment in Fürstenfeldbruck County from living nine years in an adjacent county. The level of environmental awareness is certainly high in this region due to a traditional connectedness to the land in the rural western areas of the county and due to the high level of education of the civil servants and high-tech employees who settle in the eastern part of the county because of the short commute to Munich. They are certainly also able to see the connection between their shopping behaviour and their self-interest in keeping the neighbourhood bakery alive. Lastly, their well-paid jobs give them some financial leeway, which enables them to purchase Brucker Land products – for whatever reason – without making heroic choices.[5] I therefore agree with Dengler who argued that the clientèle of Brucker Land is at least partly a function of social strata (via email, 31 March 2003). It is correct that those at the lower end of the economic scale cannot afford to buy Brucker Land products, but they are also not penalized by the existence of Brucker Land. Among those who can and do buy these products are probably some who exercise a pinch of altruism beyond genuine self-interest every time they purchase a Brucker Land product. But I claim that pre-existing and internal motivations outweigh heroic choices and reprogramming effects by far. In other words, Brucker Land simply provided a new opportunity to 'act out' these pre-existing preferences because previously people who wanted to buy regionally grown groceries simply could not do so.

This would be the straightforward interpretation if preferences were fixed; and some of them certainly are. Considering the dynamic notion of preferences introduced above, however, we also must acknowledge that either the development process of Brucker Land or its mere existence could have caused the questioning of old preferences. This effect is different by far from brainwashing or cajolery; it is simply an external trigger to disassemble and to reassess the factors that created preconceived preferences. A very sagacious observation by Oliver Wendell Holmes is extremely helpful in this regard: 'We know we're right before we know why we are right. First we decide, then we deduce' as Menand (2001, p353) puts it.[6] This explains why many people construct their preferences to a large extent around their available options. We try to avoid a stark mismatch between preferences and opportunities because it would create discontent. We also seek to work around a mismatch between deeply ingrained habits and social expectations because it would create a sense of guilt. And if we cannot change the external factors, or if we believe this is the case, we often adjust our preferences or the rationales behind them.[7] This explains why 'users increasingly rationalize their existing mobility patterns as if there existed an objective need to own and use a car in the currently defined and accepted ways' (Hoogma et al, 2002, p127). But a new element in the range of choices can destabilize the validity of preferences and can lead to their rearrangement. Hoogma et al put the same thought much more succinctly: 'Technology and user requirements co-evolve' (2002, p115).

From this claim they derive important implications for practitioners: it is 'important for developers to examine their assumptions about users' needs and preferences and. . . it is equally important for users to have an environment that encourages them to question their needs and preferences' (Hoogma et al, 2002, p172). Co-evolutionary processes thus have to be based on a thorough assessment of what counts as currently attractive and on a reflexive debate about what is *potentially* attractive to facilitate socially desired behaviour. The locally contingent definitions of both social desirableness and intersubjectively perceived attractiveness can either be guessed by (hopefully benevolent) designers or jointly articulated in a participatory, open-ended, dialogic process. As can be easily predicted from the normative and pragmatic considerations explained so far, I clearly recommend the latter strategy.

Participation facilitates synchronic pre-adaptation

Public participation is not at all a self-evident meme for significant changes in the public realm. After all, lengthy and messy public debates are often notorious for meagre results – the lowest common denominator between the atomic interests of Lockean individuals. The best outcome of participatory approaches, objectors argue, is patchwork improvement, but never a fundamental overhaul. A loophole out of this 'tragedy of incrementalism' (Scott Campbell, personal communication, 11 May 2002), some argue, is a wise and charismatic leader, endowed with the remit to 'get stuff done' (Moore, 2002, p11) – including bold, creative, radical stuff. This concept of bypassing public debate is essentially an undemocratic attempt to 'suppress conflict' (Moore, 2002), based on the rationale that expert and technocratic elites already know what needs to be done or on the argument that the free play of experimentation should never be hampered by the timid – because ill-informed – public.[8]

The application of an expertocratic approach to co-evolution, where technology is seen as something that makes a certain behaviour attractive, resonates strangely with behaviourism. From this theoretical perspective, a human being is seen as a mechanistically governed entity that reacts to certain stimuli in predictable ways, like rats moving toward food in a maze. If all stimuli are set right, Skinner argues, 'people will become wise and good without trying, without having to be, without choosing to be. The application of behavioural science to moral training will produce men who are good practically automatically' (1955, p60). This scenario must sound repulsively Orwellian to those who favour sustainability *and* democracy. A number of modifications to the rat-in-the-maze metaphor, however, might win their approval. First, the lab assistant is dismissed. Second, the well-informed rats agree that the current distribution of rats in the maze is undesirable. Third, a plenary assembly of rats decides in an undistorted debate that it would be best for all rats to gather in a certain corner of the maze. Fourth, the rats agree that a team should be appointed to place the food at an agreed-upon location. Fifth, the democratically elected rat government builds convenient steps and ladders on the path to that corner. In this version, the declared willingness to behave in a certain way (move through the maze) is developed simultaneously to the promise of attractive infrastructures (steps and ladders). This is what Rohracher calls 'synchronic pre-adaptation' (2001, p8). From a different perspective, this example shows that participation is productively harnessed to achieve the objectives of problem definition, solution finding, sense of ownership and sustainable citizenship. The remainder of this section investigates these objectives in further detail and examines comparable steps in the two cases studied.

The first of the four reasons why participation deserves the status of a meme of co-evolutionary projects is that it helps to identify societally relevant problems. This is important because solutions should be a function of the problems they are supposed to solve. In expert cultures, however, it is not uncommon that the selection of solutions precedes the problem definition because experts want to see their expertise in demand by framing the problem correspondingly. Hoogma et al provide case studies of experiments with:

predefined [mobility] technologies [where] the starting point was not a local
problem (of pollution, congestion, lack of accessibility, need for new types of
economic activity), but a solution. As a result, little was learned about user
needs and preferences, about the opportunities for users to change their behaviour,
or about how users could meet their perceived mobility needs in more
environmentally sustainable ways. Hoogma et al, 2002, p182

In participatory environments, experts have to account for their recommendations,
which includes the duty to make the problem definition transparent. Participation,
therefore, helps to get the order of steps straight: problem definition first, solution
finding second. Often, experts claim that they already know what the socially
relevant problems are. But just as often, there is 'an enormous gap between the
prescribed user [as assumed by the expert] and the user-in-flesh' (Latour, 1992,
p237). A 2002 Harvard-led workshop on science and technology for sustainable
development makes the same observation: 'A large gap persists between what the
science and technology community thinks it has to offer and what society has
demanded and supported' (Clark et al, 2002, p4). One of the reasons for this
incongruence is that 'elites can and do insulate themselves from problems' (Moore,
2002, p20). For instance, hardly anyone who has the choice would choose to live
in an unsafe or polluted area. By evading certain aspects of social reality and by
subduing social conflict, 'technocratic regimes. . . suppress the very information
they need most to govern wisely' (Moore, 2002, p20).

Rohracher and Ornetzeder phrase this mechanism positively: with
participation, it can be ensured 'that existing social needs and experiences are
reflected and respected' (2002, p81) in the design of technology. For this reason,
Clark et al call for a 'new contract between science and society for sustainable
development [to guarantee that science tackles the] most urgent sustainability
problems as defined by society, not just by scientists' (2002, p4). Such a contract
would have to acknowledge users as experts; if not as experts in technical aspects,
then at least in the social perception of problems. Ideally, this leads to 'interactive
learning processes' (Rohracher and Ornetzeder, 2002, p80) among and between
designers and users. This refers again to the two types of learning introduced
above: the more conventional first and the often overlooked second order type.
The car-sharing case is a lucid example of the latter because 'users . . . learned
much about their daily transport needs and how they could satisfy them by using
the new technology' (Hoogma et al, 2002, p156). A related type of second order
learning about the 'real' problem is the possibility of discovering and articulating
Radermacher dilemmas. I use this term to describe circumstances that force us to
do something we actually do not like doing. A deliberate change from positional
bargaining between social groups to candid exchange of problem perceptions
can lead to such Eurekas of shared problems. Such a dialogue requires safe speech
situations in a Habermasian sense, where the admission of a non-superficial and
perhaps surprisingly frank problem perception is never held against anyone.

Public participation can also facilitate the finding of creative solutions in several
ways – the second reason why participation should be considered a meme of co-
evolution. It provides a forum for the articulation of collective wisdom, tacit

knowledge and creativity of introverted thinkers. Even the absence of knowledge among the participants in a public debate can be beneficial as it requires the experts to re-open the black box of their expertise in order to re-present it piece by piece. A disassemblage of that sort makes the constructedness of the current range of choices transparent and thus provides a chance to envision new constructions. Grundin argues from a psychological point of view for participation because 'discovery more often waits upon those who conceive of achievement as part of a communal effort than upon those who want it as a personal prize' (1990, p31). Lastly, it is the sheer number of participants in a publicly conducted debate that can prove helpful because it represents 'a broader spectrum of viewpoints, [which] increases the odds of discovering creative solutions' (Rohracher and Ornetzeder, 2002, p81). This probabilistic and pragmatic argument has already been used by Oliver Wendell Holmes in his substantiation of free speech:

> *We do not permit the free expression of ideas because some individual might have the right one. No individual alone can have the right one. We permit free expression because we need the resources of the whole group to get us the ideas we need.* Cited in Menand, 2001, p431

A whole new strand of research has developed around this idea of the user as source of creativity. Spearheaded by people like Nikolaus Franke and Eric von Hippel (2002) this research community recently got a virtual home at <http://userinnovation.mit.edu/> where my related thoughts on the 'Citizen Innovator' are also posted. A case in point is the Austrian success story on solar water heaters, as presented in Box 5.3.

A third mechanism justifies the inclusion of participation among the memes of co-evolution. Rohracher and Ornetzeder describe an example of this mechanism in the context of green architecture: 'The possibilities for prospective users to decide on technological options and participate in the planning process has major effects on the environmentally sound operation of the building and the behaviour of its users' (2002, p76). In other words, participation can minimize 'deviant uses' (Rohracher, personal communication, 1 March 2005). This argument is especially important in the context of co-evolution and is closely connected to the preceding two sets of arguments. To recapitulate: co-evolution implies a collective change of behaviour, a goal that is easily missed given the manifold possibilities to undermine technologies that prescribe undesired behaviours. With regard to the appropriation of new technologies, which is inherently an active and not passive process, it is therefore crucial that people agree upon the desirability of the kind of behaviour that is meant to be facilitated by new technical circumstances. The best way to ensure that is to include the prospective users in defining the problem and in the development of solutions so that they feel collective ownership for the outcome. This strategy of modelling technologies very close to the potential of later adaptation – what Rohracher calls 'synchronic pre-adaptation' (2001, p8) – is simply a way to prevent misinvestments.

The fourth reason why participation has memetic qualities for co-evolution is provided by Light (2002), who observed that public involvement in projects of

Box 5.3 The Austrian success story on solar water heaters

Solar water heaters are much more common in Austria than in most other European countries. Ornetzeder (2001, 2002) explains this enormous success with reference to two main factors. First is the emergence of a self-construction movement, consisting of do-it-yourself groups that has spread throughout Austria since the 1980s. This strategy made it possible for nearly everyone to design a solar water heater system that not only comes at a very affordable price but also can be designed to suit one's existing – or future – demands in terms of water volume, usage patterns, availability of roof space, and so forth. The second crucial ingredient in the success story is the fact that most of the early adopters were rural families who not only commanded the skills to build such a system themselves, but also discovered that a self-constructed solar water heater could be an ideal opportunity to replace the often outdated heating technologies in their farm houses.

This case is thus an example of how the availability of a technological option triggered the reassessment and articulation of problems and preferences, which in turn led to the further development and improvement of the technology to suit these needs; a classic case of 'learning by using'.

Although no Austrian farmer would ever have minded the amenity of a modern bathroom, this did not gain action-relevant importance as long as there was no pushing urgency or pulling attraction. Only as the latter emerged in the form of self-construction groups did this latent preference surface. Of the solar water heater adopters surveyed in Lower Austria, 40 per cent mentioned 'added comfort' as the most important motivation for their decision; way more than those who were motivated by environmental concerns (20 per cent) or cost savings (7 per cent) (Ornetzeder, 2002). This observation backs Hoogma et al's claim that 'user demands are articulated and expressed in the process [of technology development] itself' (2002, p21). Conversely, the development, improvement and fine-tuning of a technology goes on during the diffusion stage because the users had a chance to essentially become co-innovators. Ornetzeder reports in this regard that 'the close connection between the self-construction movement and early users enabled ongoing technical improvements of the system, which were adopted by commercial producers and installation companies' (Ornetzeder, 2001, p105). Thus, the lessons learned from the self-built solar systems spilled over into the design and success of commercially produced solar water heaters with the effect that by 1995, Austria had gained second place (after Greece) in Europe for the diffusion of solar water heaters per capita.

ecological restoration bound the participants to their environment. The resulting 'ecological citizenship' made people more aware and appreciative of complex ecological phenomena at the local and the global level. Similar mechanisms are realistically to be expected if people are invited to become co-designers of technologies, which triggers learning processes that may lead by themselves to a change of behaviour. The unofficial slogan of Brucker Land 'through the stomach into the mind' (Seiltz, personal communication on several occasions) is based exactly on this expectation.

After all this theoretical reasoning the question remains whether the projects in Hasselt and Fürstenfeldbruck were in fact developed with significant citizen participation. Archival records and information from many interviews suggest that the debate over the long-term redesign of Hasselt's public infrastructure was launched by the study *Hasselt, een beeld van een stad* (Studiecentrum Willy Claes [SWC], 1990), which was commissioned by the Socialist Party (SP) in 1990. The authors of this document emphasized the necessity of citizen input, discussion evenings, hearings and exhibitions in neighbourhoods on several occasions (Studiecentrum Willy Claes, 1990). The study was professionally printed and distributed to every household, but its ambitious plans could not be realized because the SP was at that time the opposition party in the city parliament. However, the study triggered further thoughts within the ruling Conservative Party (CVP), which subsequently resulted in a new study, *Hasselt levendig stadscentrum* (SHLS [Stuurgroep Hasselt Levendig Stadscentrum], 1994). The 21 members of the steering panel consisted solely of city officials and external professionals, but no citizens, and the study was not distributed publicly. A very blunt reason for this anti-participatory strategy is given in the conclusion: 'It is the city government who makes choices for the common well-being' (SHLS, 1994, p28).

The plans of this study were not realized either because Stevaert's SP broke the several decades long hegemony of the CVP over Hasselt in the elections of 1994. The question concerning Hasselt's future traffic infrastructure was raised again under the new regime, which started with an inventory of the most problematic traffic points (*knelpuntenaanpak*) in Hasselt. This step was considered 'completely impossible without the contribution of . . . the citizenry' (Van Moerkerke, 1997, p7) and Moerkerk remembers it as 'a very interesting idea to let the people have something to say about the traffic problems in their surroundings' (Moerkerk, via email, 10 March 2003). Fifteen public hearings were organized, which led to a 232-page report enumerating traffic problems in the inner city (e.g. parking, accessibility, bike lanes), in the suburbs (e.g. speeding, public transportation, traffic volume) and along the arterials (e.g. safety, speeding, bike lanes, poor living conditions, pedestrian crossings) (Van Moerkerke, 1997). The results of this inventory of traffic problems are still used by the city of Hasselt to make its allocation of resources transparent, 'to prioritize its projects. . .[and to] tell complainers which priority their problem has' (Van Moerkerke, 1997, p7).

The next step, the search for a framework of solutions, was conducted with the explicit exclusion of the citizenry, because this 'is the business of planners, traffic experts and designers who are authorized in this regard' (Van Moerkerke, 1997, p8). This phase, it cannot be ignored, was not a model for the formal participation of future users. With more citizen input, the low usage of the strolling lane might have been averted, because citizens could have foreseen that it was less attractive to them than anticipated by professional planners. Aldo Rossi, the leading architect, was even hired without the approval of the city parliament (Jacobs, 1996f). However, the public was invited to contribute ideas to the design of the Samen Anders Mobiel campaign (SAM secretariat, undated).

The plan for the remake of the inner ring road was then presented to the public through the regional press, folders and information boards, the city newspaper, a mock-up model displayed in the city hall, public hearings, an information bus with a spokesman on board and mailings to neighbourhoods, retailers and service providers (*Mobility with*, 1999; Van Moerkerke, 1997; and MVGWV, 2001). All citizens and especially those living close to the inner ring road, were invited to voice their opinion on the plan, which led to the elimination of a fourth major bus stop along the inner ring road (Verdee, undated) and to some minor detail changes. In general, 'very little criticism' (Van Moerkerke, 1997, p17) was received, but the few critiques at that point seemed to have received serious consideration. Despite this massive effort to inform the public, it still qualifies as 'end-of-pipe input',[9] although I do not share the impression that the project was 'pushed through' (anonymous Hasselt shopkeeper, personal communication, 3 December 2001; R. Meulendijk, representative of the Flemish Blok, interview, 27 November 2001). It seems that these complaints were largely fuelled by the personal and/or political bias of the complainers. After all, Hasselt certainly does not qualify as a Foucauldian 'sanitary society. . . purged of deviants' (Moore, 2002, p19). Everybody still has all mobility choices and many still do use their cars. Two co-designers of the transport policy, Bormans (interview, 26 November 2001) and Moerkerk (via email, 12 July 2002) even declare the preservation of choices a crucial element of Hasselt's success.

The decision to make the buses free of charge, however, could not be criticized by the citizenry because it was allegedly forged behind closed doors (Jacobs, 1997h) and made public only a few days before the new public transportation system was launched. An adviser to Stevaert admits that the concept of the free buses was 'not debated on a large scale, because then I'm sure that so many people would have opposed the idea' (Duverger, interview, 6 December 2001). He justifies this strategy as a means to avoiding premature, over-pessimistic and ideological criticism. In hindsight, it is of course impossible to say whether this fear was founded. There are obviously differing opinions on Stevaert's leadership style, but it is also obvious that Hasselt's decision-makers could have pursued a more proactive approach in encouraging citizens to add their input to the development of solutions. Stevaert himself refutes the allegation that he made decisions detached from people's real desires; quite the contrary, he claims to be an 'expert in people' (interview, 6 December 2001) while his adviser assures that 'he is. . .always asking, "am I doing the right thing?" He asks other people this too, he does not include himself' (Duverger, interview, 6 December 2001). Indeed, no single interlocutor denied Stevaert's affability and empathy, which people say stems from his experience as the owner of several coffee bars. There, the uncontested account goes, 'he learned to listen to people and to know what's going on in their minds'

(Moerkerk, interview, 27 November 2001; similarly Mulders, interview, 30 June 2000). Stevaert still lives in the centre of Hasselt above one of his first cafés and everyone in Hasselt calls him by his first name. He also is a 'notorious visitor to [an] alternative rock festival' (Beckerset al, 1995, p40) and he holds open days at his private house (de Condé, 1996). The massive indications of Stevaert's affability make me inclined to conclude that he is an effective co-evolutionist because he compensates for his sporadic formal participation with a great deal of 'informal participation', as Moore (personal communication, 3 February 2003) describes what took place in Hasselt. I consider it imaginable that Stevaert's pronounced sense of the people's interests enabled him – and the designers working under his direction – to do a good job in anticipating and balancing these interests.[10] Moerkerk in fact describes the design process in this manner: 'A kind of balancing act . . . because you need to get your policies accepted by the people' (via email, 12 July 2002).

Brucker Land is 'simply a private initiative' (Langer, interview, 5 February 2002), 'developed outside of traditional political structures' (Klein, interview, 25 January 2002). It is not based on any parliamentary resolution or on any mayor's decree but on the consensual agreement of several social groups. People obviously influenced the definition of the problem as is demonstrated by the fact that Elsbeth Seiltz started her early retirement activities with a survey of the needs of the people living in small towns in the western part of Fürstenfeldbruck County. The results 'made it quickly clear that most villagers wanted a village store so that they could buy local groceries' (Krömeke, interview, 22 January 2002). Seiltz then brought this demand together with the idea of a 'county bread', which had circulated as wishful thinking among some farmers but who had never seriously pursued the idea. Her exchange with other ecologically inclined individuals led to the gathering of a group of enthusiasts, which widened and became formalized as the Brucker Land Community of Solidarity e.V. One of the official five 'columns' – as the social groups that constitute this community are called – represents consumers. Klein admitted that the creation of this column was a bit formalistic because every representative of the other four columns (farmers, food tradesmen, environmentalists and churches) is always also a consumer. But it was seen as crucial to have the voice of consumers formally represented and therefore, some people were willing to 'play the role of the consumer' (Klein, interview, 25 January 2002). This created a forum for negotiation between the supply and the demand sides, which led to a mutual agreement on 'controlled cultivation' farming, that is, a compromise between conventional and orthodox ecological farming methods. The detailed regulations regarding the production of each product are co-authored by the consumers, who have full access to the control reports. The president of the Farmers' Association of Upper Bavaria summarizes that 'the consumers are involved in all affairs. They are not only buyers but they are present at the table. They take responsibility and they co-shape the conditions for the production of their groceries' (Dinkel, cited in Brückmann and Witzel, 2001, p4). The whole of this negotiated construct seems to be the *pareto optimum* that reconciles producers' and consumers' concerns. The former need reliable prospects that their products will be bought, whereas the latter want high-quality groceries at a reasonable price.

In this regard Brucker Land is an excellent example of how participation enables synchronic pre-adaptation.

A review of the level and nature of participation in both cases seems to indicate that a combination of formal and informal participation *can* be effective to devise successful co-evolutionary projects. However, such a hybrid strategy cannot be blindly recommended to other settings because Stevaertian informal participation is anything but granted at most places. Brucker Land certainly chose the more messy, discursive path of proactive participation. It is by all accounts the more reliable and replicable means to identify societally relevant problems (and, conversely, societally meaningful definitions of desirability), to find and select creative solutions (and thus to ensure their attractiveness) and to create a sense of ownership. In short, participation and synchronic pre-adaptation are closely linked.

To summarize, user participation is a critical ingredient of co-evolution for a number of reasons. However, these potentials cannot be reaped through the token exercise of citizen surveys – although they might be a fertile starting ground – or through citizens' input on preconceived drafts after the arrow has left the bow. Wherever possible, participation means that users create or get a platform to experiment with new socio-technical reconfigurations themselves. They should be free to set their own agenda and to ask fundamental questions about preferences, necessities and constraints as defined by common sense. A context where this is not easily possible is the field of urban infrastructures; citizens cannot simply conduct their own experiments with, say, sewage systems. A certain degree of synchronic pre-adaptation can nevertheless be generated through the *dialogic* anticipation of the interplay between the design, appropriation, amendment and usage of infrastructures.

New technologies require social embedding

Every new technology that is to be sustained by a given society needs to be embedded in a narrative that suggests how to use the technology and that confirms that it is good to use it. The absence of such social endorsement can lead to the misuse of technology – in the eye of the designer – as is illustrated histrionically in Jamie Uys' movie *The Gods Must Be Crazy*. In this tale, a Coca-Cola bottle, inadvertently tossed out of a plane, lands in the Kalahari Desert, where it triggers confusion as well as creativity among Bushmen, who try to figure out the proper use of this God-sent thing. The new artefact is socially under-defined; it lacks, in Norman's words, an 'affordance . . . a perceived property . . . that suggests how it should be used' (cited in Pfaffenberger, 1992, p284). Familiarization with technology[11] is thus one of the primary purposes of social embedding, but it is also used for less educational and more political causes, namely to ensure the acceptance and maintenance of new technologies, 'to stave off antiprograms' (Latour, 1992, p248), or as Lukes calls it, to 'define away alternatives' (cited in Pfaffenberger, 1992). The most blunt approaches exercise 'logonomic control' (Hodge and Kress, cited in Pfaffenberger, 1992) by establishing standards of decorum, including rituals, legends and songs[12] – of which defiance is declared morally impolite.

I found no evidence in Hasselt or Fürstenfeldbruck of such rigorous attempts to mute criticism or to ban undesired behaviour. The people retained the choice to use cars or to buy conventional groceries. But other, more subtle strategies are used in both cases. One of them is to showcase members of an elite group who proclaim the chicness of a certain technology or technology-related practice. For this reason, the mother of Hasselt's main jeweller is reported to find the buses 'simply excellent' (Stevaert cited in *Hasselt: Stadt*, 1998, p21). Brucker Land, in turn, was able to win Alois Glück, a Bavaria-wide respected politician from the Conservative Party, as its patron. The support from a particular political party bears the risk of triggering suspicion among its opponents. This danger is usually small in the case of approval by church representatives. Brucker Land was actively supported by members, mostly lay people, of the Catholic and Protestant community in the area. Churches also helped establish some car-sharing initiatives in Switzerland, for example by 'providing cheap parking lots or by advertising the system among their members' (Hoogma et al, 2002, p151). Often, it is less the social status of people than their numbers that are harnessed to justify a technological decision, as is demonstrated by Stevaert's claim that 'now, the buses have become sexy in all of Flanders' (Stevaert, interview, 6 December 2001).

While prominent endorsement might be one element of an embedding strategy, it is absolutely mandatory to address the expected users through inter-subjective reasoning. After all, people prefer to adopt a new technology because they were 'educated rather than simply reprogrammed' (Rorty, 1989, p89). It is therefore not surprising that most explanations I heard for the innovations implemented in Hasselt and Fürstenfeldbruck were heavily based upon instrumental arguments, such as 'strategy X solves problem Y'. In theoretical lingo, people like to interpret their achievement as a Habermasian project of collective self-enlightenment, rather than the creation of a dominant leader. These rational substantiations are often condensed in slogans that serve as arguments-in-a-box, which are easier to print on t-shirts or billboards than a voluminous expertise. The effectiveness of this strategy is demonstrated by the steep increase in sales of Philips' energy-saving light bulb, formerly called the 'earth light', after it was renamed the 'marathon bulb' (L. Winner, personal communication, 7 March 2002). An even more powerful catchphrase was Kennedy's 'man on the moon', which stirred enthusiasm for a new technology and which 'transform[ed] the US identity from a nation of God-fearing people to space-race people' (Spinosa et al, 1997, p3). Others try to rationally reconcile religion with space research by saying that it is God's will to explore the Universe (see Pope John Paul II, 1997). This example highlights another function of social embedding, namely the portrayal of a discontinuation of a certain practice as the continuation of an overarching principle. Rorty describes logical arguments in this context as 'not much more than ways of getting people to change their practices without admitting they have done so' (1989, p78). This mechanism can be identified in Fürstenfeldbruck, where 'Matthias Kugler' told me that 'now you can approach every county politician and he will praise Brucker Land and claim to be its co-inventor' (interview, 16 January 2002).

Slogans and catchphrases are also used in the two cases studies because 'getting the name right' is said to be one of the secrets of successful innovations (Young, cited in Albery et al, 1996, p276). The name 'Green Boulevard' already had a positive connotation in the minds of Hasselt's citizens as the name of the circular park that was constructed where the original city walls had once stood. Stevaert resuscitated this name[13] (Peperman, interview, 26 June 2000) and explains in hindsight 'history was an instrumental thing to sell [the project] to the people. . . You can take history to explain a crazy idea to the people' (Stevaert, interview, 6 December 2001). The name Brucker Land has also been around for many decades, most prominently in an old song praising the beauty of the area. The positive connotation of this expression is also documented by its use as the title of a local soccer club, an association for the protection of animals, a shooting club, the regional Yellow Pages and as a demarcation of historic settlement patterns to the west of Munich (www.google.com).

More modern slogans were also used to articulate the intent of the respective projects. In Hasselt, *Samen Anders Mobiel* (Together Differently Mobile) invites everyone to make use of every means of transport; *Hasselt fietst* (Hasselt rides a bike) promotes the use of bicycles in general; *Met Belgerinkel Naar De Winkel* (Shopping with bicycle bells) promotes the use of bicycles for shopping; *Hasselt graag traag* (Slowly through Hasselt please) asks car drivers to reduce their speed. Moerkerk points to another important expression that gathered meaning and was communicated in Limburg's capital: 'The Hasselt experience brought meaning to the term "*duurzame mobiliteit*" [sustainable mobility]' (via email, 10 February 2003). Stevaert in particular is praised among many Hasselters (many personal communications), criticized by members of the Conservative Party (see Martens et al, 1994; Rutten and Gybels, 1995; Gybels, 1995) and even envied (Schonk, interview, 7 December 2001) for his talent in coining catchy slogans.[14]

The marketing strategy of Brucker Land, in general, relies more upon rational arguments as well as the utilization of some deft slogans. 'From the region, for the region' is one of these slogans that concisely sums up the primary concept in one short sentence. The term 'Milky Way' was used as a publicity slogan during the introduction of Unser Land milk. A more subtle linguistic technique is the distinction between *Lebensmittel* and *Nahrungsmittel*; both words can almost interchangeably be translated as groceries, but only the former is used in Brucker Land promotional materials due to its explicit reference to *Leben* (life), whereas *Nahrung* merely stands for nutrition.

These phrases have to be transmitted to the public. Editorial coverage in the news is not only a cheap but also a credible way to achieve this. Chapter 3 contains some benchmark data for the overwhelming media attention given to the Hasselt project.

Brucker Land was equally lucky to gain the support of the regional press, which 'always accompanied us benevolently' (Herrwig, interview, 30 January 2002). The national and international press is also considered a helpful if not a necessary success factor because 'if you have light from the outside, people will prick up their ears' (Klein, interview, 25 January 2002). In this regard it was useful that CNN broadcast a documentary about the free buses in Hasselt (MVGWV, 2001), while almost 100 articles appeared in the national press about the city's transport policy (*Hasselt: Stadt*, 1998). Awards are a good stimulant for such external news coverage. Hasselt experienced this effect after it received a special recognition in the European Prize for Public Transport in 1998. Brucker Land, in turn, was honoured with the European Nature Conservancy Award in 1995 and with the European Solar Award in 1999. Klein remembers the painstakingly prepared award events as milestones in the history of Brucker Land. 'I think that this was a real eureka for many supporters. . . And I think this swept along very many people. They said "Wow, there's something going on here!"' (interview, 25 January 2002). The growth of car-sharing initiatives in Switzerland was also a frequent topic in the Swiss news. It is estimated that the free publicity for car sharing through the media was 'equivalent to several million Swiss Francs' in a period of ten years (Hoogma et al, 2002, p159).

The experience of these cases also suggests that it would not be advisable to exclusively rely on media coverage to communicate a project's intent and justification. The content, design, date and scope of the distribution of self-managed publications and advertisements can be much better controlled. Schonk, a representative of the Conservative Party in Hasselt, admits that this is exactly where his party was lacking: 'We are also good, but our marketing and communication was very, very bad. That opened a great opportunity for Stevaert' (interview, 7 December 2001). A tangible example of this insight is the aesthetic difference between the Conservative Party's study, *Hasselt levendig stadscentrum* (SHLS, 1994), which featured hand-coloured thematic maps and the Socialist party's study, *Hasselt, een beeld van een stad* (Studiecentrum Willy Claes, 1990), with its appealing 3-D renderings printed on high-gloss paper. The same professional approach was taken in the marketing of the Green Boulevard and the other elements of Hasselt's transport policy. An advertising agency created attractive pamphlets and brochures, a public relations officer was available on a free telephone hotline, radio spots were broadcast on a local station and a friendly logo canvassed for approval.

The decision-makers of Brucker Land also knew that their logo would be a crucial element in their marketing strategy. Therefore they invested over €5100 in its design, which seems to have paid off because 92 per cent of customers in Fürstenfeldbruck County are able to recognize it (GALB, 2001). The logo adorns posters, air balloons, stickers, tote bags and billboards that are placed on the fields of participating farmers. Brucker Land also has published a comic strip for children and a number of flyers, which were distributed to all 80,000 households in the county. The presentation of the products themselves is also an indication of Brucker Land's professional image: 'Every single. . . product, from the potato bag to the honey jar, is completely styled-through and carries a bar code. "We don't want to be known for a granola image," says Elsbeth Seiltz, "we have a professional design that is a match for every Nestlé competition"' (cited in GALB, 2000).

There is also a danger of over-professionalization because too much high gloss can appear sterile and impersonal. Therefore, Hasselt and Fürstenfeldbruck pursued the additional strategy of what can be called a straightforward vocabulary. Both translate complex facts into everyday language in order to ensure that everyone can grasp the message. Stevaert, the gregarious ex-owner of several coffee bars, who has no university degree and who knows the names of the latest rock bands (Beckers et al, 1995), is famed for this skill. He says about himself, 'I am very simple. I am not intelligent enough to make things complicated' (Stevaert, interview, 6 December 2001). Almost every Hasselter I talked to confirmed and praised this quality of their ex-mayor: 'Sometimes when you see politicians talking on TV you don't know what they say. Steve, however, speaks very clearly' (owner of a bed and breakfast; similar comments were made by: Mulders, interview, 30 June 2000; Moerkerk, interview, 27 November 2001; Schonk, interview, 7 December 2001). An example is Stevaert's vivid explanation of global warming, which can be found in the official prospectus of his energy policy: 'More greenhouse gases in the atmosphere make the insulating "blankets" around the earth thicker' (Stevaert, 2000a, p7). Brucker Land relies less on individual translators and more on the everyday language of its many members, including farmers, housewives and retirees. Many of them volunteer for so-called shelf missions (*Regaleinsätze*) in supermarkets, where they explain the details of Brucker Land to interested customers in their uncontrived vocabulary. Around 2000 of these missions have been conducted since the founding of the initiative (Seiltz, via email, 2 March 2002), which underlines the importance Brucker Land gives to direct contact with customers. Other occasions for such encounters are systematically sought and organized: 'Thanksgiving services, school events, eco-festivals, [and] regional fairs' (GALB, 2000).

Apparently both approaches, Stevaert's talent in Hasselt and the straightforward communication in Fürstenfeldbruck, have managed to convey social embedding contents to the populace. It therefore cannot be concluded that the more inclusive approach pursued by Brucker Land is a necessary condition for effective communication. I think, however, that this strategy is the more reliable and advisable one because there is no guarantee that exceptionally gregarious translators are available in every community. In addition, an explanation from the guy next door always has a credibility bonus compared to the statement of a politician or a glossy leaflet.

The above deliberations should make it clear that there are various – additive, not alternative – effective methods of social embedding. The main strategic lesson of this section, however, is that the intended usage of a new range of choices in a co-evolutionary project has to be publicly articulated and approved in some way.

Strategic alliances are more productive than ideological purity

A strategic alliance is defined as 'an agreement between two or more individuals or entities stating that the involved parties will act in a certain way in order to achieve a common goal' (InvestorGuide, 2003). Despite the attractive prospect of such an alliance, both technophilic and technophobic pursuers of sustainability tend to prefer strategies that do not involve significant cooperation with 'the others', mostly because the looming compromise might threaten the purity of their own respective mission. Besides, the unfettered and competitive pursuit of individual ideas is the prevailing rule of the game in most parts of the world. Neoclassical economists might argue that it is actually not a rule – because rules are man-made – but rather a law of nature because it can be observed anywhere, even in the animal kingdom. This view is rooted in the works of Adam Smith (1723–1790) who argued that 'if we want society to grow and prosper we need only get out of the way' (according to Frank, 1997, p63). If we follow this call for *laissez faire*, the admittedly simplified argument goes, we will reach the best of all possible outcomes because human intervention cannot produce better results than a law of nature.[15] A concrete application of this law would be to let individual farmers compete in a free market, which would reveal the most talented farmers, who generate the largest yield per acre. Those who have more manual skills would become cobblers and trade shoes for corn. Eventually, the whole of the society would get the maximum amount of food and shoes from the given amount of human labour available.

Among the major disadvantages of a free market, however, are at least two related to common assets. First, it creates incentives to maximize the use of free resources and free sinks, usually common goods such as water and air – a strategy known as 'externalization of costs'.[16] Second, it fails to create incentives to join forces and build new common assets, such as a community-wide irrigation system, which would provide synergistic benefits for all. For these reasons, a range of authors retorts that competition in a free market is not a law of nature but simply a meme that has proven to be fairly successful in organizing the efficient allocation of *individually* owned resources. However, it is apparently not the best of all possible memes for the safekeeping and creation of common assets. Kelbaugh observes in this context that the free market is 'such a genius at establishing price but such an idiot at dealing with externalities' (2000, p7).

If we assume that most people agree on the desirability of common assets and if deliberate and proactive collaboration is required to safeguard or reap them why, then, are these strategies not more widespread? One way to explain this discrepancy uses the metaphor of the prisoners' dilemma.[17] In essence, it describes the fact that unilateral cooperative behaviour does not pay back directly and quickly enough to make it economically rational. A farmer, for example, who unilaterally lowered the use of pesticides in order to do less harm to the ground water would lower his yield and hence his income in relation to other farmers.[18] Most sober-minded farmers would therefore prefer a sub-optimal status quo to the heroic pains of a forerunner. Many traffic participants find themselves in a similar quandary. They know that public transport is better for the local air quality but they don't want to sacrifice an hour each day by switching from their car to an under-invested transit system. They even are aware that the transit system is underdeveloped *because* most people in their situation make the same decision. I suggest calling this bottom-up inertia, because people (users) legitimize their passivity with the failure of the government (supplier) to take the first step. The latter, however, transfers responsibility to the people, who have to first prove their willingness to use – and thus finance – an investment in public transport. This might be termed a form of top-down inertia.[19] The self-suggesting remedy to this mutually stabilizing pair of inertias is often phrased like this: 'I would do my share if I had the guarantee that the others would do theirs.'

Box 5.4 The love–hate supermarket

Sometimes one can learn as much from failure as from success, for example, from Gerrards Cross, Buckinghamshire. The supermarket chain Tesco sought planning permission to build a tunnel over an existing rail line in order to create space for a large new branch. Gerrards Cross' residents fiercely opposed these plans arguing that the supermarket would drain all purchase power from small shops, greengrocers and the modest shopping centre in the town's high street. In addition, people were concerned about the environment, the amount of traffic generated by the new store and about various problems related to the huge construction project. Not surprisingly, 'a referendum of the 8600 locals . . . saw 93 per cent of voters oppose Tesco's original planning application' (Wainwright, 2005). The local authorities, including the parish council, South Buckinghamshire District Council and the county, shared the residents' views and refused planning permission. The final arbiter, however, Deputy Prime Minister John Prescott, approved the whole project. The doors of the new Tesco, meanwhile upgraded to a superstore, were expected to open in summer 2005 if the collapse of parts of the tunnel had not delayed the grand opening. Sooner or later, however, the new Tesco will open and at the same day a prisoner's dilemma will start to challenge the people in Gerrards Cross.

Their straightforward reaction would be to simply boycott the store. This way, they could save the commercial base of their cherished high street by their own actions. This is exactly the reasoning of a Tesco spokesman who was interviewed in a BBC documentary on the case. He could easily make this seemingly disinterested statement because he knew that the people *will* come and shop at the new store. They won't be strong enough to weather through their dilemma between shopping in high street at slightly higher prices and shopping at Tesco at Tesco prices. It is impossible to overemphasize that the residents of Gerrards Cross are not to blame – everyone would do what they will do. But this is not a problem of individual failings, rather that of structures. This particular structural dilemma is hard to tackle ex post, even with strategic alliances. But it is important to note that attempts had been made to prevent the dilemma from emerging in the first place and strategic alliances across various interests and certainties were forged for this purpose. However, this case also shows that alliances are not necessarily a panacea against power, especially if it is backed by an alliance itself.

Sources: Wainwright, 2005; Wolmar, 2005.

Some ideas have been developed in the history of thought to overcome this deadlock. One of them tries to overcome the systematic discrimination against forerunners by doing without them completely. A strong state, for example, could coerce its citizens into simultaneous cooperative behaviour by means of prohibitions and commands or by assigning a stiff price tag to every unit of common goods. The epitome of such an intervenor has been described by Thomas

Hobbes (1588–1679) as Leviathan, the ideal sovereign, entrusted with the power to enforce socially compliant behaviour for the good of all. The shortcomings and undesirability of this approach, however, have already been addressed at several points throughout the preceding chapters.

An alternative to noble-minded despotism is consensual agreement to move collectively and simultaneously thus avoiding heroic choices on anyone's part.[20] The findings of Taylor (1976), Axelrod (1984) and others, who have quantitatively modelled the implications of the prisoners' dilemma, support this conclusion: 'Voluntary cooperation. . . is nevertheless rational under certain conditions' (Taylor, 1976, p85).[21] Equipped with this information, 'we ought not to be surprised when rational, well informed people try to improve matters through collective political action' (Frank, 1997, p68). I include these approaches under the expression *strategic alliance* as defined above. Such agreements are based on negotiation and are often codified in binding contracts. Concrete manifestations can be seen 'in several cities, [where] citizens voted to tax themselves for new parks' (Steiner, cited in Mazzola, 2001, p100). The alliance in this case has been hard-wired into the local tax ordinance.

From my observations in Hasselt and Fürstenfeldbruck, I conclude that these cases also made use of this strategy. I even argue that the willingness to cooperate among designers, providers and users of the new infrastructures was crucial to the implementation and appropriation of co-evolutionary decisions. Bormans, spokeswoman of De Lijn, made the unsolicited comment that 'working together is the key. Get everybody on the table' (interview, 26 November 2001). Seiltz made a very similar statement about the five 'columns' of Brucker Land: 'We understand ourselves as partners who have jointly plucked up the courage to take our fate into our own hands' (cited in GALB, 2002). Langer's definition of solidarity is an extension of this logic: 'Solidarity is cohesion. And the participating social groups act in solidarity in order to reach a certain goal. Only together we can succeed' (interview, 5 February 2002).[22] The goal of such collaboration is that 'everybody benefits from it' (Haberkorn, interview, 22 January 2002; Stevaert cited in Jacobs, 1997c), a situation that has come to be known as win–win.

Bormans expound the list of winners among the users of the new mobility infrastructure, namely 'cyclists, pedestrians, user of the bus and of the car; everyone' (Bormans, interview, 26 November 2001). The providers of the new infrastructure are also listed as winners: 'The Flemish Community had wanted to remake the inner ring for a long time because of its traffic danger . . . De Lijn already had commissioned a study of how to run the buses more smoothly through the city centre. . . the city government wanted a higher quality of life in the city' (Verdee, undated, p18). Van Moerkerke also reports that these three players found their interests well met by the new mobility policy (1997, p10). The bottom line for retailers seems to be positive, too, as can be taken from a statement of the chairman of the local retailers' association: the free buses are a 'direct hit for the publicity of our city' (Franssen, cited in Jacobs, 1997i, p1). In short, all three 'Es' of the sustainability triangle – economy, ecology and equity – are among the winners of Hasselt's new transport policy, whose purpose was 'to make the commercial centre more accessible, to reduce the carbon dioxide emissions of individual motorized traffic, to improve the mobility for elderly, young and handicapped people and to avoid the construction of new roads, namely of a third ring' (Jacobs et al, 1997, p1).The empirical evidence I encountered permits the conclusion that these goals have been largely met.

Win–win mechanisms are also cited in Fürstenfeldbruck. 'All participants – from the producer to the consumer – benefit from this project,' said the Bavarian Minister for Agriculture and Forestry about Unser Land (Miller, 2001). Dengler expresses this concept even more explicitly: 'Win–win is also a motto of Brucker Land. . .The environment wins . . . farmers win because they gain a higher price; trademen win because they stabilize their clientèle; consumers win because they get more safety, more quality, more freshness' (interview, 28 January 2002). In other words, the willingness to cooperate pays for each of the five 'columns'.

The question remains, however, how these win–win options can be identified and how social groups who are not traditionally known for their amicable interaction can cooperatively work toward them. This question is especially interesting because technologies are, according to Bijker and Law, 'born out of conflict, difference, or resistance' (1992b, p9). Campbell (1996) makes a similar statement regarding sustainable development, which he claims is by its very nature the subject of conflicts of interests, particularly between advocates of ecological, economic or social issues. Each of these authors, however, suggests similar ways to resolve such conflicts: through 'negotiation and mediation' (Campbell, personal communication, 11 April 2002) and through 'some kind of accommodation . . . compromise . . . [or] negotiated settlement' (Bijker and Law, 1992b, p10).

It cannot be the purpose of this book to present a summary of the vast literature on alternative dispute resolution (ADR), but I do not want to fail to emphasize the kinship between ADR and cooperative, co-evolutionary approaches to sustainable development. It is widely acknowledged that a discussion climate that permits a frank and non-hostile exchange of ideas and fears is a crucial condition for a mutually beneficial resolution of conflicts. Healey's strong argument for 'collaborative planning' (1997) for example is all about the synergistic effects of an undistorted dialogue of all possible stakeholders. Hasselt seemed to have succeeded in this regard, as can be taken from Moerkerk's recollection of the atmosphere in the transport commission that strategized the plans for the Green Boulevard: 'We were not bothered by all the political things.We could speak openly. Sometimes we talked straight against what our bosses said. . . There was not a strict line along which we had to walk' (interview, 27 November 2001). The experience from Fürstenfeldbruck suggests that sometimes it is necessary to help the communicative process along. Seiltz, for example, reports that she practised shuttle diplomacy for half a year between the farmers and the environmentalists in order to bridge the strong initial reservations between the two groups. 'I always carried the message back and forth until we had a seedling of trust and until everyone said "Actually, we all want the same. Let's get together"' (interview, 15 January 2002).The aforementioned strategy to shed light from outside on a project was also used to suspend the opposition-reflex of certain interest bearers. Klein remembers the intention he pursued for Brucker Land's application to be featured at the 'Green Week', the most important national trade fair for agriculture. 'If the

Fürstenfeldbruckers see their own people in Berlin on TV . . . this will cause a stir among the farmers here' (Klein, interview, 25 January 2002).

A 'focus on interests, not positions' is another important trait of productive dispute resolution and, for good reasons, a chapter in *Getting to Yes*, a famous guide to ADR (Fisher et al, 1991). The disclosure of interests requires the questioning of one's own traditional, dogmatic, ready-made positions. The classic fable of two sisters who both want to have the only orange in the larder illustrates this point. After much arguing, it turns out that one sister only wanted the juice, the other the rind. With the disclosure of their intrinsic interest, both can have 100 per cent of what they want. Such a transition from ideology-based haggling to substance-based negotiation is what Stevaert saw as central to a successful environmental policy, which goes 'further than the narrow . . . shackles in which some groups try to put the world. . . This asks for an open and democratic policy, which is far away from all kinds of political games between majority and opposition' (1991, p1; translation by Gijs Moors). Overcoming preconceived perspectives is also reported in Brucker Land, where the social groups involved in the project 'abandoned stereotypical perceptions of the others [through] personal contact and personal dialogues' (Dengler, interview, 28 January 2002). They also started to ask questions about the others' situation: 'How are you really doing? What are your interests? What are the worries of a farmer or a baker?' (Dengler, interview, 28 January 2002). The findings of my previous research also showed that these close encounters led to a 'complete consensus that orthodox ecological farming must not be an end in itself' (Brand, 1997, p42).

The resulting compromise of 'controlled farming' does indeed spoil the purity of some players' missions. But missions are ideologies whose reflection is crucial to ADR and to co-evolution. What counts is that Brucker Land progressed from categorical 'no's to questions of substance, for example, whether the dough made from controlled cultivated wheat can be handled in the bakers' machines' (Krömeke, interview, 22 January 2002). Eventually, all participants understood that the Brucker Land compromise met their actual interests much better than the looming alternative of continued stalemate. Seiltz describes this point during the negotiations: 'The bakers made it very clear: "We participate, but only if it isn't orthodox ecological farming". . . The environmentalists said: "Well, we go along with that compromise if it is the precondition of moving something at all"' (interview, 15 January 2002). Examples of compromises abound in Hasselt, too. The number of parking spaces, for example, was a much contested issue, especially between the shopkeepers and a coalition of the Flemish Ministry for Transportation and De Lijn (Moerkerk, interview, 27 November 2001). Eventually, the shopkeepers agreed to decrease the number of parking spaces in the inner city in exchange for parking garages close to the outer side of the inner ring. The abandonment of ideological positions also made Stevaert advertise an intelligent compromise regarding car access to the inner city: 'I think it should be possible to get close to a store or to the city hall on a rainy Tuesday evening in February. However, on a Saturday during shopping hours, everything should be free of [motorized] traffic' (Stevaert, cited in Jacobs, 1996h, p9). In other words, effective cooperation rests upon substantial rather than formalistic compromises.

This lesson was also implemented in Switzerland where car-sharing organizations and the federal railway company SBB discovered that they are not at all natural enemies just because they both provide transport services. They found that they target people with different and often complementary types of mobility needs and that it makes sense to team up. SBB thus decided to provide car-sharing locations at its major train stations, which multiplied the number of car-sharing depots (Hoogma et al, 2002).

To summarize, I confidently declare strategic alliances, especially between designers and users of technologies, a meme of co-evolution because they are suited to overcoming the dissipative competition between conflicting ideological purities and to getting beyond 'partisan mutual adjustment' (Lindblom, cited in Healey, 1997, p24). Such coalitions require hard work – overcoming traditional prejudices, letting go of ingrained positions, disclosure of genuine interests, patience in negotiations – but are often rewarded with synergies that satisfy not only individual interests but also create new common goods.

Inventiveness enables a departure from the prevailing discourse

It may sound banal to emphasize that co-evolutionary projects are the result of inventiveness; any departure from the prevailing discourse is a way of 'thinking outside the box' and thus by definition a creative venture. I do not claim that inventiveness is a meme of co-evolution that sets it apart from other approaches to sustainable development. It is, nevertheless, a constitutive factor of co-evolutionary strategies, which is why it deserves its own section. There is no doubt that the two cases I studied qualify as outcomes of inventive or creative thinking. This is not only my personal perception but also shared within Hasselt and Fürstenfeldbruck and by external authors describing these projects. Donné, for example, explicitly refers to the Hasseltian approach as he extols the need for 'creativity to get public transport out of the hole' (De toekomstvisie, 1997, p10). A publication of the City of Hasselt legitimizes its transport policy with the 'need to search for creative solutions . . . for mobility-related problems' (*Hasselt: Stadt*, 1998, p26), while Stevaert mentions 'lots of creativity' as an important ingredient in his mobility policy as Flemish Minister of Transport (2000b, p9). Brucker Land also 'builds upon people's creativity' (Baindl, 2001) and its chairwoman Seiltz explains that 'one of the biggest lessons we learned was that it pays to bring forward creative ideas' (Seiltz, interview, 15 January 2002). While Brucker Land brings together producers and consumers of groceries, the Finnish project Mottinetti links producers and consumers of firewood as an innovative means to stimulate the usage of alternative sources of energy (see Box 5.5). If inventiveness is so important for co-evolution, then it is worth investigating where new ideas come from. Are they inspired by other projects, do they stem from the technical knowledge of experts, from the mastermind, or play instinct of an individual genius, or are they the result of collective deliberation in citizen groups? These four potential sources of inspiration are examined below with respect to both cases.

Box 5.5 Mottinetti hits several birds with one stone

'Mottinetti' combines the Finnish words for one cubic meter of firewood (*motti*) and the internet (*netti*) because it uses the latter to link producers and consumers of the former. It was set up by North Karelian Electric (NKE), the 10th largest electricity company in Finland with around 82,000 customers. Between 60 and 70 per cent of them use electricity to heat their homes. During cold winter days, the demand for electricity reaches extreme peaks that are very costly for NKE to satisfy. It is therefore in the interest of the company that their customers use firewood as an additional energy source. However, the firewood value chain from forest owners (especially small ones) via wood producers, dealers and transportation companies to the end customers proved to be quite under-developed. Information about suppliers was often spread only by word of mouth and the prices and quality of wood as well as the standard of service varied considerably. In addition, the increasingly urban Finnish population has less and less personal connections to forest owners. In order to alleviate these problems, Mottinetti was set up in 2001 as an e-marketing service by NKE in collaboration with the local forestry centres. Mottinetti is thus an ideal example of a synchronization between supply and demand because customers can find and compare suppliers much easier in a more transparent and efficient firewood market, while at the same time forest owners and wood producers can reduce their marketing costs. The system turned out to be a tremendous success and gained massive news coverage. Mottinetti is now known by 75 per cent of the Finnish population and over 65,000 people use it each year with an annual growth rate of 25–30 per cent. It is expanding rapidly from North Karelia to other parts of Finland so that its services are now available to 1,500,000 Finns.

The benefit for NKE is a better predictability of energy demand and accordingly a higher profitability of their operation. It also gains additional revenue from Mottinetti and enjoys increased visibility and consumer loyalty. Mottinetti also helps the forestry centres to fulfil their mission of securing rural jobs and promoting forest fuels and silviculture. In addition, firewood has environmental advantages because it is a CO_2 neutral source of energy. Mottinetti thus manages to hit several birds with one virtual stone; a truly innovative approach, especially given the very earthly nature of its product and the traditional way wood was sold for centuries.

Sources: Tahvanainen et al, 2003; Tolvanen, via email, 23 June 2005

Although no interviewee in Hasselt formally alluded to earlier projects in other cities as a source of inspiration, it becomes clear from looking at related publications that most groups had indeed looked beyond the city limits. The SP study *Hasselt, een beeld van een stad*, for example, commends the mobility plan of Freiburg, Germany (Studiecentrum Willy Claes, 1990) and the Conservative Party borrowed analogous backing for its counter-study from a strategy that was implemented in

Eindhoven, Netherlands (SHLS, 1994). Eddy Baldewijns, former Flemish Minister of Transport, expressed his hope that Hasselt might become traffic safe 'just as the model Bruges, where the use of public transport is 30 per cent higher' (cited in Jacobs, 1996j, p17). Stevaert also uses the traffic concept of Aachen, Germany, to corroborate his idea of how to keep through traffic out of Hasselt's inner city (according to Cloostermans, 1995). A representative of the BTTB concludes that the 'fresh visions . . . [were] developed on the basis of foreign paragons' (Meukens, cited in Jacobs, 1996g, p12). The idea of the free buses had its precursors, too, which were portrayed as 'expensive foreign experiments' in a lengthy article in the regional newspaper (Dure buitenlandse, 1997, p9). Therein the author reports Lenin's failed attempt to provide free public transportation in 1921 and about a number of projects in the 1970s[23] that were discontinued after a maximum of two years because of financial problems. Sint-Truiden, a town 11 miles to the southwest of Hasselt, offered one free bus line on eight market Saturdays in 1996 but was dissatisfied, too; not for financial reasons but because of low acceptance (Thuwis, 1997). From these indications it can be concluded that best practice examples were not – and should not – be consulted for project blueprints, but they may still serve as proof that alternatives can be viable. This is how Moerkerk imagines the impact of external examples: 'Probably smart people told him [Stevaert] that . . . outside Belgium, there are projects where public transport is a real success' (interview, 27 November 2002).

Dengler points in the same direction in his statement that 'these [ideas] are better conveyed by human beings than by hardcopy guides' (interview, 28 January 2002). But for Brucker Land, he continues, neither source of external information played much of a role in the generation of the basic idea. However, some interlocutors mentioned two other projects that had an impact, not as models but as examples of initiatives that could be improved upon. The Bauernquelle (Farmers' Source) was one of them. Fifty farmers founded this association in 1988 to promote direct marketing in Fürstenfeldbruck County. Their main activity is the organization of a farmers' market every Saturday between 8am and noon in the grounds of a monastery in Fürstenfeldbruck. What is interesting is that consumers can also become members of this organization – just as in Brucker Land. Krömeke describes the Bauernquelle as the 'basic structure' upon which Brucker Land was built but also criticizes its members as 'lone fighters' (interview, 22 January 2002). Their treasurer, Matthias Heitmayr, quit his post in 1993 because his 'proposals for the further development of the association beyond the farmers' market were not adopted' (O. H., 1993, pFFB3). Kugler, who also served on the board of the association, explained that Heitmayr's ideas were geared toward quantity buyers like restaurants and factory canteens. However, the winning argument was that no one had time to implement these ideas.

The other project that might have inspired the creation of Brucker Land was Mutters Brotkorb (Mother's Bread Basket), an initiative launched by the Bavarian Bakers' Guild (Bäcker Innungsverband) in 1993. It was also a regionalization strategy, but only for grain and on a much larger geographical scale. It covered all of Bavaria, which is 162 times larger than Fürstenfeldbruck County. The cultivation guidelines for farmers who wanted to produce for Mutters Brotkorb were strikingly similar to those developed shortly after by Brucker Land (for example, no pesticides in the actual cultivation year). Herrwig, a baker himself, was familiar with Mutters Brotkorb at the time he joined the Brucker Land network but he also witnessed its subsequent failure. 'It didn't last. . .The identification with it on such a large scale was too little. That could not be communicated to the consumer' (interview, 30 January 2002).

Krömeke, who was not actively involved in the design of Brucker Land's concept, is the only one who remembers a third possible source of external inspiration. He states that, upon his suggestion, Seiltz established contacts with the Verein für ländliche Kultur in Hessen (Association for Rural Culture in Hesse), which pursued regional marketing by reactivating abandoned village stores (Krömeke, interview, 22 January 2002). Seiltz does not remember this well, however. 'I had been in contact [with said association] but unfortunately, I don't remember anything . . . therefore, it couldn't have been that important' (Seiltz, via email, 9 June 2002). All other interviewees leaned toward Seiltz's account, with Haberkorn, Kugler and Langer explicitly negating inspiration by other projects (interviews, 22 January, 16 January and 5 February 2002 respectively); Langer affirmatively answered my question whether Brucker Land was invented from scratch. Seiltz's description of these early stages sounds a little more differentiated: 'I enquired everywhere about regionalization concepts, but one like our "community of solidarity" was not among them' (via email, 9 June 2002). In our interview, she elaborated, 'I think we really chose new paths of togetherness. . . Sure, there were other small and neat [regionalization projects]. . . but our collaboration with tradesmen was uniquely new and so was the concept that consumers become active on their own behalf' (Seiltz, interview, 15 January 2002). Exchange with other initiatives only became important in the expansion stage, when such questions arose as, 'What is the next step? Where can we get further suggestions?' (Dengler, interview, 28 January 2002). In that phase, Kellermann recalls, 'we visited a mill, but that was a lone fighter. . .There are many direct marketers and you can fetch ideas from everywhere' (interview, 25 January 2002). It seems clear, then, that the authors of both cases did not rely heavily on external sources for inspiration. They rather used the example of other projects to clarify certain questions of detail and maybe even as encouragement to exceed them.

If idea-import alone does not explain the emergence of new visions, then there must be a source for home-made ideas. This leaves the task of investigating the role of experts, individuals and the public in the creation of new ideas. These roles are of special interest because they affect the likelihood of finding co-evolutionary solutions. A predominance of experts and individuals tends to overlook the input of citizens, that is, the future users, because both groups are often inclined to consider debate and theory as dispensable; experts due to their unquestionable expertise and geniuses due to the irresistibility of their ideas.

Experts are often praised for their beneficial knowledge, as in the case of Curitiba, where 'credit [for success] is invariably given to . . . a small "team of planners, technicians and architects"' (Moore, 2002, p13, citing Lerner according to Di Guilio). Technical know-how was also instrumental in the design of Hasselt's mobility policy, starting with the SP's visioning study in 1990 (Studiecentrum

Willy Claes), followed by the CVP's draft for a redesign of the inner ring road (SHLS, 1994) and also in the last and eventually implemented concept during Stevaert's first mayoral term. *Hasselt, een beeld van een stad* (Studiecentrum Willy Claes, 1990) was authored by the Studiecentrum Willy Claes in collaboration with the SP faction of Hasselt's city council. I could not obtain details about the exact composition of this group but it can be assumed that it consisted of technical experts and city politicians only. The 3-D renderings in the published report are also clearly the product of a professional designer.

The new ideas introduced by this group include a two-lane one-way street on the outer half of the inner ring road, exactly as it was later implemented. The inner half was to be used for pedestrians, cyclists, for generous green spaces and for 230 new and free parking spaces, whereas the number of parking spaces in the inner city was to be reduced. Some areas there were to be made completely free of car traffic and 'every dead angle should be refilled or dedicated to green space' (Studiecentrum Willy Claes, 1990, p12) in order to attract new residents to the inner city. As part of this strategy, the weekly market was to be brought back into the city, the governor's garden opened to the public and another small park connected by a greenbelt to the woods around Hasselt. The idea to keep the outer ring road free of further development was not yet present in this draft, nor was any mention of improving public transportation, let alone bus lanes. The steering group that devised the study *Hasselt Levendig Stadscentrum* (SHLS, 1994) consisted of Hasselt's then-Mayor Roppe, five city deputies, four delegates each from the railway company and from architectural consulting firms, three employees of De Lijn and two representatives each from the Flemish department of transportation and police. This assembly of experts adopted a number of ideas from the 1990 study, such as splitting the inner ring road to create two one-way lanes on the outer side and to use the inner side for parking, bicycles, pedestrians and 'a lot of green (comparable to the previous "boulevards")' (SHLS, 1994, p26). In general, however, the proposals of this steering group dealt almost exclusively with traffic issues. In fact, Moerkerk remembers that 'there was no focus on green, on city building, nothing. It was all about traffic' (interview, 27 November 2001). But these issues were addressed quite thoroughly in the 'holistic approach' of the planning process (SHLS, 1994, p15) that included not only the remodelling of the inner ring road but also a stringent parking policy, the construction of parking lots for carpoolers, bicycle lanes and a sophisticated traffic information system on the outer ring. The genuinely new idea of this approach, however, was the strong focus on public transportation. One concrete implementation of this vision would have implied the construction of 'large, very large I should say, concrete bus lanes' as Bormans put it (interview, 26 November 2001). Other elements of this concept were a central public transport hub near the train station, the expansion and construction of bus stops, a redesigned bus network, shuttle buses to and from the park and ride lots, and more. Nothing was said, however, about the total number of bus routes, bus frequencies or bus fares.

After the elections of 1994, it became clear that the new city government continued to support the one-way solution on the inner ring, but that it would not approve the concrete bus lanes due to their negative impact on the sense of place in the city centre. In addition, the new mayor, Steve Stevaert, was not known as a fervent friend of public transport (Moerkerk, interview, 27 November 2001). Nowadays, he proclaims that he was only 'against empty buses' (Stevaert's press officer, interview, 6 December 2001; confirmed by Stevaert's nodding). De Lijn therefore commissioned new technical expertise to demonstrate the continued need for improvements in the public transport system and to avoid buses coming from the south, bound for the train/bus station, having to go three-quarters around the city on the one-way ring. Utilizing computer-based traffic modelling software, a consulting company constructed several scenarios for bus routings on the inner ring and ultimately suggested creating some kind of bus-only lane between the Sint-Truidersteenweg and the station. The study is remembered as 'a valuable contribution, which helped to prepare a more thorough analysis by the Dutch consulting company Goudappel & Coffeng' (Van Moerkerke, 1997, p4). This company conducted a traffic count and fed the results into another traffic model, but generated very few new ideas. Their suggestions for the outer ring, the radial access roads and the inner ring road were almost identical to the cumulated concepts of the Studiecentrum Willy Claes and SHLS studies. However, the idea of lengthy concrete bus lanes was abandoned in favour of several short stretches of differently coloured bus lanes near intersections or bus stops. For more information on this study see Verdee (undated) and Van Moerkerke (1997).

In May 1996, the engineering office Lebost accepted a bid to work on the final details of the remodelling of the inner ring. Four months later, it presented a preliminary draft, which basically refined the proposals of Goudappel & Coffeng, including the re-routing of most bus lines, three major transfer stations and a remote-controlled priority for buses at traffic lights. Among the few newly introduced ideas were shuttle buses on the boulevard at five minute intervals and the possibility of 'extending the bus lanes over the total length of the Boulevard if De Lijn succeeds in increasing the number of bus users considerably at the expense of car traffic' (Van Moerkerke, 1997, p13). In September 1996, Aldo Rossi, a famous Italian architect, was entrusted with the final design of the public spaces along the Green Boulevard. With his work, the design of the infrastructural aspects of Hasselt's new transport policy was practically completed.

In recapitulating, it seems that almost all of these ideas stemmed from the pencils or drawing boards of professionals, politicians, experts or consultants. Despite this impression, Mulders states: 'No, there were not too many consultants involved in this traffic concept' (Mulders, interview, 30 June 2000). His assessment becomes clearer from an elevated position that shows Hasselt's transport policy as more than the sum of its infrastructural elements. After all, the success of Hasselt is also due to free bicycle rentals, school programmes, art in public spaces, bicycle pools, car-free days, informational brochures, the encouragement of companies to provide provide showers for their bicycling employees and the like; not to forget the free buses. None of these measures was proposed in any of the aforementioned studies, which helps us to understand Luwel's opinion that 'Hasselt doesn't come from the brain – it comes from the heart' (interview, 26 June 2000). Hence, there must be yet other sources of creativity that were at work in Hasselt.

I argue elsewhere that 'one of the main factors that sets Brucker Land apart from other regionalization initiatives is the consistent professionalism in every phase. . . At certain strategic points, external technical expertise is indispensable' (Brand, 1997, p83). A considerable amount of this knowledge was contributed, often pro bono, by the environmental management consulting company BAUM Consult GmbH, whose CEO is also one of the founding members of Brucker Land. He therefore usually offered his knowledgeable opinion as a private person in the many brainstorming sessions that led to the foundation of the Community of Solidarity. Other external know-how was requested from a design expert in the creation of the logo and from a lawyer to indemnify Brucker Land's legal status. Most of the remaining need for specialized knowledge was met by various members of the volunteer network, most notably by Seiltz, who contributed the mercantile experience she had gained as the owner of a tow-bar-producing company. Related comments about the necessity of this kind of competence were made by Seiltz (interview, 15 January 2002), as well as by Dengler, Kellermann, Haberkorn and Klein (interviews, 28 January, 25 January, 22 January and 25 January respectively). Business-related skills, however, were not most relevant for brainstorming new ideas; they were rather used at their best during the implementation phase, which is not the focus of this section on inventiveness. Similar considerations apply to advice given in regard to financial planning, funding applications, conduct with state agencies, calculation of profitability, trademark rights and the like (information obtained from interviews with Kellermann, Herrwig, Klein and Langer).

Thomas Carlyle's Great Man theory of history (1841) credits individuals such as Heracles, Shakespeare, Luther, Rousseau and Napoleon with the invention of new ideas. In some cases, this might be justified, but often such great men end up in the spotlight simply because the work of a genius is easier to communicate – and sells better – than the product of a network of complex, incremental inspiration. The opposite effect, however, occurs as well when an individual makes a brilliant comment in a meeting that trickles into the final report of a consulting company. If someone spearheads the diffusion of such seemingly anonymous suggestions, he or she might, again, appear the genius hero. We know from the preceding pages that many ideas came out of collective fermentation processes, but in my analysis of *ex post* perceptions of the source of creativity, I still came across quite a few Carlylean statements.

Among those who have influenced Hasselt's transport policy behind the scenes are clearly Guido Moerkerk, Dirck Luwel and Odine Bormans, to whom I spoke in person and certainly many others whose names are not prominently recorded in documents or memories. Those already in the limelight of public perception are remembered best. The head of the Flemish Administration for Traffic Infrastructure in Limburg, Herman Swillen, for example, is said to have originated the one-way concept for the inner ring (Mulders, interview, 30 June 2000). Toon Hermans, a Green Party member of Hasselt's city council, is also categorized under 'people without which the transport policy in Hasselt would not be the same today' ('Sibyll Beuzenberg', letter, 16 June 2002). But by far the most references are made to Steve Stevaert, who is also called 'Steve Stunt'[24] (anonymous shopkeeper, personal communication, 3 December 2002; Kindhäuser, 2000, p64) because of his allegedly many spectacular ideas. His political allies and opponents alike confirm this public perception through a variety of statements.[25] It is also uncontested that the idea to make the buses completely free of charge stems from Stevaert's ingenuity. Two of his advisers ('Lieben-Claes', interview, 29 June 2000 and Duverger, interview, 6 December 2001) conveyed this view, as did Moerkerk, Bormans and Mulders (interviews, 27 November 2001, 26 November 2001 and 30 June 2000 respectively). He in fact pursued this idea despite the vehement and continued warnings of transport experts (De toekomstvisie, 1997; Peperman, Lieben-Claes, Duverger), 'without much deliberation, without much planning. He simply made a calculation. . . what is this going to cost us? 20, 30, 35 million Belgian Francs and four years later we'll see' (Mulders, interview, 30 June 2000).

This lack of interest in established practices has been identified as a potential source of creativity because it can enable a person to see things uninhibited by the blinders of conformity (see Butzer, 1992; Menand, 2001). This is not to say that Stevaert does not value factual knowledge; on the contrary, 'he really studies his dossiers, he has knowledge of what he says' (Moerkerk, interview, 27 November 2001). Stevaert's political career is rooted in the intellectual circles that met in his student cafés where 'the working class youth did not gather so much' (Stevaert in de Condé, 1996, p27). Later, in his role as Flemish Minister of Transport, he asserted that 'the search for solutions for traffic problems has to be scientifically underpinned' (Stevaert, cited in Vandenreyt, 2001, p19). He also referred to tedious political documents (the Kyoto Protocol and Agenda 21) (Stevaert, 2000a), even though he scoffed at my question concerning the Rio process, sustainable development and Agenda 21 as something 'for the intellectuals'[26] (Stevaert, interview, 6 December 2001). This anti-intellectual flavour was relatively strong in our conversation. It contained the following passage that developed in response to my question as to why no other city has come up with the idea of free buses if it is supposedly so simple:

Stevaert: *'Because they are intellectuals, they are not foolish. . . Intellectuals won't change anything, crazy people change the future. Intellectuals come into play later'.*

Duverger: *'You have to have foolish ideas. But foolish doesn't mean that they aren't targeted. . . A fool with a vision'.*

Mulders suggests that Stevaert's vision probably lies in his capacity as a 'social democrat and [as an] environmentally conscious guy' (interview, 30 June 2000). This opinion is also expressed by Lieben-Claes, who calls him 'a green social democrat' (interview, 29 June 2000) and Moerkerk: 'He is green and red together and he is proud of that' (interview, 27 November 2001).

There is consensus that Elsbeth Seiltz is the mastermind of Brucker Land. Kellermann remembers that 'all the ideas came from her' (interview, 25 January 2002) and Haberkorn agrees when she says that 'she [Seiltz] would probably say "it was me. I had the idea"' (interview, 22 January 2002). 'It would have never happened without her' is the way Klein (interview, 25 January 2002) puts his appreciation of Seiltz's input. But the basis of the idea of a County Bread is said to have stemmed from Mr Assam, a member of the County Parliament. 'The idea was his. Ms Seiltz took over from there and pursued the implementation' (Herrwig, interview, 30 January 2002). Seiltz's own version contains yet another Ur-originator:

> *The idea of starting with bread came up when I went to the head of the Office of Agriculture and I said: 'Well, Dr Stangelmeier, we would like to do something hands-on. We want to show our responsibility for God's creation with something practical'. Then he told me – I will never forget this – 'Our farmers have been trying to bake a County Bread for three years . . . but they didn't get it together. Couldn't you join forces?'. . . And I went out and I called everybody and I said 'I've got the idea, I think I know now how we can really go forward.'* Interview, 15 January 2002

From this point on, the details of the concept were hammered out by a number of people whose individual inventive contributions can hardly be traced.

With respect to the fourth source of creativity – collective deliberation in citizen groups – the 'Panamarenkos of Hasselt'[27] deserve special mention because they conducted the earliest brainstorming sessions with tangible impacts on Hasselt's current transport policy. Stevaert refers to the customers of his cafés, who gathered there in the 1970s, by the name 'Panamarenkos of Hasselt' (de Condé, 1996). These were 'some very critical architects . . . artists, journalists, a little green, a little alternative . . . who cared about the spatial development of Hasselt . . . Steve comes from that milieu' (Mulders, interview, 30 June 2000, combined with email, 31 May 2002). Another place where ideas could congregate was the so-called traffic commission, consisting of representatives of the city, De Lijn, city planners, the police and the Flemish Department of Transport. It was established in the late 1980s, helped devise the mobility plans of the Conservative Party, then fell idle after the publication of *Hasselt Levendig Stadscentrum*, but was revived after Stevaert's election victory. Moerkerk remembers that phase: 'We met almost every week. . . Everybody had their say. Everybody had their ideas' (interview, 27 November 2001). The city parliament and certainly informal meetings of the governing coalition were yet other forums for the exchange and accrual of ideas. How else could it be that the Green Party and SP's coalition partner 'AGALEV contributed a lot to the mobility concept' (Beuzenberg, letter, 16 June 2002).

The path to what Brucker Land is today was also lined with countless meetings. It is hard to say which was the first that influenced the design of Brucker Land. Several of its activists mentioned '*Das bessere Müllkonzept*' (The Better Waste Concept)[28] in this context, because this initiative brought together a number of people who continued their communication and momentum even after the *Müllkonzept* failed in 1992. Haberkorn (interview, 22 January 2002) and Langer (interview, 5 February 2002) report that the impetus of these people was soon afterwards rededicated to a regionalization project in the food sector, an idea that ripened in the ambiance of a project called Dorf 2000 (Village 2000). One of its organizers, 'Daniel Suttner', remembers that the County Centre for Adult

Education (Kreisbildungswerk) facilitated four such visioning workshops (via email, 7 June 2002). Detailed questions were delegated to caucuses, of which those dealing with food and agriculture were the most active, among other reasons due to the 'enormous commitment of Ms Seiltz' (Sutter, via email, 7 June 2002). She allegedly transferred these energies to a follow-up process, a lecture series about 'responsibility for the creation', organized by Seiltz for the Catholic Continuing Education Organization (Katholische Erwachsenenbildung) in the county. These events did not produce concrete results but, according to several other accounts, created a readiness for action. The brainstorming continued in late 1993 in the Office for Agriculture, 'where we sat together to figure out how to build the whole thing. . . And so a group of seven or eight people gathered there two to three times per week and discussed the next steps' (Kellermann, interview, 25 January 2002). Other, more informal and strategic meetings were held at people's homes, as Klein remembers: 'Three or four of us sat around my kitchen table and talked' (interview, 25 January 2002). Dengler refers to these meetings as the 'germ cell, a nucleus of people' (interview, 28 January 2002). Formal meetings, the results of which required the approval of the member associations, were held at a frequency of every few weeks (Herrwig, interview, 30 January 2002), while new ideas were in fact forged over cups of coffee at informal gatherings: 'There was my kitchen table again,' says Klein, recalling such brainstorming sessions (interview, 25 January 2002). From this personal experience, Klein confirms what he has read: 'The power of innovation doesn't rest with transnational structures. It lies no doubt in small structures. . . at the regional dimension' (interview, 25 January 2002).

The attempt to retrace the origins of creative ideas in both cases resembles the search for the source of the Amazon. At many bifurcation points, it is hard to tell which tributary is bigger or more important; the conclusion must be that a plethora of springs makes the Amazon what it is. What corresponds to confluence points are uncounted formal and informal meetings, caucuses and get-togethers where 'one man starts a new idea, [which] is taken up by others and combined with suggestions of their own; and thus it becomes the source of further new ideas' (Marshall, cited in Bishop and Lisheron, 2002). In hindsight, then, most ideas have to be seen as the result of accumulated and diffuse authorship by skilled experts, creative individuals and openly searching people.

Experts ideally serve as 'valuable strangers' (Harding, 1991, p124) that counterbalance the tendency of insiders to incrementally improve what has outlived its usefulness. Experts should offer – rather than impose – their knowledge in the way Clark et al suggest: 'Given the inevitably unpredictable and contentious course of social transitions toward sustainability, Science and Technology needs to see its role as one of contributing information, options and analysis that facilitate a process of social learning rather than providing definitive answers' (2002, p4). Individual visionaries need a chance to speak out; those who are present as well as those who are not at the rostrum of the social discourse. Stevaert is said to have provided this chance for his 'colleagues and advisers. . . It must have been him who made the ideas come out of the others' (Moerkerk, interview, 27 November 2001). In this sense, he – and certainly Seiltz too – acted according to Holmes' aforementioned rationale for free speech: 'We need the resources of the whole group to get us the ideas we need' (cited in Menand, 2001, p431). This point leads to the third ingredient, public participation, an important contributor to solution finding as described above.

It is the cross-fertilization of these elements that counts. This process requires coordination and spaces for articulation, where fools can dream while experts explain and citizens contribute their concerns and ideas as future users. This exchange can and needs to be manifest in various forms: on traffic commissions, in cafés, city council meetings and at kitchen tables. The crucial task of organizing these encounters may be called the management, diplomacy or facilitation of creativity[29] – and I am sure it can be learned as any other craft. All of this communication and facilitation is most effective in an atmosphere that is 'ready for new ideas' (Mulders, interview, 30 June 2000), where change is in the air, or, in Grundin's words, 'in "charged" moments' (1990, p35). One cannot artificially create these situations, but it is possible to train oneself to detect and articulate disharmonies (Spinosa et al, 1997) that common sense tends to overlook.

Critical mass is crucial to overcome path dependencies

As many STS studies have shown, our current technological regime is not God-given and neither are our behaviours that are facilitated by it. However, we are rarely aware of the constructedness of our technologies or of how they create corridors for our daily choices. Pfaffenberger, among others, eloquently describes this phenomenon:

> *What was once the conscious product of human cultural and political action, passionate and meaningful, is now a silent material reality within which we lead our daily lives, mutely acting out patterns of behaviour that once had obvious connections to the root paradigms of our culture.* 1992, p309

This statement does not refer to one single technology, like a certain brand of valve heads, to a complex of mutually reinforcing elements, like cars, parking lots, highways, mall-lined urban fringes, tax cuts for SUVs, neighbourhoods devoid of stores, repair shops, and so forth. Any attempt to shield the ubiquitous 'momentum' (Hughes, 1994) of such a mature technological regime to a degree that routine and/or deliberate behaviours change requires no doubt more than optimizing valve heads. Therefore, successful co-evolutionary projects need a critical mass to break free of the rail tracks along which we live our normal lives.

To stay in the tracks[30] is the most convenient option for mere mortals, who cannot be blamed for avoiding the heroic pains of a forerunner, even if they grasp the detrimental direction of the journey. Dengler describes the situation of the farmers in Fürstenfeldbruck in similar words. They are:

Box 5.6 The 'best cycling city in the world'

A good example of critical mass is the mobility policy of Groningen, the Netherlands' sixth largest city with a population of 170,000. Since the 1980s the city gradually turned away from its previous car-friendly traffic policy until in the early 1990s it adopted an ambitious and 'integrated urban renewal, planning and transport strategy' (GlobalIdeasBank, 2005). As part of it, cycling has been made as attractive as possible by means of advanced stop lines for cycles at traffic lights, right of way for cyclists to do right turns at red lights, tens of thousands of parking spaces for bicycles, many of them with security guards (including 3000 at the central railway station), cycle lockers at rural bus interchanges to allow suburban dwellers to bike and ride and, of course, a dense network of bicycle routes consisting of two-way usage of one-way streets, specially built bridges, overpasses and short-cuts and bike-lane arterials into the city centre for commuters. The £18 million that the city has invested over ten years in the cycling infrastructure has paid off well. With 57 per cent of its inhabitants travelling by bicycle (compared to 4 per cent in the UK) (GlobalIdeasBank, 2005) the city was rewarded with the title 'Best Cycling City in the World' by the Bicyclists Magazine (GlobalIdeasBank, 2005).

In addition, new city centre buildings must provide cycle garages, some new houses are only accessible by bicycle, a pleasant open-air environment is created through high-quality architectural design and upgraded public spaces with generous greenery and restored monuments. Roads were also narrowed all across the city, out-of-town shopping centres are banned, inner-city parking was seriously restricted (for example, one space for every ten employees maximum), electronic transmitters ensure the right of way for buses at traffic lights, and a speed limit of 30km/h extends over the whole city centre. Free buses run between the city centre and park and ride facilities, a call-a-car borrowing system provides an alternative to car ownership, the central market square was converted from a roundabout to a public space with markets and street cafés, and the pedestrian area was extended. Employers are assisted in the drawing up of a company transport plan and special arrangements with freight transporters help them combine deliveries in fewer trips. The latest trick is the establishment of the Kolibri public transport network throughout the region of Groningen Assen with its characteristic 'transferias', strategically located connection hubs between light rail, trams and buses (www.kolibri-ov.net).

Gerrit van Werven, a senior city planner emphasized that all these measures were not primarily part of an environmental mission, rather of a down-to-earth economic regeneration programme. Its goals have been reached as the city has become more attractive for visitors, the city centre has strengthened its role as the core retail area and more people moved back into the city. This was only possible because changes were made to the whole urban infrastructural regime, not just to some of its elements here and there.

Sources: European True, 2000; Bardou, 2002; Jones, 2003; Smile Project, 2005; GlobalIdeasBank, 2005;

> *by and large dependent on the industry, in terms of information but also in*
> *terms of necessary supplies. . . And many have the feeling that this situation*
> *might not actually be that good – but they defend it at the top of their lungs*
> *because they have no alternative.* Dengler, interview, 28 January 2002

Schedler says, on the grounds of the same logic, that 'it would be unfair to assign all the guilt [for the contamination of groundwater with pesticides] to the farmers. They are often forced by a failed agricultural policy which forces them to produce higher and higher yields' (cited in P. S., 1993, February 3, pFFB6). Here we re-encounter the phenomenon of the technological treadmill or, in more general terms, the feeling of being coerced into doing something that one does actually not want to do. Dengler and Haberkorn confirm exactly this analysis with respect to the situation of the farmers (interviews, 28 January and 22 January 2002, respectively).

How hard it is to turn such structures around is demonstrated by a relatively small example from a German university that attempted to introduce recycled paper for its official letterhead stationery. Eventually, the proposal was dropped because 'the gray shade of the paper mismatched the colours [of the corporate design], which was developed only a few years ago, so one was unwilling to change it again' (Eickhoff, 2002). Beinhocker describes this example of 'technological momentum' in more general terms: 'Big decisions are hard to reverse. . . Once a company [or a community] is heading down a particular path, it may be very costly, time consuming, or simply impossible to change' (1999, p96). Overcoming this dilemma would require cannibalizing prior investments, which few are willing to do.

The difficulty of redirecting the momentum of centralized structures in the food production and distribution chains is illustrated in the case of Fürsten-feldbruck. Many interviewees lamented that almost all of the previous structures have been supplanted: 'We don't have a sizeable grain mill any more. . . There's no sizeable sawmill any more' (Krömeke, interview, 22 January 2002). Langer complained about the absence of a dairy in the county (interview, 5 February 2002), Herrwig reports that before 1995, 'there was no one left in the county who cultivated rye' (interview, 30 January 2002) and Haberkorn was concerned that 'bakers were not any more able to process wholewheat flour' (interview, 22 January 2002).

The situation in Hasselt possessed similar traits. The tramway tracks from the early 20th century had long been disposed of, the trees and the wide unpaved lane that lined the inner ring since the late 19th century had to give way to the automobile in the 1960s, 'large retail businesses are located outside the city centre' (Lieshout, interview, 27 November 2001) and sprawl is deplored among city planners (SHLS, 1994). The question, then, is how Hasselt and Fürstenfeldbruck managed to break the momentum of these regimes if the authors of both projects were aware of this aspect and whether they tackled it deliberately with a critical mass approach.

For Hasselt, there is evidence that clearly negates the above question, for example Stevaert's announcement not to initiate 'mega- or luxury-projects' (cited in Stas, 1995, p13) during his mayoral term. A representative of the Green Party also states that during the election campaign in 1994, they did not focus on 'grand and bloated ideas [because] the citizens don't care much about them; they are rather annoyed by the many little things' (Beuzenberg, letter, 16 July 2002). On the other hand, it is clear that Stevaert was never short of boldness. In 1991, while provincial deputy for environment, he wrote: 'I am clearly aware of the fact that this provincial environmental policy statement. . . has something ambitious and unrealistic' (Stevaert, 1991, p1; translation by Moerkerk). With regard to the revival of the inner city, he refused to 'fight only symptoms' (cited in Meuris, 1996, p1) and he promised in 1995 that the reconstruction of the inner and outer ring would be 'no patchwork' job (Cloostermans, 1995, p14). The Green Boulevard is, then, consequently described as a 'gigantic project' (Andere, 1996, p16) by a journalist of the local newspaper. Stevaert also explains his recipe for public transport in ambitious terms: 'When you opt for good public transport, you have to do it 100 per cent' (interview, 6 December 2001). It is thus not surprising that his adviser describes Stevaert as saying, 'I am going to take three steps at a time. I am not going to do what the technicians said was possible; no, I am going to reduce speed much more drastically[31]. . . [and I want] a very high frequency for the shuttle bus' (Duverger about Stevaert, interview, 6 December 2002).

In hindsight, a report on Hasselt's transport policy uses the language of force, concluding that the city council 'decided to break through this vicious circle' of road construction, increased traffic and more road construction to absorb the increased traffic (*Mobility with*, 1999, p1). Revisiting Chapter 3 (section entitled 'Hasselt') should make it clear that the reconstruction of the inner ring and the radical improvement of the bus system deserve the adjective *bold*. The cumulative effect of the many other, maybe less spectacular, elements of the project does not rank far behind. In regard to the latter measures, a then-city employee told me 'we don't unwind an algorithm; we rather implement many ideas step by step with a trial and error approach' (Peperman, interview, 26 June 2000; similar statement by Mulders, interview, 30 June 2000). I would argue that the lack of a master plan for these sub-projects does not derogate their combined weight. Stevaert's successor as mayor of Hasselt, Reynders, declares in this context that 'the proverb "many small steps add up to a big one"[32] [is] certainly appropriate' (cited in Rutten, 1995a, p12).

Brucker Land's early aspiration to introduce a County Bread was rather modest compared to the vision Klein suggested about six months after Seiltz' initial proposal:

> *I always told her [Seiltz], 'think big'. It's not enough to just make some bread and see what happens. Instead, we must consider what this thing will look like in ten years. . . In ten years, this must be known all over the world, there must be 1000 dissertations about it and we must have won 20 awards. This must be the scope of our vision and what do we have to do to get there? I think it was really important that we did not only think in these itsy-bitsy dimensions.* Klein, interview, 25 January 2002

As of now, Brucker Land still has a long way to go towards this goal but it has also definitively overcome the petite dimension. An important element that led to its current size is the inclusion of supermarkets in its distribution strategy. Of 21 key persons I interviewed, 17 ranked this factor within the highest 20 per cent on a scale ranging from 'very low' to 'very high' relevance for success (Brand, 1997). Seiltz elaborates that a distribution strategy that relies only on the remaining small stores in villages and neighbourhoods would only reach a small portion of the population because the majority of people now shop in supermarkets and do not want to run extra errands. Thus this was the only way to reach an order of magnitude which really makes a difference (Seiltz, via email, 2 March 2003).

Another indicator for ambitious goals is the resolution of the Brucker Land Energy Forum to make the County of Fürstenfeldbruck completely independent from energy imports by the year 2030 (Umweltinstitut München, 2002). This said, the dreams of Brucker Land activists are not yet exhausted:

> *There is the idea, at least among the core people of Brucker Land,. . .what if we managed to establish such regional structures that work according to the same methods and regulations all over Germany?. . .My vision towards globalization is to have a global network of thriving sustainable regions cooperating with each other. . .And this is where it gets exciting and we would have to say, 'OK, we combine all regions that have their regional products to a nationwide or worldwide corporation and each particular region is defined as a profit centre, with very strict specifications of its spatial scope'.* Klein, interview, 25 January 2002

Klein's daring dreams pose a very interesting question: is co-evolution secretly wed to modernist ideology, mass production and the suppression of local particularities? Is the size-matters meme of co-evolution a deliberate affront to Schumacher's (1973) claim that 'small is beautiful'? Such concerns deserve our attention because the transplantation of one successful co-evolutionary project to the rest of the world *can* be steamrollering. This is not what I propose, however. My suggestion is to disengage from the dichotomous discourse about sustainable development in every locale anew, to search for co-evolutionary solutions and to implement them in one particular location at a scale large enough to overcome path dependencies. If this principle is applied all over the world as a tool in the search for locally specific, co-evolutionary options, there is no reason for objection. I assume that even Schumacher would have liked to see his proposal catch on everywhere.

Definition of co-evolution

At this point, I conclude the list of memes of co-evolution. To say less would have left the idea of co-evolution under-defined, too prone to misunderstanding. To say more would run the risk of leaving too little leeway for interpretation and adaptation to specific circumstances. In other words, the above description may be appropriate to give readers from different backgrounds a sufficiently overlapping idea of co-evolution, thus permitting meaningful communication about this concept. With this said, I suggest the following definition of co-evolution to sustainable development:

> *Co-evolution seeks to transcend the common dichotomy between technology- and behaviour-orientated approaches to sustainable development. It does so by means of strategic alliances between and among providers and users of technologies who jointly define socially perceived problems and jointly seek innovative solutions. The result of this venture is a new, sufficiently large, technological regime that establishes a new range of realistic behavioural choices, including those that make the socially desired behaviour attractive. Like every successful innovation, the outcome of a co-evolutionary process must be socially embedded in local narratives and rituals.*

Notes

1 In this context, it is remarkable that the full name of AGALEV, the Flemish Green Party, which is part of the governing coalition in Hasselt, is Anders gaan Leven, which translates as 'to live in another way'.
2 Or to facilitate the 'rediscovery' of traditional needs, as some would put it.
3 'You can only reach the consumer if you argue "it tastes good. You are spoiling yourself"' (Haberkorn, interview, 22 January 2002). 'I eat less meat twice a week and in return I buy a really good piece of meat, one that really tastes different' (Haberkorn, interview, 22 January 2002).
4 'There [at a discount grocery] I get really lower quality products. . . [whereas from Brucker Land] I get products that are fresher, less contaminated . . . simply healthier food' (Dengler, interview, 28 January 2002).
5 The following calculation may support this claim: German households with three members spend about €115 per person per month on groceries, excluding luxury items (Krebs, 2002). People who purchase Brucker Land products every other shopping trip have additional expenses of €17.24 per person each month (calculation based on the price scheme presented in Chapter 3). This increases the percentage of annual income spent on groceries from the current 11 per cent (Trotz Agrarwende, 2001) to 12.7 per cent. This change appears rather insignificant, bearing in mind that this figure was almost 50 per cent in 1950 (Maxeiner and Miersch, 2001) and that the French and Italians still spend about 30 per cent of their income on groceries (Trotz Agrarwende, 2001; Bürgerstiftung Zukunftsfähiges München, 2002).
6 Holmes' original statement was: 'It is the merit of the common law that it decides the case first and determines the principle afterwards' (cited by Menand, 2001, p217).
7 Especially people with low revolutionary inclinations tend to make use of this mechanism. Or they honestly don't see the need for revolutionary acts because they have internalised this yielding mechanism. The term 'revolutionary' in

this context does not refer to a grand political upheaval; simply to a change of well-established habits, preferences and so forth.

8   Postrel uses the latter argument most prominently. She holds that:

> *the ostensibly antitechnocratic ideal of 'participatory democracy' became in fact a new form of technocracy. . . Such forms of 'democracy' require the time to sit in meetings and the attention to master specialized issues. They recreate bureaucratic governance by giving self-appointed activists the power to veto other people's experiments.* 1998, p21

9   Following Guy and Shove's term '"end-of-pipe" social science' (2000, p71).

10 I recently witnessed a related example when the chairperson of a meeting asked the participants to jot down spontaneous comments with a pencil so they can be erased afterwards if we wished. On similar prior occasions, most people used a pen despite such a request because they did not have a pencil handy. This time, however, the chairperson provided a set of pencils so that no one had to rummage for one. She did not need our participation to come up with this idea; she simply knew us well.

11 The familiarization of existing members of a given society with new technologies and of new members with existing technologies (socialization).

12 Because, as Bloch states, 'You cannot argue with a song' (cited in Pfaffenberger, 1992, p284).

13 The study group Hasselt Levendig Stadscentrum commissioned by the former, conservative city government envisioned a new traffic infrastructure and also strategized that 'the small ring can become a "boulevard" again' (SHLS, 1994, p28). Their concept lacked the adjective 'green' in substance and language, however.

14 A few examples of Stevaert's linguistic adroitness may suffice to support this observation: he initiated the Flanders-wide renaming of the Socialist Party from SP to SPA (A for anders = different) (Moerkerk, interview, 27 November 2001). He also promoted Hasselt's shopping district as an 'open-air shopping-center' (Jacobs, 1995a, p13), and came up with the name 'rainbow coalition' for the alliance of all but one party in the Hasselt city parliament (Moerkerk, interview, 27 November 2001). Stevaert even renamed himself; his given name was not Steve but another disyllabic and rather Germanophone name that did not have the chantable alliteration of the double 'st'. (Mulders, interview, 30 June 2000; I promised Mr Stevaert I would not reveal his original name).

15 Feenberg describes this position as a relict of times when 'the forces of the market were believed to transcend the will of peoples and nations. The economy was treated as a quasi-natural system with laws as rigid as the movements of the planet' (1999, pviii).

16 Supporters of both cases lamented this mechanism. Langer complained about the false costs for conventional groceries, arguing that 'if you look at the consequential costs then you'll see that the cheap products are actually the expensive ones. But the general public has to bear the costs. The general public has to bear the air pollution' (interview, 5 February 2002). An analogous

argument is made by Donné: 'From a macro-economic point of view, public transport is much cheaper than private traffic. . . We pay much too little for car-bound mobility. The extra costs. . . are borne by the government. The societal advantage of public transport is clear (less consumption of gasoline, less pollution, more safety, etc.)' (De toekomstvisie, 1997, p10).

17 'The story about two prisoners, which gave the game its name, can be found in R. Duncan Luce and Howard Raiffa, *Games and Decisions* (New York: John Wiley, 1957), p95' (Taylor, 1976, p13, footnote 8).

18 In addition, he would still have to drink the water contaminated by other farmers, whereas his small contribution would be enjoyed by everyone, even by non-cooperating free-riders.

19 The same problematic is at work in the industrial sector, where people claim they would buy certain environmentally friendly products if they were cheaper. The industry, in return, argues that without advance-purchase guarantees it would be overly risky to invest in large-scale production facilities, which could lower the price per unit.

20 An example of how contracts can protect early movers from the heroic fool status is the Kyoto Protocol, an international agreement intended to reduce greenhouse gas emissions. It only became legally binding after 55 countries had ratified it and after the ratifiers' cumulative carbon dioxide emissions had accounted for more than 55 per cent of the global emission. The practice of illegal cartel agreements (for example, to raise prices) is based upon the same mechanism and shows that even capitalist enterprises do not always abide by the 'law' of the free market.

21 These conditions have primarily to do with the discount rate of future payoffs, that is, the degree to which a player values immediate profits more than future profits (Taylor, 1976).

22 This comment was made in response to my question whether the word solidarity in the full title of the project (Brucker Land Community of Solidarity e.V.) means that members are expected to do something for others that is beyond their egoistic self-interest. Dengler's response to the same question was similar: 'Beyond sounds too altruistic. . . Self-interest is certainly not left aside' (interview, 28 January 2002).

23 Bologna, Italy (1972–1973) pursued an integrated approach including bus lanes, pedestrian zones and significant improvements to the public transport system; buses were free during rush hours. Car traffic in the historic centre reduced by 20 per cent and Bologna became one of the traffic-safest cities in Italy. Eventually, fares were reintroduced to cover the costs.

Compiègne, France (1976) intended to improve the traffic link between the inner city and residential areas on the outskirts. After the buses became free, passengers increased by 150 per cent and stayed at a satisfying level when fares were reinstated.

Rome, Italy (1972) experimented twice with free buses over a total period of nine weeks. The sobering result was that bus passenger numbers rose sharply during rush hours, which made it logistically impossible to continue the free service. In addition, almost no effects on car traffic were recorded.

Denver, Colorado (1978–1979) tried to attract customers to its commercial centre by providing free buses during off-peak hours. Private car traffic is reported to have decreased by 23 per cent, while the turnover in stores located in the centre is said to have risen noticeably

24   The meanings of the Flemish and of the English words 'stunt' are almost identical. A Flemish dictionary explains it as 'unexpected, striking action or accomplishment, daring escapade, brilliant coup' (http://www.vandale.nl).

25   'People in Hasselt say so, that he has many ideas. . . Well, it's quite possible that he has not too bad ideas, but most of them are not affordable' (Lieshout, interview, 27 November 2001).

'Well, he has his ideas, he's very clever . . . Stevaert is famous for that. He has very simple, stupid, straightforward ideas and he implements them' (Mulders, interview, 30 June 2000).

'What Steve does in Hasselt is brilliant' (Vermassen, cited in Thuwis, 1997, p11).

'My personal view always was . . . he must get everything from his assistants around him, who give him the ideas. . . But lately in the national politics, I don't believe this any more, I think I was wrong. Much of the things came from himself and I think the ideas came from him' (Moerkerk, interview, 27 November 2001).

26   Stevaert might actually be right. A professor at the Diepenbeek Academy told me that 'people don't talk about Rio. Well, the professors do, but. . .' (Mulders, interview, 30 June 2000; he did not complete the original sentence).

27   Panamarenko is a Belgian artist who is 'propelled by dreams of flight – the longing to escape the bounds of gravity, both physically and metaphorically [and who] creates machines for looking at the world from new angles' (Noble, 2000).

28   *Das bessere Müllkonzept* proposed an improved waste policy for Bavaria through the official plebiscitarian channels provided by the Bavarian constitution. The county of Fürstenfeldbruck was a major hotspot of this initiative, which gathered many environmentally inclined people. The draft of an improved waste law was presented to the Bavarian electorate in a referendum in 1992 but failed by a narrow margin.

29   Klein reconfirmed the importance of this task in his 'member check' and suggested the term 'communication brokers' for individuals who rendered these services to Brucker Land (via email, 14 April 2003).

30   What I call 'staying in the tracks' has been addressed previously by other scholars, albeit under different terms: to 'follow the drift' (Spinosa et al, 1997), to accept 'path dependencies' (Edquist, 1997), or to follow 'technological trajectories' (Dosi, 1988).

31   Moerkerk reports on this matter: 'In the previous year, Steve Stevaert put the issue of speed on the political agenda in Flanders. . .He has brought the general speed limit on many roads from 90 down to 70km/h. He even would like to change the law to make 70 the maximum speed outside villages, instead of 90' (via email, 10 February 2003).

32   Flemish original: *vele kleintjes maken een groot.*

6

Anticipation of Criticism

This chapter is structured in relation to a series of hypothetical or actual criticisms against the concept of co-evolution. In each section I attempt to develop a response that demonstrates the continued validity, relevance, usefulness, viability, appropriateness and realism of the co-evolution hypothesis. In addition to the critical arguments dealt with in this chapter it would certainly also be worth addressing the plausible criticism that Hasselt and/or Brucker Land are sustainable by themselves. Since this would not necessarily be lethal for the concept of co-evolution proper, this discussion has been made available on the website of the co-evolution initiative at www.coevolution.info.

Co-evolution is old wine in new bottles

A number of people working in the field of sustainable development might argue that the concept of co-evolution is not really new. To some it might even appear banal because they can identify a plethora of existing approaches that already call for better technologies *and* for a change of behaviour. The Wuppertal Institute, a German sustainability think-tank, could be proffered as an example because it accommodates a research group on 'Factor Four' resource efficiency *and* a task force on 'New Lifestyles' (www.wupperinst.org). Even the *Brundtland Report* contains passages that demand efficient technology (for example, Chapter 8, entitled 'Producing More with Less') *and* 'painful choices' (World Commission on Environment and Development, 1987, p9). The United Nations Conference on Environment and Development (UNCED), which was convened in response to the *Brundtland Report*, declares in its core document, Agenda 21, 'Achieving the goals of environmental quality and sustainable development will require efficiency in production *and* changes in consumption patterns' (UNCED, 1992, Chapter 4.15; emphasis added). Ten years later, at the World Summit in Johannesburg, Ricardo Navarro, chairman of Friends of the Earth International, said in a live broadcast on the PBS television network that 'we don't only need eco-efficiency but also eco-sufficiency' (NOW, 2002). And recently, Members of the European Parliament called for a programme to cut energy consumption through measures like 'subsidies for energy efficiency programmes and a public awareness campaign' (PLANNING, 2005, p3).

It would be untenable indeed to claim that no one has ever before looked at both the technical and behavioural side of the sustainability challenge. But it seems fair to maintain that few have done so in the stereoscopic manner that is suggested by the co-evolution hypothesis. Other authors share this view, for example Kemp and Rotmans, who observe that 'environmental policy has been unsuccessful in changing behaviour and bringing about societal transformation, involving a change in both technology and behaviour' (2001, p1). Hoogma et al criticize a similar phenomenon with regard to sustainable transport: 'The co-production (or co-evolution or con-construction) of the technical and the social, has not been recognized well. . . Hardly any policy instruments try to exploit and work upon the socio-technical features of transportation systems' (2002, p3). A few pages later they state that traditional policies 'do not seek to exploit synergies because they fail to see how the factors are interrelated, especially how technical aspects are related with social and institutional ones' (Hoogma et al, 2002, p17).

Seen in this light, the aforementioned quotes from political documents are based upon an additive logic, where the best we can do is to split the national budget for sustainability issues – if there was one – equally among eco-efficiency laboratories and groups that campaign for sophisticated simplicity. To cite Hoogma et al again, this approach 'address[es] barriers one by one' (2002, p17) while they should be tackled in a synchronized manner. Upon closer inspection, many political measures like regulation, taxes, market incentives and so forth indeed boil down to the two main halves of the sustainability discourse. For example, policy measures are often geared towards speeding up the development of new technologies without much consideration for their societal embedding. Political carrots are often used to speed up the adoption of eco-friendly technologies and sticks are used to quicken the phase-out of old ones. But such policy schemes still run into non-technical problems such as vested interests and habitual fixations. One case introduced above is an example of this problem: subsidising energy-efficient air conditioners remains an uphill battle as long as employees have to use their private space heaters to heat their offices. On the behavioural-only side, taxes and market incentives are often intended to stimulate behavioural changes against the grain of the prevailing technological or infrastructural regime. For example, introducing stiff parking fees is not very effective if no realistic public transport alternatives or bicycle infrastructure (bike lanes, showers, bike shelters) are available.

Co-evolution aspires to go further and is therefore new wine in new bottles. It proposes a synergistic, rather than additive relationship between technology and behaviour; not a little bit of each, but concerted action between them; not mixing black and white to an amorphous shade of grey, but an engraving that cultivates the artful composition of black and white. Latour's eloquence proves, once more, well suited to distil my own thoughts in one striking paragraph:

> *What appears in the place of the two ghosts – society and technology – is not simply a hybrid object, a little bit of efficiency and a little bit of sociologizing, but a* sui generis *object: the collective thing, the trajectory of the front line between programs and antiprograms. It is too full of humans to look like the technology of the old, but it is too full of nonhumans to look like the social theory of the past.* Latour, 1992, p254

While the above arguments illustrate the conceptual reasons why state-of-the-art policy instruments have not yet superseded co-evolutionary ideas, it must also be noted that both types of activities operate at different spatial scales. Policy interventions like taxes, regulations, incentives and subsidies fall in the realm of international, national or regional governing bodies whereas co-evolution has its strength primarily at the local level. Co-evolution is therefore not meant as substitute for, but as addition to, policy measures at higher spatial levels. Subsidies, taxes, standards, penalties and co-evolutionary approaches 'all have a role to play, depending on the circumstances' (Hoogma et al, 2002, p200).

Where city administrations in collaboration with their citizens already turn both screws (the technical and the social) in a coordinated fashion I am more than happy to acknowledge the co-evolutionary nature of such initiatives – regardless of whether they use this label. If, for example, the money raised from road tolls is used to improve public transport infrastructures, such an approach has undoubtedly co-evolutionary traits.[1] Such highly integrated and holistic forms of socio-technical policies are, fortunately, being developed but they seem not yet widespread enough to make co-evolution appear old in fancy new clothing. For now, the co-evolution concept still seems useful as a descriptive and prescriptive tool because it provides lucidity in the engine room of cases where new technologies make socially desired behaviour attractive. In this sense, the memes of co-evolution are like chapters in a car repair manual. They help to clarify how things work and why they sometimes don't work.[2]

Despite these attempts to defend the relative novelty of the concept of co-evolution, I would like to emphasize that the general purpose of this book does not rest anyway on the non-existence of other co-evolutionary projects. The value added by the word co-evolution alone seems to justify its existence. It is useful as a linguistic tool or, with Joerges, an expedient 'LogIcon . . . a picture to think with' (1999b, p427). The availability of such a conceptual proxy makes it easier to communicate, to imagine and to pursue projects where technologies make socially desired behaviour attractive in a systematic fashion.

Established professions will undermine co-evolution

Critics of co-evolution could argue that established professions will attempt to consciously or unconsciously badmouth the concept of co-evolution in order to nurture a socially perceived necessity for their own specialized knowledge and expertise. After all, the promise to produce value for society depends upon funding opportunities, social status and the availability of jobs for any discipline. Therefore, the imaginative argument continues, established professions will drown co-evolutionary voices by means of lobbying, presentations to the public and, most importantly, by teaching students the 'proper' practices. In the end, the dichotomy between technology and behaviour orientated approaches will be perpetuated.

In its essence, this point addresses the sociology of science and its derivative, the sociology of sustainable development. It has primarily to do with the fact that the definition of a problem can be preceded by either interests or beliefs as explained earlier. Schön formulates this phenomenon as 'cutting the practice situation to fit professional knowledge' (1983, p44). This professionalism trap appears in two manifestations: one results from conscious manoeuvres performed by 'discourse coalitions'[3] (Hajer, 1996, p26) such as professional associations or even by individual inventors who 'construct problems suited to their unique skills and ideas'[4] (Carlson, 1992, p175). The second manifestation is an unreflective but candid conviction in the value of one's profession. No doubt many engineers, for example, really believe in sweeping technological solutions, which is why they continue their technology push. Experts in social and behavioural sciences are certainly no less prone to analogous pursuits. This professional myopia is often referred to as solipsism, a 'theory that locates reality entirely in the mind of the beholder' (Heylighen, 1998). The disciplining effect of a technological regime falls exactly within this line of reasoning because it 'implies a set of rules [and] prestructures the problem-solving activities that engineers are likely to undertake' (Hoogma et al, 2002, p19). Dosi observes similar effects of a technological paradigm. It 'consists of an exemplar (an artefact that is to be developed and improved) and a set of (search) heuristics, or engineering approaches, based on technicians' ideas and beliefs of where to go, what problems to solve and what sort of knowledge to draw on' (according to Hoogma et al, 2002, p18).

I fully agree with Hajer that 'different [scientific] cultures imply "contradictory certainties" [and that] nobody stands above such cultural preferences' (1996, p29). The looming resignation fed by this assessment can only be avoided with resort to pragmatism: we should judge competing positions by their *outcome*. Thus, if the vanguard of this game is determined by 'what works', I would argue that the concept of co-evolution is well equipped, with Hasselt, Fürstenfeldbruck and others as trump cards. But before further co-evolutionary experiments can be conducted, we still face the professionalism trap of mayors, developers, consultants and the like. Two main strategies appear suitable to overcome this hurdle.

A first possibility is to cognitively approach those who trust their profession by educational default and to make them mindful of missed co-evolutionary opportunities through straightforward information, best practice guides or other related readings. However, it is quite possible that solipsists-by-routine change into solipsists-by-interest when they begin to think that their own and their peers' position is at stake. This deliberate and strategic scepticism against co-evolution is probably the hardest to cope with but it might be susceptible to a core principle of alternative dispute resolution: taking interests seriously. What becomes visible from such a position is that specialized professions can actually gain something as partners in a co-evolutionary project. After all, their expertise in either technology or behaviour related issues is still necessary in a co-evolution-bound strategic alliance. In addition, they will have a more satisfying job because they can rightly expect less vehement opposition, that is, better adaptation of their findings or products. This is identical to the prospect for success, which certainly ranks among the strongest motivations. In other words, members of established professions should be invited to develop a widened conception of self-interest beyond ideological purity. This will imply an unavoidable amount of 'unlearning and undoing . . . of dissociating old ideas, assumptions and habits [which] proves to be very difficult but is central to a regime-shift' (Hoogma et al, 2002, p197) and could turn out to be quite satisfying.

A second and additional strategy – not an alternative one – is less patient with professionals; it rather confronts them with facts that they have to react to. This approach is basically a remedy for Hajer's analysis that 'politicians, policy makers at the local level, environmental NGOs and citizens are initially kept out and are not seen as relevant actors for the phases during which technologies are composed' (1996, p33). Therefore, he demands that politics[5] – not government – be brought back so that 'policy makers could become active in the *creation* of problem definitions' (Hajer, 1996, p29) again.

A bottom-up version of this strategy is to allow citizens to make policy. This is what happened in Hasselt, as its citizenry was systematically involved in the inventory of the most problematic traffic points in Hasselt. This questioned the professional wisdom about the allegedly obvious definition of Hasselt's traffic problems. In general, citizens' questions can be very powerful in forcing experts to re-open their professional black box and present its contents before a curious audience. 'A disassemblage of that sort makes the constructedness [and interest-ladenness] of the current range of choices transparent and thus provides a chance for new constructions' is how I described this mechanism earlier. Fürstenfeldbruck escaped the professionalism trap mainly for the following reason: its founding team consisted of a variety of social actors who mutually balanced and questioned each other's professional and personal biases. In addition, they had to explain their strategy to members like Ulrike Haberkorn, who admits her non-expertise: 'I did not contribute any know-how' (interview, 22 January 2002).

The top-down version of this strategy interprets the primacy of policy in its traditional sense, that is, the competence of elected politicians to define the direction. This is certainly a partial explanation of why Hasselt escaped the professionalism trap. After all, the decision to involve the citizenry in the definition of the problem in the first place was made by the top-ranking officials of the new SP/Green city government. And although the honour and the task of developing solutions to these problems was assigned to professionals, they were guided by political specifications. Lieben-Claes made this very clear: 'You have to guide the consultants . . . the vision has to be there at first so it does not mutate into mere technical rationality' (interview, 29 June 2000). Moerkerk describes how such mutations usually come about: 'We were trained for making a road, making a highway according to the norms. "We need it three meters wide and so on". . . . [But] we are not city-builders. We are not trained to look at public space, to look at green' (interview, 27 November 2001). It was ultimately fortuitous for Hasselt that the vision of a Green Boulevard brought together experts from a broader array of disciplines: 'engineering, mentality, environment, city building, social issues, [and] communication' (Moerkerk, via email, 16 June 2002). In this context, it may be noteworthy that the team that authored the *Flemish Mobiliteitsconvenant* (see www.coevolution.info) consisted of 'engineers, social scientists and even a philosopher' (Duverger, interview, 29 June 2000).

The top-down strategy to overcome the professionalism trap has one more twist: governmental funding policies. Quite often, policy makers ask only the standard questions – often literally on funding application forms – and thereby receive only standard answers (see Spinosa et al, 1997). More freedom to create locally meaningful problem definitions could reduce the common practice of feeding locally specific data into the never-changing optimization algorithm and of presenting the results always on the same report template in the solipsistic language of the expert who happens to fill it out.

If I take my deliberations about professional bias seriously, I have to face up to possible allegations of creating my own professionalism trap in my work. Such a reproach could claim that I prefabricated the technology–behaviour dichotomy as a problem definition that would make me appear valuable as the saviour who proffers co-evolution as the solution. From this perspective, my suggested solution would be completely self-referential because I did what humans usually do in the eyes of a pragmatist: 'We know we're right before we know why we are right. First we decide, then we deduce' (Menand, 2001, p353). As support for this allegation one could refer to Campbell, who mentions six – not just two – disciplines that dominate the current sustainability discourse: economics claims to lead to sustainable development through better market incentives; engineering through better technologies; public policy through better policy programmes; communicative action through better community dialogue; spiritual community through better environmental ethos; and better planning through better plans (Campbell, 2002). In this enumeration, 'engineering' and 'spiritual community' clearly represent what I see as the two constituents of the technology–behaviour dichotomy. The other four, one could argue, are inadmissibly ignored in my concept – for all too obvious reasons. My binary interpretation of the sustainability discourse would then be unmasked as interest-driven, undue generalization. I do not claim that my perception is better or more correct than Campbell's; I merely think that they operate on two different abstraction levels. Public policy is, as far as I can see, usually intended to create the right incentives, which in turn are supposed to lead to the 'right' behaviour or to the development and application of the 'right' technologies. Economic incentives are also primarily an intermediate step to trigger either certain behaviours and/or the market success of certain technologies. Political and economic incentives thus fall mostly into the *carrot and stick* category as discussed in Chapter 2. Communicative action, too, is hardly an end in itself. It is rather a process that could lead to the acceptance of a certain technological regime or to a consensus about socially desirable behaviour and can thus be seen as an ingredient of co-evolution. Planning is probably the least prone to the technology–behaviour dichotomy, or, in other words, closest to what I call co-evolution.

The above lines of argument may clarify why and how I interpret the dichotomy of technology and behaviour orientated approaches as a legitimate aggregation of Campbell's six disciplines. I am aware that these arguments, plus those I have already presented in Chapter 2 under the heading of 'Ringing bells', cannot vitiate the most enduring sceptics. From such brave colleagues, I retreat to the position of a liberal ironist in a Rortyan sense: 'People who combin[e] commitment with a sense of the contingency of their own commitment' (1989, p61). But I stand by my assertion that we should at least try co-evolution and assess it by its results.

Common sense is not susceptible to co-evolution

Not only members of established professions tend to think in dichotomous categories but also the public at large. In democratic societies this can be an obstacle to co-evolution because people tend to elect politicians and approve of projects that appear straightforward, non-verbose, low-dimensional and action orientated; co-evolution does not necessarily fall into this category. To preserve the potentials for sophisticated but effective action that lie within the complexity of co-evolutionary projects would require more time, more energy and a willingness to look more closely. In our media-mediated world, however, small chunks of highly aggregated information sell better and fit better into the predefined boxes on the layout templates of certain newspapers. Besides, with all the information overflow, things have to look or be made to look straightforward, either black or white, if they want to retain their chance of being perceived at all. This is why the higher slogan-value of the presumably simpler technology or behaviour message makes such a difference. In other words, both meet the demand for neat and clean information and the media partially creates and certainly caters to this taste.

This observation does not stem from intellectual chauvinism and its disdain for the intellectual capabilities of the electorate but from an awareness of socialization effects in a world that is largely split in two respective camps: positivism and its derivatives versus constructivism and its affinity; quantitative versus qualitative doctrines; modernism versus antimodernism; technophilic versus sociophilic; state-of-the-art GMOs versus all-out awareness campaigns. In other words, socialization casts the techno–socio dichotomy into a common sense trap, which is basically the popularized and internalized version of the professionalism trap, but without the intentional component of the latter. I assume that readers who do not share this assessment also do not see the public as a noteworthy obstacle to co-evolution and might well proceed directly to the next section.

To do justice to the phenomenon of common sense, it deserves praise as a very useful device to cope with our complex world, as it 'makes our lives intelligible' (Spinosa et al, 1997, p29). Postrel notes in this context that 'rules of thumb help us navigate the world' (1998, p111), while Fisher remarks rightly 'a cliché saves time' (Fisher, 2002). A life without this 'technique of selective inattention' (Schön, 1983, p69) would be quite troublesome, as Bijker and Law describe. If we began to wonder why and worry how our artefacts – our saucepans, cars, refrigerators, bridges – work it would take us hours to brew coffee in the morning. The conduct of daily life surely demands a tactical lack of curiosity (Bijker and Law, 1992b).

Conversely, common sense always has a built-in blind spot for alternatives: 'A Westerner cannot help thinking that the sensible (healthy, civilized, natural) way to sit, for example, is on chairs, at tables and so forth and not on the floor' (Spinosa et al, 1997, p29). Such certainties gain momentum as they are handed down from one generation to the next, they become 'institutionalized and . . . [are] no longer examined, evaluated, or criticized' (Innes, 1995, p186). Criticism would even be considered immodest because some things are simply off intellectual limits and the emperor cannot be naked even though the rationale behind such rules has long been forgotten. In Feenberg's words: The 'general assumptions [that make our] cultural horizon . . . seem so natural and obvious that they often lie below the threshold of conscious awareness'[6] (1995b, p11).

Our perception of the world falls into corresponding preconceived categories and so do our perceptions of problems. This has far-reaching consequences because 'when we set the problem,. . . we set the boundaries of our attention to it and we impose upon it a coherence which allows us to say what is wrong and in what directions the situation needs to be changed' (Schön, 1983, p40). This trick allows us to efficiently encircle the one seemingly correct, logical and appropriate solution. But when we trace the chain of our reasoning for more than a couple of links, we will notice that its origin lies somewhere in an opaque mist.[7] At this point, we would have to acknowledge 'that there is no right way of doing things' (Spinosa et al, 1997, p29), only various ways that differ in their effectiveness of delivering the desired result. This proviso applies to technology and behaviour orientated approaches as well as to co-evolutionary projects.

The good news is that it is obviously possible to depart from such ingrained automatisms. Hasselt, after all, is literally described as a 'path-breaking project' (Jacobs et al, 1997, p1). But *how* is it possible to convince people to back-pedal if they are about to say, 'of course we need better technology (alternatively: better behaviour) to reach sustainable development. Therefore, I vote for mayor X; this is why I advocate a third ring around Hasselt; hence, everybody should cycle the extra mile to the eco-farmer'? How is it possible to challenge the adjectives *clear, obvious, self-evident,* or *commonsensical,* that often are used to fortify such proposals for action? The following four thoughts might provide a strategic handle on this problem.

An almost obvious first lever is to make people aware of the contingency of their 'logical answers'. Dengler raises the issue of socialization and 'education. . . The question [of] how people become what they are, how they grow up, or how they develop' (interview, 28 January 2002). This does not imply that we should re-educate or reprogramme people to a new truth. Rather they should come to understand that 'the framing of a problem excludes certain solutions' (Dengler, interview, 28 January 2002) and they should be encouraged to 'question the way they look at a problem, whether it is the real problem' (Dengler, interview, 28 January 2002). This could make them a little more humble[8] in regard to the obviousness of their solution. It would be welcome if such approaches trickled into school and college curricula; but for a particular community, this is too oblique a task. Andragogy might be a more feasible path and is indeed a prominent element in the toolkit of Brucker Land and Unser Land. The latter even carries the official subtitle 'educational network' (Brückmann, 2002b). The educational setting, however, often looks less like a classroom than an aisle in a supermarket. If, in the end, people agree with Seiltz that 'Brucker Land is rooted in common sense' (cited in Brand, 1997, p114), the goal is either achieved or overachieved, as the case may be.

A second and additional approach to challenging commonsensical reflexes is to address influential individuals so they become 'careful not to think with the same logic as others', as Stevaert exhorts himself (cited in Jacobs, 1996b, p1). Thus immunized, they can become the agents of what I call the diplomacy of creativity à la Seiltz or they can suggest alternative futures themselves. A direct outcome of this stance is Stevaert's response to the 1500 employees of Hasselt's hospital: 'The personnel demanded its own parking lot, which would have meant sacrificing some green space. Now, I disposed of that discussion because they can and do use the free buses' (cited in *Hasselt: Stadt*, 1998, p20). I admit that I lack an easy answer as to how to achieve this aforementioned 'immunization'. The idea of providing more formal education to more people – based on the probabilistic hope that future leaders might be among them – will cause eyebrows to rise because neither Stevaert nor Seiltz has a university degree. I am unsure about the lesson this teaches; it might well be that college education can backfire if it merely converts common sense into a professionalism trap. On the other hand, my notion of 'great (wo)men' views them as the torch-bearers of ideas that ferment in circles with at least some academically trained members. I am sure it would not hurt if young people, who will play that role one day, were exposed to more noetic thinking, such as STS, during their college education. Exposure to critical art could also trigger reflective thoughts among individuals, because art can propose bold and even provocatively unrealistic alternatives. Thus expressed, utopia 'becomes a rationality that can be thought, liberated from the burden of declared impossibilities and accepted alienation'[9] (Baudson, 1996).

A third possibility in questioning taken-for-granted certainties is to facilitate encounters with competing common senses. Non-experts like children are very well suited for this task because they have or take the liberty to pose disarming questions to bearers of established wisdom, who usually perceive them as largely unthreatening.[10] Postrel, even though she is interested in creativity within the technological paradigm, testifies in this context: 'We rarely think about [rules of thumb] except when reminded by children' (1998, p111). Even though Hasselt and Fürstenfeldbruck did not systematically seek children's input, this strategy still seems worth raising, as the experiences of communities with official children's parliaments (for example, Luzern, Switzerland) demonstrate. It appears feasible to emulate children's curiosity through public participation. Here, non-expert citizens can play the role of the disarmer. This is not to say that average citizens are childish or of a lower status in such discussions, but it is obvious that one cannot be an expert in every discipline. I, for example, would make a very good child on a number of issues. 'Valuable strangers' in the sense of Harding (1991) are perhaps the most applicable possibility in questioning preconceived opinions. In her words, the stranger brings 'just the right combination of nearness and remoteness, concern and indifference, that are central to maximizing objectivity. . . The stranger can see patterns of belief or behaviour that are hard for those immersed in the culture to detect' (Harding, 1991, p124, building on the work of Collins). Here, the valuable stranger is helpful by deconstructing (in its best sense) our constructed common sense and reconstructing the pieces into a widened horizon.

Fourth and lastly, it appears feasible that academia can contribute to over-coming the common sense trap through engaged research. Spinosa et al call our attention to this option:

> *Disharmonies are practices in which we engage that common sense leads us to overlook. . . We should beware of the Cartesian tendency to imagine the skill of noticing and holding on to disharmonies as primarily intellectual, as noticing a problem in one's life and stepping back to analyse it, to puzzle through it, in one's mind. Rather, the skill of uncovering the tension between standard, commonsense practices and what one actually does is a skill of intensified practical involvement.* Spinosa et al, 1997, p23

The concept of co-evolution, derived from nine weeks of research in both Hasselt and Fürstenfeldbruck, might be perceived as my own humble contribution as an academic. It may permit me to 'escape the traps of common sense set by everyday speech' (Bijker and Law, 1992d, p202). A combination of these four strategies – education, immunization, disarmament and involvement – seems suitable to lift common sense from muddy waters to the reach of tactical handling. The sanguine corollary is that co-evolutionary projects are not doomed to get stuck in the common sense trap.

Co-evolution is not radical enough

The allegation 'co-evolution is not radical enough' would not be very surprising and can originate from different sources. One of these objections claims that co-evolution takes too long, that 'we'll all die waiting for utopian conditions', as Moore puts it in a deliberate provocation (S. Moore, personal communication, 17 August 2002). My counter-argument largely rests on the sobering assessment of the results achieved so far by either the technology or the behaviour orientated approaches. To avoid misunderstandings: I am talking about their real, not about their idealized implementation,[11] which I in turn consider utopian. The value added by co-evolution is actually the synergistic combination of technological and behavioural change which still makes it the best and fastest game in town. I admit, however, that this is only visible from a long-term perspective because the 'synchronic preadaptation' (Rohracher, 2001, p8) process between designers and users is always locally specific, it has to be negotiated anew in every locale and cannot be imported as a universally applicable template. In other words, the search for a co-evolutionary project can take quite some time, which is a disadvantage compared to the promise of instant implementation that representatives of the technology or behaviour orientated approaches can make.

What feeds the argument that co-evolution is too slow is therefore impatience with the messy discourse on democratic decision-making. This is not a new phenomenon as Menand shows. He reports on Henry Maine, a legal historian in the 19th century who was 'an enemy of majoritarianism [because] he considered popular prejudice an obstacle to progress' (2001, p304). In the late 20th century, Hawken et al posit a very similar argument with explicit reference to sustainable development: 'Society can work toward resource productivity . . . without waiting to resolve disputes about policy'[12] (1999, p20). Campbell describes the target of this position as 'the tragedy of incrementalism' (2002) but he does not subscribe to this pessimistic stance himself. Instead he shares a Deweyan 'theory of democracy that dispensed with Lockean assumptions' (Menand, 2001, p304). To avoid repetition, readers may refer to Chapter 5, where I describe such a position in more detail. The bottom line is that in the long run, co-evolution seems to be the best approach we have because it avoids most conditions that make the technology and/or the behaviour orientated approaches either difficult to sustain, rife with anti-programmes, or simply marginally effective.

A second objection under the flag 'not radical enough' could actually come from colleagues who agree that a change of behaviour is necessary and possible. Despite this common point, their rejection of co-evolution can be disaggregated into at least two strands. One group might argue that I have given up hope in human self-responsibility, that my conception of human beings is too pessimistic. This stance has immense political consequences, as Menand shows when he describes the Unitarian position in the debate about slavery: 'Unitarianism . . . was a creed founded on the belief in the innate moral goodness of the individual . . . [Therefore, it] advocated a policy of moral suasion . . . as the proper means for inducing the South to give up slavery' (2001, p12). Analogously, the root of un-sustainability can be seen as immoral behaviour, which is curable through persuasion and requires more radical awareness campaigns. As a general rebuttal of this opinion, I dare simply point to the section 'The behavioural-fix approach' in Chapter 2 , where I describe and criticize this sermonizing approach.

The *Weltanschauung* of the second group, the antagonists to Unitarians, is Calvinism, 'a creed founded on a belief in the innate moral depravity of the individual. [Its followers proposed] political coercion, as the proper means' (Menand, 2001, p12) to free the slaves. In the sustainability debate, the direct descendants of this position would argue that more radical policies can enforce a change of behaviour. This strategy makes deliberate use of prescription and domination as described and rejected above. A hypothetical construct of *liberal* Calvinism could lead to an interesting twist in the discussion of how to make people do what they 'ought to' do. The best example for this position is a stomach bypass as a means to control obesity. It does not trust in human self-responsibility to eat less, nor does it resort to coercion. It is a genuinely new approach – in the tradition of the technological quick fix – that uses technology to exert a rigorous but *self-imposed* prescription. A stomach bypass meets surprisingly many criteria of my definition of co-evolution. However, it does not open a new *range* of choices; rather it permits only one single choice: eat less, full stop. A more co-evolutionary way of tackling obesity would be to improve access to grocery stores, which has been found to be a crucial explanatory variable for the consumption of fruits and vegetables (see above).

Co-evolution seems to qualify as not radical enough from a third perspective, which locates the root of the problem at higher political levels. Costantini argues in this context that 'as long as the WTO [World Trade Organization] works this way, powerful nations and corporations will use it to steamroller the shelters that citizens have built against the stormy side effects of market forces' (2000). From this angle, Brucker Land might appear as such a shelter: well meaning but ineffective. The efficacy of Hasselt's mobility policy might be declared marginal as well,[13] as long as the price of gasoline does not reflect the true macroeconomic costs of its harms. I am fully aware of these mechanisms and would welcome a number of changes in the White House, World Bank, European Union headquarters and the like. But I do not pinpoint the only furcation between detriment and salvation in these locales; I rather think that the cumulative effect of community level efforts can make a difference. In addition, the conditions for reaching co-evolutionary accomplishments are ideal in a community: it must be small enough to permit the negotiation of collective and cooperative measures in face-to-face communications and big enough to reach a critical mass. Furthermore, I would like to note that the global framework evidently did not obviate what has taken place in Hasselt and Fürstenfeldbruck. I think it is even possible that such projects radiate to higher levels, where policies such as the Flemish *Mobiliteitsconvenant* (see www.coevolution.info) are devised.

Given the above deliberations, I argue that the allegation that co-evolution is not radical enough is simply based upon different definitions of the *radix*, that is, the assumed root of the problem. Which definition is correct and which is wrong cannot be determined from an Archimedean point; moreover, any such attempt would be futile because there is no single root to the problem of unsustainability. It seems that one such root – probably a major one – lies in omitting potentials for co-evolution between technology and behaviour.

Co-evolution is too radical

Postrel (1998) would probably argue that the concept of co-evolution is too radical because it undermines the roots of the ideal practice of cultural evolution. The best routine of meme development and meme selection, she would argue, is unhampered experimentation and rigorous selection in a free market. Not even in its extreme version does this argument amount to a critique of planning as a human activity. Although Hayekian theorists distance themselves on many points from their neo-liberal brethren, they too claim that market processes are better than dialogical procedures in determining the optimal allocation of resources to competing demands. From this perspective Pennington criticizes the idea of collaborative planning à la Patsy Healey for its emphasis on 'face-to-face communication and the conveyance of information via public discourse and debate. For the Hayekians, by contrast, markets are required to facilitate intersubjective learning and co-ordination' because of their superior 'communicative role' (2002, p190). Democratic discourse as a process to encircle potential strategic alliances must seem too radical and a waste of energy to free market advocates of whatever shade.

Those who do not share this impression are denounced as 'enemies of the future' (Postrel, 1998, modification of her book title). Sclove and Scheurer receive this verdict because they call for '"no innovation without evaluation", "no innovation without regulation" and "no innovation without participation"' (cited in Postrel, 1998, p22). The concept of co-evolution is subject to similar criticism because it calls for coordination, concertation, participation and negotiated agreements. In other words, co-evolution could be accused of too much state involvement. Notwithstanding the fact that Brucker Land was virtually developed without state intervention, Postrelians would still accuse it of over-regulation because of all the rules for farmers and tradesmen. Moerkerk's statement 'everything works here because of state subsidies' (interview, 27 November 2001) would be nothing short of a provocation. Those who consider co-evolution too radical would ground their allegations in the conviction that superior memes will survive by their very essence and do not need state intervention or other such memetic engineering.[14]

Assuming that a policy based on this position produced an abundance of technological innovations, they still would have to pass through technological dramas in the sense of Pfaffenberger (1991). After all, the replication of memes does not depend on the decision of their designers but on their acceptance by the meme replicators, that is, the people. Powerful authorities could organize a theoretical circumvention of this problem by imposing technologies and infrastructures onto people. Such an option is not only bluntly anti-democratic, it would also face powerful anti-programmes and would be inconsistent with Postrel's tenet of anti-intervention. But assuming further that people did accept the – hopefully resource-efficient – technologies resulting from creative anarchism, the resource-saving effect would soon be overcompensated due to the rebound effect. From a sustainability perspective, this position is therefore not feasible and cannot be accepted.[15]

My suggestion to avoid the rebound effect is to achieve a change of behaviour. This in turn is unacceptable for free market ideologists, who could marshal a statement by Oliver Wendell Holmes: 'Some kind of despotism is at the bottom of seeking for change. . . I don't care to boss my neighbours and to require them to want something different from what they do – even when, as frequently, I think their wishes more or less suicidal' (cited in Menand, 2001, p62). This argument, however, is off the mark for two reasons. First, certain practices we call unsustainable are not only suicidal for the originator, they also harm others. Second, co-evolutionists do not boss people, they rather give people a strategy to escape from what I refer to as Radermacher dilemma, a situation that forces people to do what they don't really want to do. As demonstrated earlier, it is only cooperation that can build a ramp out of this version of the prisoners' dilemma. John Locke's philosophy, its modern political manifestation as 'liberal anarchism' (Barber, 1984) and Postrel's theory of 'dynamism' fail to provide the conceptual framework for such a project. These perspectives all regard citizens as nothing more than atoms of self-interest. But atoms that stay atomized will never make molecules. John Dewey made the same point over a hundred years ago as he argued that meaningful 'democracies are not just the sum of their constituent atoms because atoms are not independent of their molecules. They are always functioning as parts of a greater whole' (according to Menand, 2001, p305) or as *zooi politicoi* as Aristotle would put it. Co-evolution does not prescribe the single best chemical synthesis for atoms to follow; it does not stipulate one golden path of how to reap potentials for synergies; it merely offers a generic manual to facilitate the assemblage of locally available components into something bigger than the sum of its parts.

This construction process is itself always a creative venture and an experiment that succumbs to the rule of memetic selection. Postrel should therefore appreciate the dynamics that are inherent in this process. Strategic Niche Management (SNM) has been developed as a tool for the design of such experiments with new socio-technical regimes. The core idea of SNM is to conduct such experiments in clearly confined real world laboratories, for example in one particular town. The purpose is not to find out whether a predefined technology works but to experiment with, learn about, alter, adjust and reassess socio-technical constellations under massive involvement of users as co-innovators and co-designers. In Hoogma et al's words, SNM 'allow[s] for working on both the technical and the social side in a simul-taneous and coherent manner' (2002, p3). Its underlying conceptual ideas thus closely resemble those of the co-evolutionary approach. Once a local socio-technical constellation between the supply and demand has ripened to a certain degree of stability it should be easier to translate the concept from its niche to larger markets as in the case of car sharing, which originated in very small circles in Switzerland.

To summarize, I can understand if and why liberal anarchists consider co-evolution too radical. But it needs to be emphasized that co-evolution is not identical to choking control or medieval-style stagnation, which they seem to perceive as the only alternatives to their ideas. My hope is that those liberal anarchists with political decision-making power can be inspired by successful co-evolutionary projects to re-examine the wiring of their opposition reflex in the black box containing their world-view.

Co-evolution sets the fox to guard the geese

Critics of the concept of co-evolution could throw a curve ball by constructing the following, not unrealistic scenario: imagine a community where the majority of people find it desirable to commute to work as smoothly and comfortably as possible. If co-evolutionists make these people co-designers of urban technologies, they will most likely end up with more roads. Exactly this could be observed in:

> *Central Texas [where the] majority . . . still believes in a 50-year-old myth that we can escape traffic congestion by building more highways. [In 2001], over 60 per cent of Travis County voted for a property tax increase to purchase right of way and construct highways.* Ascot, 2002, p3

Ascot (2002) sees the 'brainwashed society' as the reason behind such decisions, but they could also simply stem from a 'tendency of people to opt for what they already know' (S. Moore, personal communication, 31 January 2003). This is the lesson Moore drew from a study conducted in California, which revealed a correlation between ethnicity and preference for certain settlement patterns; Hispanics tend to prefer high density neighbourhoods, whereas Anglos predominantly chose suburbia type settlements (see Myers, 2001; Baldassare, 2002). This triggers the legitimate question of how participatory approaches can ever lead to bold and significant changes. Boswell casts his pessimistic answer into 'the paradox of sustainable development: public participation compromises *substantive* sustainable development' (personal communication, 23 November 2002; emphasis added). Boswell is joined by Lewellan, whose ideal of urban sustainability would self-evidently rely upon 'pedestrian modes of travel (walking and bicycling). . . [because they] are essential to the urban and suburban environment. Sacrificing the behavioural preference for lard-butt motorized travel . . . is more of a duty than an act of heroism' (2002) or a question of preference. Co-evolution, the argument could continue, is too opportunistic and shirks the duty to do what has to be done. This argument could culminate in the allegation that co-evolution sets the fox to guard the geese and worsens unsustainable practices.

It is tempting to counter-argue that co-evolutionary projects are likely to educate the metaphorical fox. After all, the designers of both projects I studied intended to raise citizens' awareness regarding the complex connections between economy, ecology and social equity. Bormans reports that the people who questioned the usefulness of a third ring around Hasselt 'said maybe it's better to invest a small part in public transport in order to change the mentality of the people' (interview, 26 November 2001). Kindhäuser confirms this effect: 'Hasselt managed to answer the question of how to infuse the "bus in the head" into the car-focused mental horizon' (2000, p67). The main goal of Brucker Land's designers is said not to be 'the creation of a product and its establishment at the market, but primarily a change of the awareness of the consumers' (Reginet.de, 2002). Seiltz encapsulates the same ideal in the slogan 'through the stomach into the mind' (Seiltz on several occasions). Provided this effect did come about, it would still be too late because the outcome of a project cannot be helpful for its creation. Thus, we are still left with the question of why we should trust people to guard the geese. In acknowledgement of some of the aforementioned concerns, I refrain from the attempt to provide a sweeping, context-free answer to this question.[16] What I suggest instead is to partition the continuum of real-world settings into three portions and to tackle them separately: ideal, conditional and imperfect circumstances for public participation in co-evolutionary projects.

Citizens can easily be trusted as co-designers if they are subject to a widely perceived Radermacher dilemma. My colleague was in such a situation when she thought about switching from a compact car to an SUV simply because she felt unsafe among all the other huge cars. The farmers in Fürstenfeldbruck were in an similar quandary, feeling unfairly accused as polluters even though the technological treadmill was not of their choosing. Hasselters, who had to drive through a congested inner city along a dangerous road just because the public transport system was not a viable alternative, knew this problem as well. In general, decisions about the reconfiguration of infrastructures are likely to induce sustainability gains if they are made collectively by people who find themselves in a situation that forces them to do something unsustainable, even though they don't like this practice. It seems fair to argue that such circumstances are fairly widespread because of the self-momentum that mature technologies tend to acquire (Hughes, 1994), to the extent that their memes take care of their own reproduction, regardless of the actual usefulness they provide for human beings. If the above reasoning is correct, it is reasonable to expect that the work environment of planners contains much potential for successful co-evolutionary projects under the co-direction of citizens.

A second type of situation might be found in a setting where people do not find themselves in a Radermacher dilemma but are receptive to factual information. For co-evolutionists, this is no reason to shower people with rational arguments about the complex ecological, social and economic effects of their life and consequently about the necessity of changing their behaviour. It should rather be seen as an opportunity to cognitively approach people with information about – or maybe just examples of – the synergistic potentials of coordinated action. ADR practitioners support this view, showing that the probability of people of making their choices from an enlightened long-term perspective increases with the amount and quality of information about known complexities, risk assessments, feedback loops and so forth (R. Paterson, personal communication, 11 December 2002). Gundersen (1995) provides empirical evidence that 'democratic deliberation' – not just tokenistic participation – of citizens is a reliable strategy to ensure that people do not base their decisions upon myopic, egoistical deliberations. Experience gained from Brucker Land justifies hope in the efficacy of education and guided reflection as well. Dengler mentions the deliberation, 'I still want a baker and a farmer [in my neighbourhood] in the years to come' as one of the main rationales behind Brucker Land and he believes that '80 per cent of the population are capable of this reasoning' (interview, 28 January 2002). This assessment of a practitioner provides reason to trust and to invest in the reflective capabilities of the public.

Co-evolution is, admittedly, not a panacea, especially not in a third type of cultural environment, where current unsustainable behaviour is considered sacrosanct[17] and where citizens have cultivated and are celebrating myopic individualism. In such a situation, it is much less likely that a co-designership of the public would lead to infrastructures that make sustainable behaviour attractive. This constellation might lead to a worsening of sustainability parameters until – very late – the socio-economic and ecological trends are declared no longer desirable. In turn, this could lead to conventional reactions such as tightening command-and-control ordinances and the accelerated development of improved technologies. If these measures are again insufficient, the trajectory could culminate either in a 'liberal realist' (Barber, 1984) regime that forces people to change their behaviour *ex cathedra* or in the discovery of co-evolutionary potentials. This scenario is not a prediction; it is merely the extrapolation of my acknowledgement that the applicability of co-evolutionary approaches is culturally limited.

To avoid misunderstanding about the scope of the applicability of participatory co-evolution: it does not end where people opt for more roads in the face of a binary choice between preconceived options like more roads versus an expensive light rail system that reaches a fraction of the population. But I admit my scepticism about the usefulness of public co-authorship in cases where people choose more roads even though they could reopen the whole box of choices. In other words, I hesitate to recommend participatory co-evolution in cases where people choose more roads even though they are assisted by well-prepared information, valuable strangers and immunized individuals, plus if they are allowed and encouraged to construct new options like a massive improvement of the bus system with free buses, a web of low-investment cable car routes, showers for cyclists in office buildings and many other possibilities I cannot think of because I can never be as creative as hundreds of people brainstorming together.

Co-evolution only works under strong leadership

Adherents of Carlyle's Great Man theory (1841) could argue that co-evolution is not a strategically applicable concept because all you can do is wait for the emergence of strong leaders who have and implement great ideas and who are strong enough to push aside the many obstacles in the way of co-evolutionary projects. I confronted Schonk, a representative of Hasselt's conservative CVP, with the related statement that the rule 'you just need an innovative, creative, charismatic mayor' does not make a good recommendation for other communities. His response was, however, simply affirmative: 'Yes, it is important' (interview, 7 December 2001). Moerkerk contributes to this potential source of resignation when he declares the charisma of a leader as 'a very important thing. . . The charisma of Steve really played a role' (interview, 27 November 2001). Dengler makes an almost verbatim comment about the 'charismatic leader figure. . . This is certainly also an important point here' (interview, 28 January 2002) at Brucker Land. Similarly, Herrwig nods to my comment that other people consider Seiltz a heroine and adds: 'Without her, it would have definitely gone to pieces' (interview, 30 January 2002).

Assuming that these interlocutors understood charisma in its prevalent sense as a divine gift, which only few possess and which cannot be learned, then it would be discouraging indeed if it were a *conditio sine qua non*. I suggest not to surrender yet but to pursue a more differentiated investigation, which Klein opens by questioning the charisma talk. He responded to the question I posed to Schonk (see above): 'I am not so sure if it is charisma. But it definitely depends on one person who pulls the strings. I guess I have to disappoint you here. It's just how it is' (interview, 25 January 2002). If 'pulling the strings' can be learned or if people who already have this skill are not too scarce, the problem would be eased.

On the way to an educated opinion on the first part of this question, I suggest a closer look at the meaning of this skill. Kugler explains the same expression 'to pull the strings' as the task of 'do[ing] all the organizational work with a lot of comprehension by all social groups' (interview, 16 January 2002). This statement suggests that leadership here does not mean to steamroller the diversity of opinions in pursuit of one's wisdom or by the power of one's charm but to coordinate and facilitate many people's creativity and dedication. In support of this interpretation, I recall Moerkerk's statement that credits Stevaert with the ability to make 'the ideas come out of the others' (interview, 27 November 2001). Spurring and motivating others seems to be a general skill of the ideal leader. Haberkorn attributes Seiltz with this talent, an 'unbelievably positive attitude, which she transmits to her interlocutors, convincing them "we'll make it. It'll work. We just have to want it. Look how easy it is"' (interview, 22 January 2002). I take it from a statement of Mulders that Stevaert was no less a motivator: the city employees 'work very enthusiastically and very dynamically because the mayor himself is such an exemplary case' (interview, 30 June 2001). Young mentions another crucial factor of successful innovations: 'A sheer dogged persistence, even a kind of benign ruthlessness . . . always taking "no" as a question' (cited in Albery et al, 1996, p276). Seiltz' half-year-long shuttle diplomacy between farmers and environmentalists (Seiltz, interview, 15 January 2002) confirms the importance of Young's point for the creation of a non-hostile communication environment. The implementation of consensual decisions necessitates this skill too; Herrwig ascribes Brucker Land's success partially to this talent of Seiltz, who 'got on someone's nerves until she prevailed. This requires the ability to assert oneself and patience' (interview, 30 January 2002). Keeping in mind these statements, I conclude that the set of skills required to guide a co-evolutionary project to success is not simply inborn charisma. Leadership, I admit, is necessary, but it seems to be of a kind Pauli describes as 'enzymatic' (2002), following the biological function of enzymes to catalyse specific reactions. The whole notion of a leader as someone who knows the way *ex ante* is therefore better abandoned in favour of the concept of a 'cooperative leader' or a 'change agent'.[18]

Now the second part of the above question can be rephrased to investigate the availability of change agents. As my previous statements show, change agency requires more than a good heart and it still is a challenge to find qualified individuals. Klein's addendum to his disappointment (see above) permits hope in this matter: 'This shouldn't let you down. There is such a person in every region, in every city and in every town. The question is rather "How do you find them? How do you motivate them?"' (interview, 25 January 2002). Landry shares this impression based upon his extensive experience as a consultant for innovative cities: 'Wherever you go leaders seem to appear out of nowhere, if conditions are right, here an entrepreneur, there a city official and there a mother driven into action by personal experience' (2000, p76). In most cases, personal experience is rooted in the particular environment, social circumstances, political decisions, environmental problems and the like. This explains the position of Stengel, who corrects 'Carlyle's wrong-headed Great Man theory of history [from] *great men make history* [to] *history makes great men* – or women' (2001).[19] Mulders confirms this stance for the situation in Hasselt: 'If it hadn't been Stevaert, it would have been somebody else. Hasselt was ready to do something new after all those years' (interview, 30 June 2000) of conservative city governments. From his experience in Fürstenfeldbruck, Dengler thinks along the same lines that 'leaders just doze' (interview, 28 January 2002). Two factors seem suitable to wake them up, one pushing, the other pulling. Klein calls the former mechanism 'a personal sense of urgency' (interview, 25 January 2002), which he describes as follows:

> *There was this small group [a Catholic andragogy organization] where people hold meeting after meeting and people talk all the time and discuss I don't know what. At a certain point, this situation became such a pain in the neck for people*

like Ms Seiltz, who have the ambition to do something. These personalities cannot endure this discrepancy between talk and walk forever and they begin to act. . . . [To activate them] I don't have to apply thumbscrews and I don't have to lure them with money. I simply have to put them into a discussion club where sooner or later they can't take it any more. Klein, interview, 25 January 2002

The pull factor that wakes up change agents can be a thrilling idea, a plan worthy of personal commitment, a window of opportunity. A combination of push and pull factors is probably what is most effective, not only to activate change agents but also to motivate the second tier of supporters. In retrospect, it seems to be a robust claim that the coordination and facilitation of co-evolutionary projects through skilled, motivating and persistent individuals does not depend on mere chance.

Notes

1 For a number of reasons, however, a less top-down approach (than the one of Ken Livingston in London) seems advisable.
2 Those who agree with this might see immediate implications for the design of curricula in planning programmes.
3 Hajer (1996) presents compelling observations and a very insightful analysis of related strategies of 'discourse structuration' and 'discourse institutionaliza-tion' in the context of sustainable development.
4 Carlson demonstrates this claim with a historical example: 'There was no "telephone problem" in 1876 waiting for Alexander Graham Bell. Indeed, Bell's genius lay in not only devising a telephone but in constructing the problem of the electrical transmission of speech in the first place' (1992, p175).
5 Feenberg argues almost verbatim and in an almost identical context for 'the return of politics' (1999, p101).
6 Seen from this perspective, common sense qualifies as a form of determinism because it pre-determines what it is decent to do. Hence, it shares an inherent teleological component with any form of determinism.
7 Or, as Rorty would likely argue, the chain turns out to be a closed loop: 'Common sense. . . is the watchword of those who unselfconsciously describe everything important in terms of the final vocabulary to which they and those around them are habituated' (1989, p74). 'It is "final" in the sense that if doubt is cast on the worth of these words, their user has no noncircular argumentative recourse' (Rorty, 1989, p73).
8 Or, as Rorty might put it, a little more ironic or a little less sure of their 'final vocabulary' (1989, p73).
9 It certainly deserves mention that this statement was made with reference to the works of Panamarenko, a Belgian artist whose name was used by Stevaert to describe the clientèle of his cafés: 'The Panamarenkos of Hasselt' (cited in de Condé, 1996, p27).

10   In 1995, British Airways appointed an official 'corporate jester' for the same reason. 'He can question management without fear of repercussions [and] therefore serve a serious role as the mouthpiece for unorthodox criticism, couched as harmless jest' (Albery et al, 1996, p60).

11   Such idealized implementations are usually presented by self-declared gurus. They usually have a clear idea of what the ideal society looks like but they can hardly provide an answer of how to get there other than through a mysterious leap.

12   I agree with Schatzberg (2002), who observes a lack of sensitivity in Hawken et al's book regarding the social and cultural mechanisms behind technological choices. This 'stunning technological enthusiasm', Schatzberg argues, displays 'only the vaguest grasp of the complex relationships among technology, society and culture . . . [it shows] no awareness of path-dependence theory . . . [and] no sensitivity to the issue of technological determinism' (2002, pp219 and 220).

13   The roughly 250 tonnes of carbon dioxide (CO_2) emissions avoided through Hasselt's transport policy could be cited in this context. This number is based on the following assumptions: trips through the city centre avoided per month: 28,529 (see Chapter 3). Average length per trip: 4km. Average fuel efficiency of a car in city traffic: 8 litres/100km. The combustion of one litre of gasoline produces roughly 2.3kg of CO_2. Dividing these 250 tonnes of avoided CO_2 by the number of citizens in Hasselt (68,0000) yields an annual CO_2 reduction of 3.6kg per capita, thus reducing the personal annual emission from 11,672kg (Belgian average in 1990, http://unfccc.int) to 11,668kg.

14   I find it interesting that there seems to be a wide overlap between those who object to 'memetic engineering' and those who advocate 'genetic engineering'. This seeming inconsistency is rooted in Descartes' distinction between 'thinking substances' and 'extended substances', between mind and body. Whereas the former is autonomous and free, the latter may be engineered as one wishes. Consequently, human actions must not be intervened, whereas mere natural material, like plants and animals, can be improved through human intervention.

15   Postrel is indeed not concerned with sustainable development, which she locates 'one or two footnotes away from the work of reactionary intellectuals such as Schumacher [whom she accuses of writing] "the central concept of wisdom is permanence"' (1998, p9).

16   Feenberg offers such optimism, arguing that 'Lay interventions into technology are shown to be "rational" and need not lead to costly tradeoffs of technical efficiency for "values"' (1999, p73).

17   This issue cannot be tackled without a remark on the following statement of Ari Fleischer, spokesman of US President George W. Bush: 'The president believes that it [the consumption of energy] is an American Way of Life and that it should be the goal of policy makers to protect the American Way of Life. The American Way of Life is a blessed one' (Fleischer, 2001, p17). I can think of two reasons why this statement should not be taken as a blow to co-evolutionary potential in the US. First, I do not think that it is the consumption

of energy per se that defines the American way of life; and second, I do not think that President Bush speaks for all US Americans. The fact that this quote was printed on the cartoon page of the Newsweek magazine provides support for the latter argument.

18 This term was first brought to my attention by Patricia Wilson.
19 Steven Moore talks in the same context about 'the structural conditions which precede and shape great men' (personal communication, 17 February 2003).

7

Conclusions

While it might appear redundant to realign all preceding conclusions at the end of this book I decided to do exactly this in a few paragraphs to provide a bird's-eye view of the whole structure of my argument. This may serve as an occasion for synthesis for those readers who have already read the main text and as a roadmap for those who read this summary first. In addition and further below, this chapter contains four caveats and corresponding advice with regard to four policy implications of co-evolutionary action.

Summary

As I have demonstrated throughout my text and in particular in Chapter 2, it makes sense to understand the prevailing discourse on sustainability as dominated by two main camps: one trusts in smart and efficient technologies and the other claims a solution can only arise from a change of behaviour, even if this requires heroic choices. Both approaches have unique advantages but also severe and insurmountable shortcomings that should dampen the often illusory hopes their respective followers attach to them. To perceive the sustainability discourse as dichotomous helps to categorize the many voices in the babble of problem definitions and proposals for action. However, this dichotomy is not *true* in the sense that it is unavoidable due to a congruence with some pre-established nature of the world. It is rather the result of certainly benevolent intentions and interests such as professional pride and zeal or impatience to reach sustainability. In other words, the structure of the discourse on sustainability is contingent upon people's perceptions of the world, their education, experience and interests. The way the technical and the social treat each other is characterized by reciprocal attempts of domination, ignorance, isolation, belittlement or sullen tolerance.

However, the technical and social realms are much more connected than the conventional players in the sustainability discourse usually admit; STS authors have described and analysed this 'seamless web' at great length and detail. This insight, then, must have implications for the debate. The concept of co-evolution utilizes this holistic understanding to suggest more productive dealings between technology and behaviour for approaching sustainable development. I borrowed the general idea that technology and behaviour can co-evolve from architectural literature, most notably from Guy and Shove (2000) and Rohracher and Ornetzeder (2002). I developed this notion further and at a larger spatial level, expanding it from buildings to cities and regions.

In its most condensed version, co-evolution signifies *the development of technologies that make sustainable behaviour attractive*. Such an approach cannot adequately be described in either the technology or the behaviour orientated vocabulary. Co-evolution, however, proves to be capable of describing related existing cases, such as Hasselt and Brucker Land, where new infrastructures indeed make a more sustainable behaviour attractive (see Chapter 3 for a 'thick description' of these two cases). In Chapter 4, I illustrated why and how limitations of description are always also limitations of imagination. This is where the main strength of the concept of co-evolution becomes most evident: its capability to suggest new projects that could avoid the shortcomings of either the technology or the behaviour orientated approach. In this role, co-evolution serves as a 'LogIcon' (Joerges, 1999b, p427), a linguistic building block that enables us to speak and think in a conceptual framework freed from a dichotomous thought-corridor. In this sense, co-evolution can serve as an inspiration for new projects.

While it might then be desirable to produce a manual for co-evolution, empirical data gathered at the two case sites show that such a project would have to ignore the idiosyncrasies of Hasselt and Brucker Land. Both cases are simply too different – and thus unsuitable as sources of formulaic advice – in regard to their financial construction, the role of elected officials, volunteers and consultants and many other factors. In Hasselt, for example, the innovative idea was developed within an existing circle (the transport commission), whereas in Fürstenfeldbruck, a new idea triggered the creation of a new alliance. Local circumstances are too specific as to permit a universally valid algorithm, a golden path to co-evolutionary projects. This is why, on the one hand, I see the ideal function of the concept of co-evolution as an inspirational device and not as a blueprint. On the other hand, I do not want to leave my readers merely with a journalistic thick description. My understanding of science compels me to seek a compromise between the two positions: a balance that does justice to interpretive flexibility but still provides meaningful and careful generalizations. For this reason, I attempted to find inter-subjectively comprehensible patterns in the empirical data and to critically examine them in light of the existing body of literature. I presented these memes – traits that all co-evolutionary projects seem to have in common – not as universally valid sufficient conditions of co-evolutionary success, but as stimulants for other communities to form their own working hypothesis, as a quarry for inspirations, as a structured call for attention to co-evolutionary potentials and as suggestion of what these might look like. In addition, these memes aided the systematic construction of a definition of co-evolution.

In the remainder of this chapter, I do not simply want to rephrase each meme; instead, I sift my thoughts through a slightly different sieve to consider the policy relevant implications of the co-evolution hypothesis. I understand *policy* in this context not just as the acts of elected officials but the entire dynamics of debate, decisions and actions in a society, thus doing justice to its etymological precursor, the ancient Greek *Polis*. The limelight in this agora constantly oscillates between various actors: communities, citizens, academia, schools, consultants, governments at various levels and local administrations. Therefore, the concept of 'actors' is not well suited to provide a tidy structure for the presentation of policy implications. Instead, and after experimenting with different structuring schemes, I found it helpful to sort such implications into four process orientated categories, which are at the same time proposals for action: *assessing structural frames, creating awareness of contingency, assisted problem definition* and the *search for solutions*.

Assessing structural frames

My highest hopes would be fulfilled if the co-evolution hypothesis inspired some local decision-makers – not necessarily politicians – to roll up their sleeves and get to work. Those who are tempted to do this should read on, not only to gain additional hands-on advice but also to learn about particular caveats. The latter are intended to provide a realistic assessment of structural conditions emanating from the financial, administrative and legal structures within which community action is framed, thus influencing perceptions of what is considered feasible.

Lack of financial resources, for example, might discourage local actors to develop alternative technologies and infrastructures. I would argue that this problem can often be alleviated through 'synchronic preadaptation', through volunteer efforts (Brucker Land) or external subsidies (Hasselt). Ultimately, however, it is people's *perception* of these constraints that makes people act or procrastinate. In addition, I acknowledge that certain circumstances exert indisputable restraints on the feasibility of certain co-evolutionary ideas. Economic and/or ideological interests in the preservation of existing structures or in the creation of radically different solutions often contribute to these problems. A hybrid example of these two factors can be seen in the case of Brucker Land, where the Bavarian headquarters of the Bund Naturschutz (Association for Nature Conservation) vetoed its local branch in Fürstenfeldbruck from participating in Brucker Land. Part of the reason lies in an ideological discontent with the 'controlled cultivation' compromise that allegedly waters down orthodox organic farming tenets (Seiltz, interview, 15 January 2002). Economic considerations seem to have influenced this decision too. According to Krömeke (interview, 22 January 2002), the Bund Naturschutz was compelled to issue this order because it is sponsored by a chain of eco-bakeries.

Other, less interest-laden problems are built into the fabric of administrative decision-making structures. Cameralistic budgeting systems and communication structures are maybe the most prominent of such kinds of problems. Some years ago I noticed that the person responsible for the maintenance of university buildings does not have to coordinate his decisions with the person who purchases oil for heating purposes. Hence, the system made it very unlikely for them to discover win–win potentials for energy saving measures. Similar phenomena can be found at all administrative levels and they often are to blame if good ideas seep away in bureaucratic jungles. A co-evolutionary idea is especially prone to face this type of problem because of its inherent complexity that makes it difficult to be processed in cameralistic decision-making structures.

Legal obstacles to co-evolution are certainly the most severe ones. The most direct kind of problem emerges when current legal standards would simply outlaw local co-evolutionary projects or if they make them excessively difficult. For example, the EU hygiene standards for abattoirs are so tight that Brucker Land almost shied away from building its own. A fictitious but highly instructional example could be constructed for Hasselt. Imagine what would have happened if Belgian laws required every store to provide x number of parking spaces. Such legal frameworks define, in Feenberg's words, the 'technical codes' (2003, p54) that govern human practices. Feenberg's example traces the historical path toward the abolition of child labour in Great Britain. Children were able to enjoy what we take for granted nowadays, a playful childhood, not because entrepreneurs calculated that better educated children make a better workforce later on but because the British parliament outlawed child labour after long debates. And it was so from that day forward. Manufacturers enjoyed the profits their better skilled employees produced despite earlier assertions that the economy would collapse without cheap child labour. In Feenberg's words, the decision of the British parliament produced the societal equivalent to a paradigm shift, a 'civilizational change'. It redefined the boundaries within which the economy may regulate itself according to the laws of the free market. In reciprocal words, it declared child labour off limits for cost–benefit calculations (see Feenberg, 2003).

There is one optimistic and one pessimistic, yet realistic lesson to learn from this example. The sobering insight is that certain regulations (or their absence) can perpetuate existing technical codes even though their results are widely perceived as undesirable. The implication for the co-evolution hypothesis is that external regulations or frames of action can hamper the development and installation even of those technologies that could make the socially desired behaviour attractive. A related version of this mechanism is the effect external, especially legal, frameworks can have on individuals. They often tempt people to settle with less than socially desired behaviour as long as their actions do not violate the law. A modern version of this phenomenon is someone who drives 70 miles per hour on a misty highway. Yes, it's legal but it's still not an appropriate speed in bad weather conditions. In other words, people may not perceive the need or desire to change their behaviour – not even through co-evolutionary means – because they are already doing their share.

The sanguine lesson of Feenberg's example is, of course, that technical codes can be changed, that technological determinism can be overcome through political will. So I should emphasize that the hopeful tone of the co-evolution hypothesis should not excuse failure to work for changes of these frames of action that are established by legislative organs, powerful corporations, influential lobby organizations, media networks, and so forth on all hierarchical levels, municipal, state, national and global. On the contrary, it is still necessary to work for improvements of these structural conditions for sustainable development *in order* to widen the structural frame within which co-evolutionary solutions are feasible. These are, of course, long-term projects. I maintain, however, that even within the current framework, there are more potentials for successful and sustainable action than advocates of technology or behaviour orientated approaches are able to see; and these potentials should certainly be exploited.

Creating awareness of contingency

I fully agree with Winner that our inattention to the socio-economic mechanisms behind the production of particular artefacts constitutes 'technological somnambulism,. . . an inherent tendency toward forgetfulness' (1977, p315). The goal, then, is to wake up or, as Feenberg argues, to 'challenge the horizon of rationality under which technology is currently designed. . . [to] demystify the illusion of technical necessity and expose the relativity of the prevailing technical choices' (1995b, pp20 and 12). A new awareness of how technological choices are *really* made has to be complemented by a heightened cognition of how technologies exert a gravitational pull upon our behaviours. With this critical faculty, we can see that the social and the technical mutually constitute one another. This double-sided awareness of the contingency of technology and social practices is a crucial precondition to 'regestalt' our perception of society, thus revealing options for an alternative society.

This theoretical reasoning leaves us with the question of *how* to become that awake. I believe that it is a long process not unlike that of learning a new language. It also implies emancipation from our conventional language and its integral way of thinking about *great inventors, expertise, necessity* and *common sense*. In an ideal case, the new vocabulary is not simply taught but jointly developed by individuals in (current or future) leadership positions as well as by the public at large. The designated locations of such a departure from simple explanations to a more complex view of the world are schools, colleges and universities. STS findings should be communicated in these settings, adapted to the specific situation. The not-at-all logical history of the refrigerator (Schwartz Cowan, 1985), for example, provides material for an exciting story as well as for cognitive reflection upon the social shaping of artefacts. It would also be instructive to expose students to interdisciplinary settings, preferably consisting of representatives of both the natural and social sciences. Moderators should emphasize that the purpose of such encounters is not for one discipline to prevail but to increase understanding of the spectrum of alternative certainties, to de- and re-construct one's own position in relation to them and to look for co-evolutionary potentials among them. Students can also be encouraged to conduct what Schön calls a 'frame experiment' (1983, p63), that is, a deliberate attempt to look at a problem from different (established or newly invented) angles.

An important strategy to create awareness for contingency on the community level is to prevent the discussants from falling into a dichotomous discussion pattern. Hajer calls this important intervention 'discourse structuration' (1996, p27), which requires, above all, professional moderation. But such mundane tasks as phrasing a newspaper article, an invitation, a banner, are also likely to have the potential to influence the structure of the local sustainability discourse. Those with the possibility and responsibility to steer this discourse are groups or individuals with a reputation as honest and impartial brokers, so-called change agents, who earned their position by mandate, charisma or achievement. A second important function of such enzymatic leaders is what Hajer terms 'discourse institutionalization' (1996, p27). This can become manifest in the formation of discussion arenas and decision-finding structures that facilitate encounters with *the others*, with unfamiliar positions, disarming questions and valuable strangers that challenge one's own horizon, thus lessening the allure of commonsensical platitudes.

Assisted problem definition

I have demonstrated earlier why and how the selection of solutions often precedes the definition of a problem and even the definition of goals. The consequence is that 'the policymaker . . . has to fight not merely thought constructs but a network of actors . . . [He] cannot freely readjust problem definitions . . . and lacks power precisely where the often decisive initial commitments are being made' (Hajer, 1996, p29). Policy in such a constellation is degraded to *end-of-pipe policy* that tries to direct the arrow of socio-technological developments only after it has left the bow. The cure for this ailment, then, must start with regaining the primacy of policy – not of government – in the creation of problem definitions. This is important because the reciprocal of a problem definition is the definition of desirability. With this as a backdrop, I call for assisted problem definition, whereby assistance is understood in two ways: first, as a project to create occasions, structures and places for original debates about problem definitions; and second, to help discussants in such debates to co-develop non-trivial problem definitions.

In regard to the first stipulation, Hajer calls for 'new institutional arrangements [that] create a prominent place for normative discussion about what sort of social ecology we really want' (1996, p34). Winner argues in the same context for 'the creation of arenas for the politics of technological choice' (1995, p82). Even Agenda 21 contains a related passage that asserts that 'the public should be assisted in communicating their sentiments to the scientific and technological community concerning how science and technology might be better managed to affect their lives in a beneficial way' (UNCED, 1992, chapter 31.1). The conclusion of a two-year consultation process of prestigious science institutions[1] accords with exactly that point: the participants call for a '"new contract" between science and society for sustainable development [under which] the S&T community would devote an increasing fraction of its overall efforts to R&D agendas reflecting socially determined goals of sustainable development' (Clark et al, 2002, p4). This task should be facilitated by so-called '"boundary organizations". . . [that] perform complex bridging roles. . . between science and policy and across scales and across the social and natural science disciplines' (Clark et al, 2002, p5). Rohracher translates these recommendations to the context of green buildings. A successful mediation of the various interests intersecting in the development and use of green buildings, he says, requires 'new processes of planning and design and new forms of integrating users' (1999, p3).

The same holds, of course, for the development of urban infrastructures as I have tried to demonstrate throughout this book. Even corporate decision-making structures could benefit from more systematic *front-of-pipe* user input in order to learn about social perceptions of problems. The 'Vision Team' of the auto manufacturer Audi, for example, at times welcomes ordinary citizens to help them brainstorm Audi's role in a wildly different society. BMW has launched a similar initiative, the 'Virtual Innovation Agency . . . which allows anyone with Internet access to submit ideas' (Tucker, 2003, p22). Why should municipal planning departments not do the same?

Once such arenas are created, the second aforementioned stipulation in the context of assisted problem definition becomes pertinent. This stipulation is intended to help discussants find consensus on non-trivial problem definitions. This can happen by persistently demanding answers to consecutive *why* questions. For example, tracing back the question 'why are some people not eating healthily?' has revealed that lack of access to grocery stores is a large part of the problem (Duenwald, 2002, pD5). Such a strategy examines the prevailing corridor of choices with a focus on how technologies and infrastructures dis- or encourage certain behavioural choices. If this helps to elicit Radermacher dilemmas and to unmask customarily overlooked disharmonies between the desirability and attractiveness of particular behaviours, then the debate is encircling problem definitions with co-evolutionary potentials. This is a 'midwifery approach' in a Socratic tradition because the questioners do not deliver the results but rather help others to do so. These questions are best asked not by the local usual suspects but by individuals unaffiliated with positions in the prevailing discourse, that is, by valuable strangers. Besides such content-related guidance, it is also important to provide process-related assistance by creating an atmosphere of frank discussion, partnership and trust. This might require Seiltzian shuttle diplomacy, coordination, moderation and a number of other techniques that are described in the ADR literature.

The search for solutions

The search for sustainable solutions is more likely to lead to co-evolutionary approaches if a community is equipped with awareness of the contingency of technological choices and with socially meaningful problem definitions. In addition, this quest can be supported through various forms of diplomatic intervention that guides attention to a certain *type* of outcome rather than a particular outcome in and of itself.

Co-evolution, by definition, demands technological or infrastructural solutions that make new behaviours attractive. In other words, the attractiveness of solutions determines the success of the entire co-evolutionary project. As demonstrated above, it is indispensable that the participants of this design process be permitted and encouraged to search for options outside the usual, off-the-shelf solutions.[2] The Flemish Mobiliteitsconvenant and its funding stipulation to develop a range of scenarios is an interesting approach in this regard. Even though this requirement did not trigger the innovative project in Hasselt, such political devices seem to deserve more frequent application because they can cultivate a readiness among decision-makers to expand their repertoire of potential solutions. I assume in this context that political bodies above the local level have a significant range of options to foster co-evolutionary thinking. This includes the formulation of grant requirements, the operationalization of performance benchmarks, the provision of information material and other possibilities that deserve further investigation.

Perhaps even more important is the expansion of *solution spaces* through on-site activities. The diplomacy of inventiveness is a principal task in this regard. Its main purpose is to organize 'spaces for articulation where fools can dream while experts explain and citizens contribute their concerns and ideas as future users', as I stated earlier. Such fora constitute ecosystems of creativity, where the daring, the considerate, the pragmatic and the challenging are all needed to make the whole function. Their habitat ranges from city council meetings and visioning teams to cafés and kitchen tables. The crucial point is that the voices of future users are effectively represented in these circles. Change agents are at their best organizing such encounters. In addition, they can provide extremely valuable services by guiding the solution-finding process, not toward a particular outcome but toward a particular *kind* of outcome. For this purpose, the concept of co-evolution demonstrates its primary strength as a 'picture to think with' (Joerges, 1999b, p427). Harnessing this strength does not require that a team of co-designers bother with the theoretical details of this concept. It might be helpful, however, to explicitly discuss the main shortcomings of the technology and behaviour orientated approaches, Radermacher dilemmas, the systematic punishment of forerunners, the unfortunate stalemate between technology and behaviour, the potentials of strategic alliances, and so on. Best practice examples, described in the language of co-evolution, can serve as an additional source of inspiration for co-evolutionary innovation. A common understanding of co-evolutionary potentials, shared by the supply and demand side of infrastructures, might then facilitate what Rohracher calls 'synchronic preadaptation'[3] (2001, p8), which is basically a set of dovetailed promises to provide and to adopt new infrastructures. Other necessary or desirable criteria of co-evolutionary projects should also be communicated to ensure successful implementation. Among these are the importance of a critical mass, the need for embedding strategies, the permission for deviation, a sense for aesthetics and non-discrimination against low-income groups.

Despite my above assertion not to structure this chapter by the various actors in co-evolutionary projects, I consider it fair – given the environment in which this book grew – to dedicate at least one paragraph to one specific actor-group, namely, academia. I have pointed out a number of implications for curriculum design throughout my text, so I will conclude here with an abridged version. Higher education should contribute to the creation of awareness of contingency, which presupposes a minimum amount of liberal irony in the sense of Rorty[4] and some effective exposure to the writings of STS authors in a wide array of departments. The deconstructing effects of this strategy ideally should be complemented by discussion of synergies between technology and behaviour, to facilitate the reconstruction of professional dispositions to include alertness for co-evolutionary potentials. Interdisciplinary classes and semester projects are well suited to contribute to this intellectual growth and to a widened conception of disciplinary self-interest.

I am aware that much more research is required before co-evolution will be regarded as an equal at the table of the sustainability discourse. To achieve this transformation of the co-evolution hypothesis from a noetic concept in the making to an established theory, at least four kinds of investigations are necessary. First, co-evolution has to demonstrate its descriptive power for many more empirical cases, which requires in-depth studies of numerous successful and even failed projects whose designers claimed to pursue sustainability goals. I consider it possible and necessary that such studies should reveal a more refined understanding of the cultural and situational limitations of co-evolution. Second, the memes I educed should be tested and refined through further studies. Future research should also turn its attention to other memes I might have overlooked, with the ultimate goal of establishing a clear understanding of how these memes are linked, whether some of them are substitutable and whether it makes sense to establish a hierarchy among them. A third research focus ought to identify other disciplines that can offer expertise valuable for the elaboration of the co-evolution hypothesis. Candidates I came across in my own research are CPTED (crime prevention through environmental design) and ADR (alternative dispute resolution). A fourth area of interest regards the possibility of translating the theoretical concept developed in this text into a more mundane language and into concrete recommendations for communities trying to solve their unsustainability problems. A practical means to pursue this objective is through immersed action research. The role of political entities and grant-making institutions above the community level also deserves research attention in regard to their possibilities to support co-evolutionary projects through monetary incentives, structural support and informational materials. Their support is obviously also required to conduct the above suggested research projects.

The reason I think the co-evolution hypothesis merits support and further investigation is not based on a claim that it replaces the false dichotomy between technology and behaviour with something of a higher truth value. To make this claim would violate my own call for a pinch of liberal irony. Rather I take a pragmatic stance and offer co-evolution as something we should try out next.

Notes

1 Participants represented the International Council for Science, the InterAcademy Panel, the Third World Academy of Sciences and the Harvard-led Initiative on Science and Technology for Sustainability. Workshop held in Mexico City, 20–23 May 2002. See Clark et al (2002).
2 This is not the same as 'reinventing the wheel'. In contrast, it can prove very useful to complement existing initiatives with the elements they are lacking or to renovate an initiative from a co-evolutionary perspective.

3   A related concept is the 'prosumer', a hybrid of a producer (or provider) and
    a consumer. I am grateful to L. Klein, who brought this concept, allegedly
    developed by Sixtus Lanner, to my attention. I suggest amending this concept
    with the 'convider', a hybrid of a consumer and a provider.
4   Liberal irony, according to Rorty, 'combine[s] commitment with a sense of
    the contingency of [one's] own commitment' (1989, p61).

References

Akrich, M. (1992) 'The de-scription of technical objects' in Bijker, W. and Law, J. (eds) *Shaping Technology/Building Society: Studies in Sociotechnical Change*, MIT Press, Cambridge, MA, pp205–224

Albery, N., Irvine, L., Buckley, P. and Pieau, S. (eds) (1996) 'How to launch a social innovation' [Young at eighty: The prolific public life of Michael Young], excerpted from Dench, G., Flower, T. and Gavron, K. (eds) in Albery, N., Irvine, L., Buckley, P. and Pieau, S. (eds) *DIY Futures: People's Ideas and Projects for a Better World*, Institute for Social Inventions, London, www.globalideasbank.org/diyfut/DIY-230.html, last accessed 12 January 2003

Albery, N. and Wienrich, S. (eds) (1999) *Social Dreams and Technological Nightmares: A Global Ideas Bank Compendium*, Anthony Rowe Ltd, Berkshire

Andere (1996) 'Hasseltse Kleine Ring moet "Groene Boulevard" worden', *Het Belang van Limburg*, 25 September, p16

Ascot, K. (2002) 'Sprawl!', *Austin Sierran*, December 2002/January 2003, pp3, 11

Axelrod, R. (1984) *The Evolution of Cooperation*, Basic Books, New York

Baindl, B. (2001) 'ZIEL 21: Zentrum Innovative Energien im Landkreis Fürstenfeldbruck', www.ziel21.de/energiewende.html, last accessed 21 January 2003

Baldassare, M. (2002) 'Public Policy Institute of California Statewide Survey: Special survey on land use, San Francisco, CA', www.ppic.org/content/pubs/S_1102MBS.pdf, last accessed 17 March 2003

Barber, B. (1984) *Strong Democracy: Participatory Democracy for a New Age*, University of California Press, Berkeley, CA

Bardou, J.-P. (2002) 'Groningen – the bicycle city par excellence', http://home.tiscali.dk/8x070493/traffic/engron.htm, last accessed 18 June 2005

Baudson, M. (1996) 'Panamarenko', www.uol.com.br/23bienal/universa/iueopa.htm, last accessed 11 February 2003

Bayerisches Landesamt für Statistik und Datenverarbeitung (1999) 'Strukturdaten Kreisfreie Städte und Landkreise', www.statistik.bayern.de/ew99/daten/index-sd-kr.html#Ober bayern, last accessed 30 September 2002

Bayerisches Landesamt für Statistik und Datenverarbeitung (2002) 'Ergebnisse der Landwirtschaftszählung 1999 im Vergleich zu 1991', www.statistik.bayern.de/daten/lwz99/index.html, last accessed 30 September 2002

Beck, U. (1989) 'Risikogesellschaft. Überlebensfragen, Sozialstruktur und ökologische Aufklärung', *Aus Politik und Zeitgeschichte*, vol 36, p13

Beck, U. (1992) *Risk Society: Towards a New Modernity* (translated by M. Ritter), Sage, London (original published 1986)

Beack, U. (1999) *World Risk Society*, Polity Press, Oxford

Beckers, J., Bernaers, D. and Meuris, S. (1995) 'De eerste Pukkelpop-inspectieronde van Steve Stevaert: "Als we niet snel drinken krijgen, bollen we 't af"', *Het Belang van Limburg*, 25 August, p40

Beinhocker, E. (1999) 'Robust adaptive strategies', *Sloan Management Review*, spring, pp95–106

Berlin Snell, M. (2002) 'The soul of green machines', *Sierra*, vol 7, no 8, pp40–45

Bijker, W. (1992) 'The social construction of fluorescent lighting, or how an artifact was invented in its diffusion stage' in Bijker, W. and Law, L. (eds) *Shaping Technology/Building Society: Studies in Sociotechnical Change*, MIT Press, Cambridge, MA, pp75–102

Bijker, W. and Law, J. (1992a) 'Do technologies have trajectories?' in Bijker W. and Law, J. (eds) *Shaping Technology/Building Society: Studies in Sociotechnical Change*, MIT Press, Cambridge, MA, pp17–19

Bijker, W. and Law, J. (1992b) 'General introduction' in Bijker, W. and Law, L. (eds) *Shaping Technology/Building Society: Studies in Sociotechnical Change*, MIT Press, Cambridge, MA, pp1–14

Bijker, W. and Law, J. (1992c) 'Strategies, resources and the shaping of technology' in Bijker, W. and Law, J. (eds) *Shaping Technology/Building Society: Studies in Sociotechnical change*, MIT Press, Cambridge, MA, pp105–107

Bijker, W. and Law, J. (1992d) 'What next? Technology, theory and method' in Bijker, W. and Law, J. (eds) *Shaping Technology/Building Society: Studies in Sociotechnical change*, MIT Press, Cambridge, MA, pp199–203

Bishop, B. and Lisheron, M. (2002) 'Patents a measure of city's success: number of inventions reflect the individual creativity that leads to economic growth', *Austin American Statesman*, May 19, www.statesman.com/specialreports/content/specialreports/citiesofideas/0519patents.html, last accessed 6 October 2005

Bisk, T. (2002) 'Toward a practical utopianism', *The Futurist*, vol 36, no 3, pp22–25

Boswell, M. (2002) 'Planning, sustainability and shifting paradigms', presentation at the annual conference of the *Association of Collegiate Schools of Planning*, Baltimore, MD, 23 November

Brand, R. (1997) *Nachhaltigkeit, Regionalisierung und Strategische Allianzen*, Diploma thesis at the Catholic University of Eichstätt, Grin Verlag, Munich

Brand, R. (2005a) 'Enforcing versus enabling sustainable social practices through urban infrastructures', *Journal of Urban Technology*, vol 12, pp1–25

Brand, R. (2005b) 'The citizen innovator', *The Innovation Journal*, vol 10, no 1, pp1–11, innovation.cc/The%20Innovation%20Journal/peer-reviewed/ralf-brand.pdf, last accessed 10 June 2005

British Columbia Cancer Agency (2002) 'Sunscreens, sun avoidance and clothing', www.bccancer.bc.ca/HPI/Education/CMESkinCancer/PreExaminationReading/SunscreensSunAvoidanceandClothing.htm, last accessed 26 September 2002

Bromley, R. and Schenk, T. (2002) 'Planning's darker side', presentation at the annual conference of the *Association of Collegiate Schools of Planning*, Baltimore, MD

Brown, D., Green, J., Hall, F., Rocchi, S., Rutter, P. and Dearing, A. (2000) *Building a Better Future: Innovation, Technology and Sustainable Development*, World Business Council for Sustainable Development, Conoches-Geneva, www.wbcsd.org/publications/building.htm, last accessed 3 May 2000

Brückmann, S. (2002a) 'Netzwerkallgemein.doc' [data file transmitted via email]

Brückmann, S. (2002b) 'Richtlinien.doc' [data file transmitted via email]

Brückmann, S. and Witzel, A (2001) 'Themenheft Erntedank', *UNSER LAND Dialog*

Brulle, R. (2000) *Agency, Democracy and Nature*, MIT Press, Cambridge, MA

Bundesumweltministerium (ed) (1998) *Nachhaltige Entwicklung in Deutschland: Entwurf eines Umweltpolitischen Schwerpunktprogramms*, Bundesumweltministerium, Bonn

Bürgerstiftung Zukunftsfähiges München (2002) 'Vom Wert der Ernährung', lifeguide-muenchen.de/index.cfm/fuseaction/tipps&theID=7466&zg=0&ml1=400& ml2=500& cfid=435496&cftoken=20038866, last accessed 18 September 2002

Bush, G.W. (2003) *State of the Union Address of the President of the United States of America*, Live TV broadcast, 28 January

Busse, T. (2002) 'Reichtum ist giftig', *DIE ZEIT*, 45, February 21

Buttimore, B. (2001) 'Recumbent bicycles: pros and cons', www.hpv.on.ca/recumb.htm, last accessed 24 October 2002

Butzer, K.-W. (1992) 'From Columbus to Acosta: science, geography and the new world', *Annals of the Association of American Geographers*, vol 82, no 3, pp543–565

Campbell, S. (1996) 'Green cities, growing cities, just cities? Urban planning and the contradictions of sustainable development', *Journal of the American Planning Association*, vol 62, no 3, pp296–312

Campbell, S. (2002) 'The promise and contradiction of sustainable development', presentation given in Topics in Sustainable Development course, *University of Texas at Austin*, 11 April

Carlson, W. (1992) 'Artifacts and frames of meaning: Thomas A. Edison, his managers and the cultural construction of motion pictures' in Bijker W. and Law, W. (eds) *Shaping Technology/Building Society: Studies in Sociotechnical Change*, MIT Press, Cambridge, MA, pp175–198

Carlyle, T. (1841) *Heroes, Hero-worship and the Heroic in History*, James Fraser, London

Carter, P. (1988) *The Road to Botany Bay. An Essay in Spatial History*, Faber & Faber, London

Center for Energy and Environmental Resources (2002) 'Center for Energy and Environmental Resources', www.utexas.edu/research/ceer/main.htmESP, last accessed 17 December 2002

Chan-Magomedow, S. (1983) *Pioniere der sowjetischen Architektur: Der Weg zur neuen sowjetischen Architektur in den zwanziger und zu Beginn der dreißiger Jahre*, Verlag der Kunst, Dresden

Churchill Center, The (2002) 'Winston Churchill quotes', www.winstonchurchill.org/quotes.htm#buildings, last accessed 29 October 2002

Clark, W. (2002) 'Science and technology for sustainable development: workshop conclusions' [Synthesis Workshop on Science and Technology for Sustainable Development], http://sustsci.harvard.edu/ists/synthesis02/output/ists_mexico _consensus.pdf, last accessed 14 July 2005

Clarke, M. (2001) 'Combat racism or political correctness', http://martinclarkenews.pwp. blueyonder.co.uk/combat_racism_or_political_corre.htm, last accessed 20 December 2002

Cloostermans, G. (1995) 'Groene boulevard Hasselt nog zeker voor deze eeuw', *Het Belang van Limburg*, 13 October, p14

Cochrane, W. (1978) *The Development of American Agriculture: A Historical Analysis*, University of Minnesota Press, Minneapolis

Cornish, E. (1999) *The Cyber Future – 93 Ways Our Lives Will Change by the Year 2025*, monograph, World Future Society, Bethesda, MD

Costantini, P. (2000) 'Trade talks without tear gas', *Sincronia*, Winter 2000, http://fuentes.csh.udg.mx/CUCSH/Sincronia/ costantini3.htm, last accessed 19 February 2003

Costanza, R. (2000) 'Visions of alternative (unpredictable) futures and their use in policy analysis', *Conservation Ecology*, vol 4, no 1, www.consecol.org/vol4/iss1/art5/, last accessed 6 October 2005

Csikszentmihalyi, M. (1997) 'Values and socio-cultural evolution' in Benedikt, M. (ed) VALUE, *Center 10*, Center for American Architecture and Design, Austin, TX, pp41–51

CSU im Landkreis Fürstenfeldbruck (2002) *Kreistagswahl am 3. März 2002, CSU: Fortschrittlich, fachkundig, bewährt, Landrat Thomas Karmasin,* Fürstenfeldbruck

Dawkins, R. (1976) *The Selfish Gene,* Oxford University Press, New York

Dawkins, R. (1989) *The Selfish Gene,* Oxford University Press, Oxford, New York, 2nd edition

de Condé, R. (1996) 'Tournee Generale: Hasseltse burgemeester Steve Stevaert had elk jaar een nieuw café: "Cafébaas en surrogaatvader"', *Het Belang van Limburg,* 8 August, p27

'De toekomstvisie van directeur Sabin 's Heeren: De rechte lijn' (1997) *Het Belang van Limburg,* 28 June, p10

Dosi, G. (1988) 'The nature of the innovative process' in Dosi, G. (ed) *Technical Change and Economic Theory,* Pinter, London, pp221–238

Doss, N. (1998) 'Roads/mobility/architecture/American dream', *Platform,* fall, www.ar.utexas.edu/publications/Navvab.html, last accessed 25 October 2002

Duenwald, M. (2002) 'Good health is linked to grocer', *New York Times,* 12 November, pD5

'Dure buitenlandse experimenten schrikken Hasselt niet af: Lenin baande de weg' (1997) *Het Belang van Limburg,* 28 June, p9

Dynamist.com (2002) Synopsis of 'The future and its enemies', www.dynamist.com/synopsis.html, last accessed 15 November 2002

Ebersole, S. (1995) 'Lewis Mumford', www.regent.edu/acad/schcom/rojc/mdic/mumford.html, last accessed 10 September 2002

Edquist, C. (1997) *Systems of Innovation Technologies, Institutions and Organizations,* Pinter, London

Educatieve Wegwijzer (1999) Adult education in Hasselt, 'Go-Between', www.pcj.be/socrates.nsf/fd56def67dd0fd27c125674600517aaf/7276b4878396169fc12567fc00 2c1573?OpenDocument, last accessed 7 February 2003

Ehrlich, P. and Raven, P. (1965) 'Butterflies and plants: A study in coevolution', *Evolution,* vol 18, pp586–608

Eikhoff, K. (2002) 'Re: Argumente pro Recyclingpapier', Message posted to eco-campus.net electronic mailing list, 30 May

Ellul, J (1964) *The Technological Society* (translated by J. Wilkinson), Vintage, New York

eNorm (2002) 'Erweiterte Nachhaltigkeitsoffensive Region München', www.enorm21.de/brucker_land.html, last accessed 15 May 2002

Erlandson, D., Harris, E., Skipper, B. and Allen, S. (1993) *Doing Naturalistic Inquiry: A Guide to Methods,* Sage, Newbury Park, CA

European Smile Project (2005) 'Groningen (NL)', www.smile-europe.org/demonstration_projects/groningen/catalogue_groningen.pdf, last accessed 18 June 2005

Evangelical Environmental Network (2002) 'What would Jesus drive?', http://whatwouldjesusdrive.org/, last accessed 20 December 2002

Fainstein, S. (2000) 'New directions in planning theory', *Urban Affairs Review,* vol 35, no 4, pp451–478

Feder, G. (1939) *Die Neue Stadt: Versuch der Begründung einer neuen Stadtplanungskunst aus der sozialen Struktur der Bevölkerung,* Springer, Berlin

Feenberg, A. (1995a) 'Preface' in Feenberg, A. (ed) *Technology and the Politics of Knowledge,* Indiana University Press, Bloomington, ppix–x

Feenberg, A. (1995b) 'Subversive rationalization: technology, power and democracy' in Feenberg, A. (ed) *Techology and the Politics of Knowledge,* Indiana University Press, Bloomington, pp3–22

Feenberg, A. (1999) *Questioning Technology*, Routledge, London, New York

Feenberg, A. (2003) 'Values and the environment', presentation given in Topics in Sustainable Development course, *University of Texas at Austin*, written and revised version, 26 February

Fisher, I. (2002) 'Ken Russel, critics and criticism', www.iainfisher.com/russkr.html, last accessed 17 February 2003

Fisher, R., Ury, W. and Patton, B. (1991) *Getting to Yes: Negotiating Agreement Without Giving In*, Penguin Books, New York, 2nd edition

Fleischer, A. (2001) 'The American way of life is a blessed one', *Newsweek*, vol 17, p21, May 21

Fleissner, P. (2000) 'Ökologische Anforderungen an das Essen (Teil 2)', www.umwelt institut.org/frames/all/m174.htm, last accessed 18 September 2002

Frank, R. (1997) 'Why the things we buy often aren't the things we really want' in Benedikt, M. (ed) *VALUE, Center 10*, Center for American Architecture and Design, Austin, TX, pp63–72

Franke, N. and von Hippel, E. (2002) 'Satisfying heterogeneous user needs via innovation toolkits – The case of Apache Security Software', *Working Paper # 4341-02*, MIT Sloan School of Management, Cambridge MA, http://web.mit.edu/evhippel/www/ApacheHeteroWP.pdf, last accessed 5 September 2004

GALB, Grüne Alternative Liste Bamberg (2001) 'Bedarf ist kaum zu decken', www.gal.bamberg.de/Zeitung/gaz-55/Brucker-Land.htm, last accessed 15 May 2002

Geiger, D. (2002) 'Coevolution', Lecture for Evolution and Population Genetics course, University of Southern California-Los Angeles, http://biosci.usc.edu/courses/2002-spring/documents/bisc313-Coevolution.pdf, last accessed 15 November 2002

GFUSA, Grameen Foundation USA (2004) 'Village Phone Program', www.gfusa.org/technology_center/village_phone/, last accessed 22 June 2005

Gillwald, K. (1995) 'Ökologisierung von Lebensstilen: Argumente, Beispiele, Einflussgrössen', *Wissenschaftszentrum Berlin für Sozialforschung Paper* FS III 95-408

GlobalIdeasBank (2005) 'Groningen, the car-free city for bikes', www.globalideasbank.org/site/bank/idea.php?ideaId=378, last accessed 18 June 2005

Grameen Communications (2005) 'Grameen Family of Enterprises', www.grameen-info.org/gfamily.html, last accessed 21 March 2005

GrameenPhone (2005a) 'Corporate Website', www.grameenphone.com, last accessed 20 March 2005

GrameenPhone (2005b) 'The Village Phone', www.grameenphone.com/modules.php?name=Content&pa=showpage&pid=3, last accessed 22 June 2005

Grameen Telecom (2001) 'Corporate Website', www.grameen-info.org/grameen/gtelecom/index.html, last accessed 21 March 2005

Grudin, R. (1990) *The Grace of Great Things: Creativity and Innovation*, Mariner, New York

Gundersen, A. (1995) *The Environmental Promise of Democratic Deliberation*, University of Wisconsin Press, Madison

Guy, S. and Shove, E. (2000) *A Sociology of Energy, Buildings and the Environment: Constructing Knowledge*, Designing Practice, Routledge, London

Gybels, L. (1995) 'Gemeenteraad Hasselt: CVP maakt brandhout van beleidsnota-meerderheid', *Het Belang van Limburg*, 8 March, p13

Hajer, M. (1996) 'Politics on the move: the democratic control of the design of sustainable technologies', *Knowledge and Policy*, vol 8, no 4, pp26–39

Hannappel, P. (2002) 'Nahrungsmittelpreise-in-Deutschland_von-1948-2001.xls', [data file transmitted via email] Statistisches Bundesamt

Harding, S. (1991) *Whose Science? Whose Knowledge? Thinking From Women's Lives*, Cornell University Press, Ithaca, NY

Hasselt: Stadt ohne Fahrschein (Busverkehr zum Nulltarif) (1998) [unpublished document]

Haus, M. and Erling Klausen, J. (2004) 'Urban leadership and community involvement: ingredients for good governance? Findings from the PLUS project', contribution to the conference *City futures*, Chicago, 8–10 July, www.plus-eura.org/public%20pdf%20files/ haus_klausen_urban_leadership_community_involvement.pdf, last accessed 16 March 2005

Hawken, P., Lovins, A. and Lovins, H. (1999) *Natural Capitalism: Creating the Next Industrial Revolution*, Little, Brown and Co, Boston

Healey, P. (1997) *Collaborative Planning: Shaping Places in Fragmented Societies*, MacMillan, Basingstoke

Hellman, L. (2002) 'Eco-bible versus techno-bible' [Graphics], *Built Environment*, vol 28, no 1, p4, www.louishellman.co.uk

Heylighen, F. (1998) 'Solipsism', *Web Dictionary of Cybernetics and Systems*, http:// pespmc1.vub.ac.be/ASC/SOLIPSISM.html, last accessed 16 February 2003

Hogeschool voor Verkeerskunde Diepenbeek (1998) *Busonderzoek Hasselt: Bevraging busreizigers stads-en streeklijnen te Hasselt*, Ministerie van de Vl. Gemeenschap, Department Leefmilieu en Infrastructuur, Hasselt

Hoogma, R., Kemp, R., Schot, J. and Truffer, B. (2002) *Experimenting for Sustainable Transport: The Approach of Strategic Niche Management*, Spon Press, London and New York

Hughes, T. (1988) 'The seamless web: technology, science, etcetera' in Elliott, B. (ed) *Social Studies of Science*, Edinburgh University Press, Edinburgh, pp281–292

Hughes, T. (1994) 'Technological momentum' in Smith, M. and Marx, L. (eds) *Does Technology Drive History? The Dilemma of Technological Determinism*, MIT Press, Cambridge, MA, pp101–114

Hunt, J. and Wynne, B. (2000) 'Forums for Dialogue: Developing Legitimate Authority through Communication and Consultation: A Contract Report for Nirex (draft)', Centre for the Study of Environmental Change, Lancaster University, http://domino.lancs.ac.uk/ ieppp/Home.nsf/ByDocID/A2A4D62EF8B046BA80256A8900751AF8/$FILE/ forums+for+dialogue.doc, last accessed 16 March 2005

Ingersoll, R. (1996) 'Second nature: on the social bond of ecology and architecture' in Dutton, T. and Mann, L. (eds) *Reconstructing Architecture: Critical Discourses and Social Practices*, University of Minnesota Press, Minneapolis, pp119–157

Innes, J. (1995) 'Planning theory's emerging paradigm: communicative action and interactive practice', *Journal of Planning Education and Research*, vol 14, pp183–190

InvestorGuide (2003) 'Strategic alliance definition', www.investorwords.com/cgi-bin/ getword.cgi?4772, last accessed 17 January 2003

Jacobs, D. (1995a) 'Stad wil slechte reputatie kwijt – 5.000 parkeerplaatsen in centrum van Hasselt', *Het Belang van Limburg*, 8 December, p13

Jacobs, D. (1995b) 'Schrijft Hasselt stadslening uit?', *Het Belang van Limburg*, 28 December, pp1 and 9

Jacobs, D. (1996a) 'Voor 700 miljoen openbare werken in Hasselt', *Het Belang van Limburg*, 2 February, p12

Jacobs, D. (1996b) 'Stadsgrond in Hasselt wordt plots goud waard', *Het Belang van Limburg*, 8 March, pp1 and 16

Jacobs, D. (1996c) 'Tolerant optreden politie zorgt voor extra last', *Het Belang van Limburg*, 5 June, p13

Jacobs, D. (1996d) 'Baldewijns legt aan gementen mobiliteitsconvenant voor', *Het Belang van Limburg*, 8 June, p24

Jacobs, D. (1996e) 'Licht op groen voor Groene Boulevard', *Het Belang van Limburg*, 25 June, p16

Jacobs, D. (1996f) 'Gemeenteraad Hasselt: Licht op groen voor mobiliteitsconvenant', *Het Belang van Limburg*, 18 September, p16

Jacobs, D. (1996g) 'BTTB tevreden me groene boulevard, maar.: "Openbaar vervoer moet door het centrum rijden"', *Het Belang van Limburg*, 18 September, p12

Jacobs, D. (1996h) 'Met je winkelkar heel de stad door', *Het Belang van Limburg*, 16 November, p9

Jacobs, D. (1996i) 'Romain Onkelinx is de bekendste schepen', *Het Belang van Limburg*, 26 November, p11

Jacobs, D. (1996j) 'Groene busjes voor Groene Boulevard', *Het Belang van Limburg*, 17 December, p17

Jacobs, D. (1997a) 'Het prille succes van de Hasseltse boulevardpendel Belangrijke waardemeter', *Het Belang van Limburg*, 12 March, p13

Jacobs, D. (1997b) 'Gemeenteraad Hasselt: Belastingverlaging wellicht voor eind 1998', *Het Belang van Limburg*, 29 May, p20

Jacobs, D. (1997c) 'Gemeenteraad Hasselt: "Gratis bussen kosten aan Hasselaar 1 frank per dag"', *Het Belang van Limburg*, 25 June, p14

Jacobs, D. (1997d) 'Dinsdag start Hasseltse stadsnet: "Tijd van mastodontbussen is voorbij"', *Het Belang van Limburg*, 27 June, p9

Jacobs, D. (1997e) 'Vanaf vandaag gratis bussen', *Het Belang van Limburg*, 1 July, p9

Jacobs, D. (1997f) 'Eerste dag gratis stadsvervoer van De Lijn een success: Een bus voor iedereen', *Het Belang van Limburg*, 2 July, p9

Jacobs, D. (1997g) 'Ze hebben onze bushalte afgepakt', *Het Belang van Limburg*, 8 July, p9

Jacobs, D. (1997h) 'Hasselts stadsnet gratis tot 2000', *Het Belang van Limburg*, 1 August, pp1 and 17

Jacobs, D. (1997i) 'Meer taxi's na 50 dagen gratis bus', *Het Belang van Limburg*, 21 August, pp1 and 10

Jacobs, D. (1997j) 'Al een miljoen reizigers voor Hasselts stadsnet', *Het Belang van Limburg*, 19 December, p14

Jacobs, D. (2001) 'Gratis bussen in Hasselt tot 2006', *Het Belang van Limburg*, 20 November, p1

Jacobs, D. (2002) '52 winkelketens zoeken plek in centrum Hasselt', *Het Belang van Limburg*, 25 July

Jacobs, D., Stas, N., Thuwis, G. and van Luyk, M. (1997) 'Gratis busvervoer voor de inwoners van Hasselt', *Het Belang van Limburg*, 22 May, pp1and 8

Joerges, B. (1999a) 'Brücken, Busse, Autos und andere Verkehrsteilnehmer – Zur Repräsentation und Wirkung städtischer Artefakte' in Schmidt, G. (ed) *Technik und Gesellschaft*, Yearbook Vol 10, Automobil und Automobilismus, Campus, Frankfurt/Main, pp197–218

Joerges, B. (1999b) 'Do politics have artefacts?', *Social Studies of Science*, vol 29, no 3, pp411–430

Jonas, H. (1984) *The Imperative of Responsibility in Search of an Ethics for the Technological Age* (translated by D. Herr), University of Chicago Press, Chicago

Jones, T. (2003) 'The Guiding Light that is Groningen', www.wolvesonwheels.co.uk/Groningen.htm, last accessed 18 June 2005

Jongeling, H. (2001) *Mobiliteitsbrief*, vol 4, no 30, September, p4

Karmasin, T. (2002) 'Agenda 21, Landwirtschaft und Naturschutz', www.karmasin.de/bilanz/agenda.htm, last accessed 20 September 2002

Kelbaugh, D. (2000) 'Preface' in LeCuyer, A. (ed) *Shelter by Michael Benedikt*, 2000 Raoul Wallenberg Lecture, University of Michigan, Ann Arbor, MI, pp6–7

Kemp, R. and Rotmans, J. (2001) 'The management of the co-evolution of technical, environmental and social systems', contribution to the conference *Towards Environmental*

Innovation Systems, 27–29 September, Garmisch-Partenkirchen, http://meritbbs.unimaas. nl/rkemp/KempRotmans.pdf, last accessed 19 February 2005

Kincheloe, J. (1993) *Toward a Critical Politics of Teacher Thinking Mapping the Postmodern*, Bergin & Garvey, Westport, CT

Kindhäuser, A. (2000) 'Gratisbusse statt Strassenbau: Das Beispiel Hasselt' in Altner, G. (ed) *Jahrbuch Ökologie 2000*, Beck, Munich, pp61–67

Koeppl, A. (2001) 'Nachhaltige volkswirtschaftliche Entwicklung', www.nachhaltigkeit.at/ bibliothek/pdf/monatsthemen2001/mainM01 _08.pdf, last accessed 12 October 2002

Krebs, T. (2002) 'Konsumausgaben privater Haushalte für Nahrungsmittel, Getränke und Tabakwaren 1998' in Statistisches Bundesamt (ed) *Wirtschaft und Statistik*, April, pp294–309

Lambrechts, D. (2000a) 'Hasselt-Aantaal busgebruikers: Vroeger en nu - 97-98-99-00.doc' [data file transmitted via email]

Lambrechts, D. (2000b) 'Hasselt-Aaantal busgebruikers, vroeger en nu: Stadsnet en regionaalnet.xls' [data file transmitted via email]

Lambrechts, D. (2000c) *Kunst in de Kijker – 93*, Stedelijk Museum Stellingwerff-Waerdehof, Hasselt

Lambrechts, D. (2001) *Duurzam Mobiliteitsbeleid op twee Sporen*, unpublished document

Landratsamt Fürstenfeldbruck (2002) 'Vorstellung ZIEL 21', www.lra-ffb.de/presse/ presag8.htm, last accessed 20 September 2002

Landry, C. (2000) *The Creative City*, Earthscan, London

Landwirtschaftsamt Dachau, Fürstenfeldbruck, Landsberg (2002) 'Daten und Fakten aus unserem Dienstgebiet', www.stmlf.bayern.de/aflue/dafflb/ duf/duf.html, last accessed 30 September 2002

Lapham, L. (1994) 'Introduction to the MIT Press edition: the eternal now' in McLuhan, M. (ed) *Understanding Media: The Extensions of Man*, MIT Press, Cambridge, MA, ppix–xxiii

Latour, B. (1992) 'Where are the missing masses? The sociology of a few mundane artifacts' in Bijker, W. and Law, J. (eds) *Shaping Technology/Building Society: Studies in Sociotechnical Change*, MIT Press, Cambridge, MA, pp225–264

Latour, B. (2004) 'Which politics for which artifacts?', *Domus*, June, www.ensmp.fr/~latour/ presse/presse_art/GB-06%20DOMUS%2006-04.html, last accessed 14 June 2004

Laurent, J. (1999) 'A note on the origin of memes/mnemes', *Journal of Memetics: Evolutionary Models of Information Transmission*, vol 3, no 1, pp20–21, http://jom-emit.cfpm.org/1999/ vol3/laurent_j.html, last accessed 15 November 2002

Ledbury, M. (2004) *UK Car Clubs: An Effective Way of Cutting Vehicle Usage and Emissions?* MSc dissertation at the Environmental Change Institute, University of Oxford, www.carclubs.org.uk/Resources/pdf/final%20dissertation%20complete.pdf, last accessed 13 June 2005

Levidow, L. and Carr, S. (1997) 'How biotechnology regulation sets a risk/ethics boundary', *Agriculture and Human Values*, vol 14, no 1, pp29–43

Lewellan, A. (2002) 'Hi-tech low-tech sustainability' (Comment to op-ed), *Planetizen*, 18 November, http://planetizen.com/oped/ cmt_item.php?id=805, last accessed 22 February 2003

Light, A. (2002) 'Restoring ecological citizenship' in Minteer, B. and Taylor, B. (eds) *Democracy and the Claims of Nature*, Rowman & Littlefield, Lanham, MD, pp153–172

Lincoln, Y. and Guba, E. (1985) *Naturalistic Inquiry*, Sage, Beverly Hills, CA

Lovins, A. (1979) *Soft Energy Paths*, Harper & Row, New York

Luce, R. and Raiffa, H. (1957) *Games and Decisions*, John Wiley, New York

Ludwig Stocker Hofpfisterei GmbH (2003) 'Brot per Mausklick', www.hofpfisterei.de, last accessed 12 March 2003

MacKenzie, D. and Wajcman, J. (1985) *The Social Shaping of Technology*, Open University Press, Milton Keynes

Martens, P., Thuwis, G. and Gybels, L. (1994) 'TT-wijk opblazen en er een park van maken', *Het Belang van Limburg*, 8 October, pp16–17

Maxeiner, D. and Miersch, M. (2001) 'Zukunft der Landwirtschaft. Gesunde Rinder im gläsernen Stall', *Die Welt*, 13 January, www.maxeiner-miersch.de/standp2001-01a.htm, last accessed 18 September 2002

Mazzola, M. (ed) (2001) 'Planning in the age of prosperity', *Planning Forum*, vol 8, pp97–106

McLuhan, M. (1964) *Understanding Media: The Extensions of Man*, McGraw-Hill, New York

Mehaffy, M. (2004) 'The kind of problem architecture is', *Katarxis*, vol 3, www.katarxis3.com/Jacobs.htm, last accessed 2 April 2005

Menand, L. (2001) *The Metaphysical Club*, Farrar, Straus and Giroux, New York

Meuris, S (1996) '90 frank om foldertje op te halen', *Het Belang van Limburg*, 12 October, pp1, 12

Miller, J. (2001) 'Unser Land' [Speech at the launch of the Stadt-Land-Partnerschaft UNSER LAND, Benediktbeuern], in *Bayerisches Staatsministerium für Landwirtschaft und Forsten*, www.stmlf.bayern.de/publikationen/ministerreden/2001/re23-01.html, last accessed 16 January 2003

M. L. (1993) 'Resistentere Arten gefragt: Klares "Ja" zu Gen-tests beim Zuckerrübenanbau', *Fürstenfeldbrucker Tagblatt*, 6/7 February, pFFB8

'Mobility with an eye to the environment: Hasselt, an example for Europe' (1999) unpublished manuscript

Moore, S. (2001) *Technology and Place: Sustainable Architecture and the Blueprint Farm*, University of Texas Press, Austin, TX

Moore, S. (2002) 'The miracle of Curitiba and the sustainable city', unpublished manuscript

Mugerauer, R. (1996) 'Theories of sustainability: environmental ethics, mixed-communities and compassion', presentation at the conference *Environment and the New Global Economic Order*, April, Austin, TX, www.utexas.edu/depts/grg/eworks/proceedings/engeo/mugerauer/ mughtml.html, last accessed 10 October 2002

MVGWV, Ministerie van de Vlaamse Gemeenschap, Afdeling Wegen en Verkeer Limburg (2001) *De Groene Boulevard in Hasselt –Vlaanderen. Een duurzame oplossing voor mobiliteit in de stad*, no location

Myers, D. (2001) 'Demographic futures as a guide to planning: California's Latinos and the compact city', *Journal of the American Planning Association*, vol 4, no 67, pp383–397

Nelson, R. and Winter, S. (1977) 'In search of a useful theory of innovation', *Research Policy*, vol 6, pp36–76

Newcomb, S. (2001) 'Re: the tragedy of the commons', *XML Community Portal*, 4 September, http://lists.xml.org/ archives/xml-dev/200109/msg00038.html, last accessed 17 December 2002

Noble, K. (2000) 'Flights of fantasy: obsessed by dreams of flying, Belgian artist Panamarenko creates surreal machines to transport the imagination', *Time International*, www.time.com/time/europe/magazine/2000/0320/panamarenko.html, last accessed 24 January 2003

NOW with Bill Moyers (2002) [Television broadcast from the World Summit on Sustainable Development, Johannesburg, South Africa] Public Broadcasting Service, 30 August

Oeyen, J. (1997) 'Lezersbrieven', *Het Belang van Limburg*, 12 September, p37

O. H. (1993) 'Bei Bauernquelle wirft Kasier Matthias Heitmayr Handtuch', *Fürstenfeldbrucker Tagblatt*, 15 April, pFFB3

Ornetzeder, M. (2001) 'Old technology and social innovations. Inside the Austrian success story on solar water heaters', *Technology Analysis & Strategic Management*, vol 13, no 1, pp105–115

Ornetzeder, M. (2002) 'Old technology and social innovations. Inside the Austrian success-story on solar water heaters' in Jamison, A. and Rohracher, H. (eds) *Technology Studies and Sustainable Development*, Profil, Munich, pp365–381

O'Toole, J. (1995) *Leading Change: Overcoming the Ideology of Comfort and the Tyranny of Custom*, Jossey-Bass, San Francisco

Pauli, G. (2002) 'Las Gaviotas' [manuscript to be published by *Whole Earth Magazine*] www.urbanecology.org/gaviotas/ article.htm, last accessed 24 February 2003

Pennington, M. (2002) 'A Hayekian liberal critique of collaborative planning' in Allmendinger, P. and Tewdwr-Jones, M. (eds) *Planning Futures: New Directions for Planning Theory*, Routledge, New York, pp187–205

Peuskens, B. (1997) 'Lezersbrieven', *Het Belang van Limburg*, 12 September, p37

Pezzoli, K. (1998) 'Human settlements and planning for ecological sustainability' in Gottlieb, R. (ed) *Urban and Industrial Environments Series*, MIT Press, Cambridge, MA

Pfaffenberger, B. (1992) 'Technological dramas', *Science, Technology and Human Values*, vol 17, no 3, pp282–312

Pinch, T. and Bijker, W. (1984) 'The social construction of facts and artifacts: or, how the sociology of science and the sociology of technology might benefit each other', *Social Studies of Science*, vol 14, pp399–441

Pippin, R. (1995) 'On the notion of technology as ideology' in Feenberg, A. (ed) *Technology and the Politics of Knowledge*, Indiana University Press, Bloomington, pp43–63

PLANNING, The Journal of the Royal Town Planning Institute (2005) 17 June

Planning Group, Mobility Plan for Hasselt (undated) *Mobiliteitsplan Hasselt, Fase 2*, Synthesenota Kartenboek, Hasselt

Pope John Paul II (1997) 'Science serves humanity only when it is joined to conscience', *L'Osservatore Romano*, The Cathedral Foundation, Baltimore, MD, www.ewtn.com/library/PAPALDOC/JP970111.htm, last accessed 11 January 2003

Postrel, V. (1998) *The Future and its Enemies: The Growing Conflict Over Creativity*, Enterprise and Progress, Free Press, New York

P. S. (1994) 'Scheinlösungen bringen kein besseres Trinkwasser', *Fürstenfeldbrucker Tagblatt*, 3 February, pFFB6

Pursell, C. (1994) *White Heat: People and Technology*, University of California Press, Berkeley

Quinn, D. (1996) *Ishmael*, Bantam/Turner, New York (original published 1992)

Quintiens, L (undated) *Groene Boulevard wandeling Hasselt*, unpublished document

Radermacher, F. (1998) Presentation as part of the Umweltringvorlesung of the Student Government, Catholic University of Eichstätt, Germany

Radermacher, F (1999) 'Population development, globalization and environment: crisis points', www.faw.uni-ulm.de/deutsch/publikationen/radermacher/population_development.html, last accessed 10 October 2002

Rand, D. (1999) 'Coevolution' [material for course Bio 48] Brown University, http://biomed.brown.edu/courses/bio48/27.Coevolution.html, last accessed 28 July 2002

Reginet.de (2002) BRUCKER LAND, www.reginet.de/regio_vor_brucker.htm, last accessed 15 May 2002

Rip, A. (1994) 'Science & technology studies and constructive technology assessment', *EASST Review*, vol 13, no 3, pp11–16, www.easst.net/review/sept1994/rip, last accessed 6 October 2005

Rohracher, H. (1999) 'Sustainable construction of buildings: a socio-technical perspective' in Rohracher, H. and Bogner, T. (eds) *Proceedings of the International Summer Academy* on *Technology Studies: Technology Studies and Sustainability*, Inter-University Research Center for Technology, Work and Culture, Graz, pp307–318

Rohracher, H. (2001) 'Between innovation and diffusion: the importance of users in shaping environmental technologies', *Proceedings of the International Summer Academy on Technology Studies: User Involvement in Technological Innovation*, www.ifz.tu-graz.ac.at/sumacad/01/sa01_rohracher.pdf, last accessed 13 November 2002, pp223–234

Rohracher, H. and Ornetzeder, M. (2002) 'Green buildings in context: improving social learning processes between users and producers', *Built Environment*, vol 28, no 1, pp73–84

Rorty, R. (1989) *Contingency, Irony and Solidarity*, Cambridge University Press, Cambridge, MA

Rosen, P. (2002) 'Up the vélorution: appropriating the bicycle and the politics of technology' in Eglash, R., Bleecker, J., Croissant, J., Fouché, R. and Di Chiro, G. (eds) *Appropriating Technology: Vernacular Science and Social Power*, University of Minnesota Press, Minneapolis

Roth, I. and Altwegg, D. (2001) 'Structure of indicator system and selection of indicators: Consultation document', Provisional version, MONET project: Monitoring of sustainable development, Neuchâtel, Switzerland, www.statistik.admin.ch/stat_ch/ber21/dev_dur_e_files/structure.pdf, last accessed 18 December 2002

Rutten, R. (1995a) 'Hasseltse ambtenaren krijgen rubbervergoeding', *Het Belang van Limburg*, 19 August, p12

Rutten, R. (1995b) 'Haalbaarheidsstudie over KGA-ophaling aan huis', *Het Belang van Limburg*, 27 September, p13

Rutten, R. and Gybels, L. (1995) 'Hasselt alleen nog in nieuws met prullaria', *Het Belang van Limburg*, 22 February, p11

Rybczynski, W. (1983) *Taming the Tiger: The Struggle to Control Technology*, Penguin, New York

Sachs, S. (2000) 'Arts abroad: honoring a visionary if not his vision', *The New York Times* Internet Edition, 4 April, www.nyt.com, last accessed 11 March 2001

SAM, Samen Anders Mobiel secretariat (undated) *Heb je een idee dat past binnen de Samen Anders Mobiel filosofie?* [brochure], City of Hasselt, Hasselt

Sandberg, J. (2003) 'Cold, hard truth: office thermostat might be a fake', *The Wall Street Journal*, reprinted in the *Austin American Statesman*, 16 January, www.austin360.com/statesman/editions/today/ news_6.html, last accessed 16 January 2003

Schatzberg, E. (2002) 'Natural capitalism: creating the next industrial revolution' [book review of *Natural Capitalism: Creating the Next Industrial Revolution*], Technology and Culture, vol 43, no 1, pp218–221

Schön, D. (1983) *The Reflective Practitioner*, Basic Books, New York

Schot, J. and Rip, A. (1996) 'The past and future of constructive technology assessment', *Technological Forecasting and Social Change*, vol 54, pp251–268

Schumacher, E.-F. (1973) *Small is Beautiful: A Study of Economics as if People Mattered*, Blond and Briggs, London

Schwartz Cowan, R. (1985) 'How the refrigerator got its hum' in MacKenzie, D. and Wajcman, J. (eds) *The Social Shaping of Technology: How the Refrigerator got its Hum*, Open University Press, Milton Keynes and Philadelphia, pp202–218

SHLS, Stuurgroep Hasselt Levendig Stadscentrum (1994) *Hasselt levendig stadscentrum* [limited-circulation report], 1 February

Shove, E. (2002) 'Sustainability, system innovation and the laundry', Working paper series of the Department of Sociology, Lancaster Univeresity, www.comp.lancs.ac.uk/sociology/papers/shove-sustainability-system-innovation.pdf, last accessed 16 March 2004

Skinner, B.-F. (1955) 'Freedom and the control of men', *The American Scholar*, vol 25, pp47–65

Sloterdijk, P. (1999) 'Regeln für den Menschenpark. Ein Antwortschreiben zum Brief über den Humanismus: die Elmauer Rede', *DIE ZEIT*, 16 September, pp15–17

Snell, B. (2001) 'The streetcar conspiracy', *Tom Paine*, 10 September, www.tompaine.com/feature.cfm/ID/4518, last accessed 26 October 2002

Snoeckx, L. (1997) 'Onderzoek naar profiel Hasseltse busgebruikers', *Het Belang van Limburg*, 10 October, p11

Spinosa, C., Flores, F. and Dreyfus, H. (1997) *Disclosing New Worlds*, MIT Press, Cambridge, MA

Stad Hasselt (1999) *Mobiliteitsplan Hasselt, Fase 2 – Opbouw van het mobiliteitsplan*, final revision by V. Donné as of October 1999

Stad Hasselt (2001) 'Het stads- en streeknet te Hasselt anno 2001', *De nieuwe Hasselaar*, vol 25, no 5, October, p1

'Stad trekt De Lijn helemaal doorledereen gratis de bus op' (1997) *Het Belang van Limburg*, 30 June, p12

Stappen, R. (1995) 'Das Altmühltalprojekt' in Deutsches Nationalkomitee für das Europäische Naturschutzjahr (ed) *Naturschutz außerhalb vom Schutzgebieten: Abschlußbericht*, Bonn

Stas, N. (1995) 'Hasseltse opcentiemen dalen met 200 eenheden', *Het Belang van Limburg*, 15 September, p13

Stas, N. (1996) 'Week van de zachte weggebruiker in Limburg: Opnieuw 226 miljoen voor nieuwe fietspaden', *Het Belang van Limburg*, 14 May, p9

Steger, U. (1995) 'Konsens ohne Wert', *DIE ZEIT*, 27 November, p26

Stengel, R. (2001) 'It's all downhill from here', *Time* Internet Edition, 22 March, www.time.com/time/columnist/stengel/article/0,9565,103592,00.html, last accessed 14 February 2003

Stevaert, S. (1991) *Provinciale Milieubeleidsverklaring 1991*, Hendrickx, Hasselt

Stevaert, S. (2000a) *Energie, Beleidsnota 2000–2004*, Vlaamse Regering (ed) Die Keure, Brugge, www.vlaanderen.be/regering/beleidsnota, last accessed 21 December 2001

Stevaert, S. (2000b) *Mobiliteit en openbare werken, Beleidsnota 2000–2004*, Vlaamse Regering (ed) Die Keure, Brugge, www.vlaanderen.be/regering/beleidsnota, last accessed 21 December 2001

Strong, M. (2001) 'Reforming the United Nations', *The Futurist*, vol 35, no 5, pp24–25

Studiecentrum Willy Claes (ed) (1990) *Hasselt, een beeld van een stad: Zo kan Hasselt worden met de SP van Willy Claes* [SP brochure, WESP series special issue] SP, Hasselt

Szoboszlay, A. (1999) 'Conflict of Transportation Competitors', www.trainweb.org/mts/ctc/index.html, last accessed 5 June 2004

Tahvanainen, T., Sikanen, L., Karppinen, H. and Tolvanen, K. (2003) 'Mottinetti – marketing chopped firewood and services via the Internet', Proceedings of the *International Bioenergy 2003 Conference* [data file transmitted via email by K. Tolvanen on 24 June 2005]

Taylor, M. (1976) *Anarchy and Cooperation*, John Wiley & Sons, London

Thuwis, G. (1997) 'Verkeersdeskundige Valère Donné over gratis busse in Hasselt: "Interessante test voor heel Europa"', *Het Belang van Limburg*, 23 May, p11

'Trotz Agrarwende kein Öko-Schub: Ein Jahr BSE-Krise' (2001) *Schweriner Volkszeitung*, 16 November, www.svz.de/forum/bse/, last accessed 19 September 2002

True, K. (2000) 'Groningen gears up: bicycle-friendly urban planning is good for business', *In Context*, vol 39, fall 1994, p7, www.context.org/ICLIB/IC39/TruePP.htm, last accessed 18 June 2005

Tucker, R. (2003) '7 strategies for generating ideas', *The Futurist*, vol 37, no 2, pp20–25

Umweltinstitut München e.V (2002) 'Die AGENDA 21 im Landkreis Fürstenfeldbruck', www.umweltinstitut.org/stadtgespraeche/archiv/frames/agenda/ms20_8.htm, last accessed 20 September 2002

UNCED, United Nations Conference on Environment and Development (1992) *Agenda 21: Programme of Action for Sustainable Development*, United Nations Department of Public Information, New York

United Nations General Assembly Fifty-fifth Session (2001) 'Ten-year review of progress achieved in the implementation of the outcome of the United Nations Conference on Environment and Development', Document A/RES/55/199, http://daccess-ds.un.org/doc/UNDOC/GEN/N00/571/15/PDF/N0057115.pdf?OpenElement, last accessed 1 October 2002

United Nations Office for Project Services/Afghanistan Rural Rehabilitation Programme (2001) 'Afghan education drama "New Home, New Life"', www.pcpafg.org/appeal/appeal1999/compendium_of_project_proposals/sub_empowerment/subfolders/unops_bbc_aed.htm, last accessed 10 October 2002

Vandenreyt, C. (1995) 'Alle auto's op de bon op de Hasseltse wegen', *Het Belang van Limburg*, 6 October, pp1 and 10

Vandenreyt, C. (2001) 'Prof Stevaert geeft verkeersles', *Het Belang van Limburg*, 25 September, p19

van Moerkerke, B. (1997) 'Hasselt – Een mobiliteitsbeleid in ontwikkeling' in *Het Mobiliteitshandboek*, Kluwer, Mechelen, ppHasselt/1–Hasselt/18

Verdee, E. (undated) *Groene Boulevard – Stedelijke Analyse Hasselt*, unpublished manuscript

Vitaliano, F. (1998) 'The PC DVD wars: show me the money! Show me the money! Show me the money!', *21st Impact*, www.vxm.com/21R.124.html, last accessed 20 December 2002

Wainwright, M. (2005) 'Tesco project gets Gerrards really Cross', *The Guardian* Internet Edition, 4 January, www.guardian.co.uk/supermarkets/story/0,12784,1382891,00.html, last accessed 17 June 2005

Weizsäcker, E.-U. von, Lovins, A. and Lovins, H. (1997) *Factor Four: Doubling Wealth, Halving Resource Use*, the New Report to the Club of Rome, Earthscan, London

Whittenburg, C. and Shedletsky, L. (undated) 'Technological determinism of Marshall McLuhan', www.usm.maine.edu/ com/techdet/tsld002.htm, last accessed 26 October 2002

Winner, L. (1977) *Autonomous Technology: Technics-out-of-control as a Theme in Political Thought*, MIT Press, Cambridge, MA

Winner, L. (1980) 'Do artifacts have politics?', *Daedalus*, vol 109, no 1, pp121–136

Winner, L. (1995) 'Citizen virtues in a technological order' in Feenberg, A. (ed) *Technology and the Politics of Knowledge*, Indiana University Press, Bloomington, pp64–84

Winner, L (2002) 'Sustainability', presentation given in Topics in Sustainable Development course, *University of Texas at Austin*, 7 March

Wischermann, M. (2002) 'Umweltethische Bezüge des FAKTOR VIER-Konzepts', www.wupperinst.org/FaktorVier/FaktorVier_ethik.html, last accessed 8 October 2002

Wolmar, C. (2005) 'The scandal of Gerrards Cross', *Evening Standard*, 4 July 2005, p13

Woolgar, S. and Cooper, G. (1999) 'Do artefacts have ambivalence? Moses' bridges, Winner's bridges and other urban legends in S&TS', *Social Studies of Science*, vol 29, no 3, pp433–449

World Commission on Environment and Development (1987) *Our Common Future*, Oxford University Press, Oxford

WHO, World Health Organization (2001) 'Country reports (Mental Health, Suicide Prevention)', www5.who.int/mental _health/main.cfm?p=0000000515, last accessed 17 October 2002

Index

For Product Safety Concerns and Information please contact our
EU representative GPSR@taylorandfrancis.com Taylor & Francis
Verlag GmbH, Kaufingerstraße 24, 80331 München, Germany